# THE MARK OF THE SOCIAL

# THE MARK OF THE SOCIAL

## *Discovery or Invention?*

Edited by
JOHN D. GREENWOOD

ROWMAN & LITTLEFIELD PUBLISHERS, INC.
Lanham • Boulder • New York • London

ROWMAN & LITTLEFIELD PUBLISHERS, INC.

Published in the United States of America
by Rowman & Littlefield Publishers, Inc.
4720 Boston Way, Lanham, Maryland 20706

3 Henrietta Street
London WC2E 8LU, England

Copyright © 1997 by Rowman & Littlefield Publishers, Inc.

British Cataloging in Publication Information Available

**Library of Congress Cataloging-in-Publication Data**

The mark of the social : discovery or invention? / edited by John D.
   Greenwood.
      p.   cm.
   Includes bibliographical references and indexes.
   ISBN 0-8476-8307-9 (alk. paper). — ISBN 0-8476-8308-7 (pbk. :
alk. paper)
   1. Sociology—Philosophy.   I. Greenwood, John D.
HM24.M287   1997
301'.01—dc20                                             96-28254
                                                            CIP

ISBN 0–8476–8307–9 (cloth : alk. paper)
ISBN 0–8476–8308–7 (pbk. : alk. paper)

Printed in the United States of America

∞ ™ The paper used in this publication meets the minimum requirements of
American National Standard for Information Sciences—Permanence of Paper
for Printed Library Materials, ANSI Z39.48—1984.

# Contents

# Introduction: The Mark of The Social

## John D. Greenwood

Some years ago I reviewed Margaret Gilbert's book, *On Social Facts* (1991), for the journal *Social Epistemology*. Although I disagreed with her analysis of social collectivity in terms of what she called 'plural subjecthood', I was struck by the fact that most contributors to recent debates on social theory had effectively ignored the essentially Socratic question that Gilbert raises in the first chapter:

> We think of certain phenomena as 'social' phenomena. Here are some examples: two people talking on a street corner; a football game; a meeting of the Town Council; the mob storming the Bastille. But what do we mean by 'social'? What restrictions are there on what we would consider a social phenomenon? How is the everyday, intuitive concept of a social phenomenon to be explicated? (pp. 1–2)

Many scholars had been stressing the importance of recognizing the social dimensions of this, that, and the next thing, but few (myself included) had paused to explicate those properties or relations that are held to be attributed when apparently diverse phenomena such as actions, groups, crowds, institutions, persons, language, development, emotion—and more recently, science, epistemology, and identity—are characterized as social in nature.

I was also struck by the fact that this was neither a recent nor obvious phenomenon. Even a classic theorist such as Durkheim, who seemed ostensibly concerned with questions about the demarcation of social phenomena, effectively ignored it in his discussion of 'social facts'. In the *Rules of Sociological Method*, Durkheim (1895/1982:50)

1

avowed that "it is important to know what are the facts termed 'social'," to delineate those 'distinct characteristics' that distinguish social phenomena from biological and psychological phenomena, in order that the distinctive subject matter of sociology might be identified. However, the two properties that he cited as common to all instances of 'social facts'—externality and constraint[1]—are not properties by virtue of which certain facts are social in nature. These properties are not 'distinct characteristics' of social phenomena: they are properties shared by the various objects that form the subject matters of the natural sciences. That is, Durkheim only cited properties by virtue of which social phenomena can properly be counted as *appropriate objects of a scientific sociology*—those properties that are constitutive of the "reality" or "thinghood" of social phenomena,[2] not those properties by virtue of which certain phenomena may themselves be characterized as social in nature.[3]

This tendency seemed to have been maintained by generations of theorists after Durkheim, who have offered either characterizations of social phenomena that justify their treatment as objects of social scientific analysis; or characterizations that purport to demonstrate that social phenomena cannot be studied in the manner of natural sciences but require some alternative and essentially interpretative methodology; or characterizations that purport to cite some theoretically significant dimension of social phenomena. Given the relative dearth of attempts to explicate those properties by which social phenomena are intuitively characterized as social, I thought it might be illuminating to ask a number of contemporary theorists from a variety of social scientific and social theoretical disciplines to directly address this neglected question about the demarcation of social phenomena. The present collection of essays is the result.

# I

Despite our apparent familiarity with the use of the term 'social', it is no easy task to demarcate those properties that we hold to mark the essence of the social. This may be illustrated by noting the difficulties faced by a variety of putative suggestions that may be gleaned from the writings of many classical and contemporary social theorists. For although few theorists have been explicit in articulating just what dimensions they take to be constitutive of the social, many have offered suggestive characterizations en passim, and most have implied answers in the paradigms of social phenomena they employ as their objects of theoretical analysis. The list of such phenomena is remarkably various, and includes, for example, the following: states, families, armies, religious organizations, literary societies, mobs, street brawls, people chatting on a street corner, the Roman Catholic Church, the Renaissance, insect communication, dominance hierarchies among primates, language, financial instruments, and traffic flow in a city.

One type of account that retains a certain appeal is the one offered by Durkheim himself, in terms of some form of unified structure, which, if not itself organic in nature, is held to be at least analogous to the structure of organisms. Structured social entities, like biological organisms, are held to be 'greater than the sum of their parts', and the laws governing social phenomena are held to be different from, and not reducible to, the psychological or biological laws governing their human or animal components. This 'holistic' account has the purported virtue of maintaining the explanatory autonomy of social scientific disciplines (in relation to biological and psychological disciplines) and enables us to extend social scientific categories to many animal 'societies'. This account seems to work best for organized groups and institutions, such as professional psychologists and stock markets, but does not readily extend to phenomena such as mobs and people chatting on a street corner, which appear to lack structure, and doubtfully applies to those animal 'societies' whose organization seems to be entirely determined by chemical signaling devices, such as those of ants and bees.

The primary problem with such accounts is that in emphasizing the causal autonomy of social structure, they are naturally exposed to the charge of reification and mystification, particularly given the miserable failure of 'holistic' theorists of the past hundred years to accommodate the generally acknowledged fact that any causal claim about organized groups or institutions seems to depend heavily upon truths about the psychology of the individuals who compose them. We naturally suppose that if the psychology of humans were different, the social truths about professional psychologists and stock markets would be different too. This criticism seems particularly apt in the case of social phenomena because of serious doubts about the applicability of the organic model or metaphor. For whatever exactly social structure is, it would appear to be intrinsic to or immanent in the psychology (or biology) and practices of individual persons (or other animals), in a fashion in which the structure of a cell or honeycomb is not—the structure of a cell or honeycomb would appear to be extrinsic or external to its components.

There is also a more fundamental problem about the very notion of social structure itself. Even if we agree that groups such as professional psychologists or institutions such as the stock market are structured entities, this does nothing to explicate the concept of social phenomena. It is only to acknowledge that *social phenomena* such as groups of professional psychologists or institutions such as stock markets are structured. It is to recognize a (theoretically interesting) property of phenomena that are characterized as social by intuition or some independent criterion. No theorist maintains that structure is the distinguishing characteristic of the social, since it is a property common to many biological and chemical phenomena.

Metaphysical doubts about reification and the organic analogy have led others to suggest that social phenomena—including so-called 'social collectives'—are nothing more than special sequences of human action. The most famous exponent of this "bottom-up" approach is Weber, who defined social action as any behavior whose "subjective meaning takes into account the behavior of others and is thereby oriented in its course" (1922:4) and proceeded to define all other social phenomena—such as social relations or social collectives—in terms of sequences of actual or potential social actions.

It is in fact doubtful if such a reductive analysis is possible for all social phenomena, since sequences of Weberian social actions do not seem sufficient for social collectivity or social relations: persons or animals taking steps to avoid each other—or avoid colliding with each other—on the pathway do not seem to constitute a social collectivity and cannot properly be said to be socially related. Moreover, the characterization of social action itself, while it undoubtedly does cover a large class of intuitively recognized social actions, such as the rule-governed activities of interviewing a job candidate and waving to a friend across the station platform, seems to include both too much and too little. It seems to include too much, because by essentially identifying social action with *interpersonal action*, it includes a whole range of interpersonal actions that are less than obviously social, such as some acts of aggression and sexual harassment (which at best may be described as antisocial). It seems to include too little, because there seems to be no significant difference between the interpersonal rule-governed action of depositing a check with a bank teller and the impersonal rule-governed action of depositing a check at an automated teller machine, or between the interpersonal rule-governed action of

holy communion and the personal rule-governed action of solitary gen-
uflection.

That is, Weber's analysis highlights the interpersonal nature of many
social actions but unjustly restricts the social to the interpersonal.
Moreover, there is no obvious reason for restricting the subjects or
objects of social action to persons. Again, there seems to be no
significant difference between acts of coordination or aggression
among primates and among humans, or between intentional behaviors
directed by persons to their spouses, dogs, or car stereos, or by
animals to their prey, watering holes, or human masters. The Weberian
analysis seems unduly restrictive and chauvinistic.

Another paradigm appealed to by some theorists is the sorts of mass
behavior exhibited by mobs or crowds. This paradigm has the apparent
advantage of seeming to fit the Durkheimian notion of the transcendence of social phenomena with respect to the individual psychologies
of the persons who comprise them. It has the further advantage that it
seems clearly applicable to interesting forms of animal behavior, such
as the well-documented tendency toward aggression as population
density increases. Yet closer analysis suggests serious limitations of
this paradigm. The most interesting types of phenomena on which it
focuses are *abnormal* human and animal behaviors, and these seem
entirely explicable in terms of individual psychology when this takes
into account our perception of others' behavior, and familiar mechanisms of cognitive labeling and interpersonal communication (including
chemical signals). Although Durkheim himself did appeal to crowd
behavior as an exemplar of collective behavior, the impulsive behavior
of persons in the grip of a crowd emotion or carried along by the
aggression of the mob seems to have very little in common with the
controlled and mundane social activities of the banker, curate, or
conversationalist on the street corner. Of course, many social actions
are done with passion, but it is a contingent matter whether any
particular ones are.

Another related paradigm of the social is represented by forms of
coordinated and cooperative behavior such as that displayed by drivers
who keep to the right (or left) or by civil-minded citizens who refrain
from watering their lawns in a time of drought and who elect representatives to pursue their interests in the legislature. However, although
an analysis of social phenomena in terms of forms of coordinated or
cooperative behavior does seem to include a great many forms of
intuitively social phenomena, this analysis also seems to include too
much. It includes, for example, those instances of Weberian 'social

action'—such as the interpersonal behaviors of persons or animals avoiding each other on a pathway—that are doubtfully instances of social action. And, as Weber himself noted, not all instances of coordinated actions appear to be social: many persons open their umbrellas together on rainy days and wake up, yawn, and stretch in the morning, but neither seems the product of any 'consensual order' (1922: 113).

Such an analysis has the apparent advantage that it includes the organized behaviors of nonlinguistic animals, since it usually includes forms of cooperation and coordination achieved unintentionally and without linguistic vehicles such as articulated rules. Yet this is a mixed blessing. For such an analysis is so broad that it appears to include the mechanically regulated and regimented behaviors of bees and termites, not to mention microbes and gas molecules.[4] It also appears to exclude precisely those forms of aggressive and destructive mass behaviors discussed earlier.

An alternative suggestion is that it is those collections of individuals who often engage in coordinated, cooperative, and destructive forms of behavior, rather than these forms of behavior themselves, that represent the primary social phenomena—that is, those populations of individuals that are characterized as social groups by virtue of the common or shared properties of their members, including shared beliefs, interests, and goals. This analysis does seem adequate to capture what is common to a diverse range of phenomena recognized as social in nature, such as persons chatting on a street corner, motorcycle gangs, families, political parties, and states. In itself, however, this analysis seems too broad: it includes not only the populations of Republican supporters, Bruce Springstein fans and African Americans, but also the populations of persons who are five feet ten inches tall, who occupy Bryant Park on the last Thursday in June, who want to live in a warmer country, and who have a mole on their left arm. For this characterization to furnish an account of the social, we need some explanation of why some populations that share common properties are characterized as social groups, such as members of the Republican Party and the local PTA, while others are not, such as the populations of persons who are five feet ten inches tall or who were born on July 12, 1953.

Moreover, within those populations delineated as social groups, we also need some way to distinguish between those groups that themselves appear to be social in nature—such as Russian speakers, gangs, and professional psychologists, whose members are bound by sets of rules, conventions, and perhaps shared goals and values—and those that are not—such as the populations of persons who have AIDS, are of a particular gender, or are unemployed—whose members do not appear to be bound by any rules or conventions distinctive of that population and may not share any distinctive goals or values. These latter groups seem to be characterized as social only *derivatively*, by virtue of the collective fiat of some other *intrinsically* social group, which determines, for example, that properties such as gender and having AIDS are socially significant but those such as common spatiotemporal location and left-arm moles are not.

Furthermore, whereas one naturally expects coordinated and cooperative forms of behavior from members of intrinsically social groups like motorcycle gangs and the local PTA, there is no a priori reason to anticipate such forms of behavior between members of gender groups or persons who have AIDS. Attempts to mark this difference between intrinsically and derivatively social groups in terms of the presence and absence of feelings of association or identification do not seem to do the job, because members of derivatively social groups, such as the populations of women and persons with AIDS, may have strong feelings of association or identification, and members of intrinsically social groups, such as English speakers or professional psychologists, may not.

However, the notion of some form of psychologically grounded interpersonal relation as the mark of the social seems to point in the right direction. My own view, which I have developed elsewhere (Greenwood 1994), is that the essential mark of the social is to be found in the sets of arrangements, conventions, and agreements that members of certain populations are bound by and party to. One virtue of such an analysis is that it suggests the possibility of an integrated account of social groups and social behavior, in terms of parties to sets of arrangements, conventions, and agreements, and actions in accord with arrangements, conventions, and agreements. On this analysis, it comes as no surprise that members of populations that are bound by and parties to sets of arrangements, conventions, and agreements—members of intrinsically social groups—regularly engage in forms of coordinated and cooperative behavior among themselves—one form of social action.

It also has the advantage that it leaves open the question of whether some animal populations and behaviors are social in nature, since it allows that some forms of animal behavior may be governed by nonlinguistic arrangements, while denying sociality to those behaviors that are mechanical products of physiological or chemical processes. This analysis, I believe, illuminates some traditional questions and has some significant implications, but at the end of the day it only relocates the fundamental question to the explication of the nature of arrangements, conventions, and agreements, and the subtle differences between them. Moreover, it begs two critical questions.

First, this analysis is based on the assumption that a unified account of the social can be given, because social phenomena are essentially homogeneous: that those phenomena we characterize as social share some common property or relation. Yet, at least on first inspection, phenomena such as mobs, poetry clubs, financial markets, insect communication, cashing a check, and the like, form a rather heterogeneous set. If any concept looks like a prime candidate for a Wittgensteinian (1953) analysis in terms of 'family resemblances' rather than in terms of essential properties (in terms of necessary and sufficient conditions), it is surely the concept of the social (which is a nice irony, since the concept of the social plays such an essential and unifying role in Wittgenstein's later philosophy). Second, it also assumes that those types of actions, groups, and relations that were the focus of Enlightenment social theorists remain the dominant and sustaining dimensions of advanced technological and postmodern human life— that, for example, the forms of democracy characteristic of the city-states of ancient Greece and modern Europe remain alive and well in 'representative' postmodern democracies whose business is to an ever increasing degree conducted in cyberspace.

## II

The essays in this volume reflect the variety of positions adopted to the demarcation question by contemporary theorists. Some contributors attempt to address the question directly. Others find it problematic. Others wonder whether there is (or remains) any distinctive class of phenomena that are uniquely characterizable as social.

Margaret Gilbert, in "Concerning Sociality: The Plural Subject as Paradigm," provides a characterization of essentially social phenomena in terms of 'plural subject' phenomena: a phenomenon is social if and only if—or to the degree that—participants consider themselves as 'plural subjects' who are jointly committed to an action, belief, set of values, and the like. Such joint commitments create a special kind of 'bond' between individuals that involves a 'new and constraining motivational force'. What Gilbert does is to identify a paradigm case of sociality—namely, plural subject phenomena—and characterize other candidates as more or less social according to the degree to which they approximate this paradigm.

In contrast, Walter L. Wallace, in "A Definition of Social Phenomena for the Social Sciences," defines social phenomena as any form of 'interorganismic behavior regularity', in which organism B regularly manifests a behavior given the manifestation of a behavior by organism A. Although his analysis would include many if not all the characteristically human behaviors that Gilbert characterizes as social, it is equally clear that it also includes many phenomena Gilbert would reject as genuinely social phenomena, such as some interpersonal human acts of aggression and the interorganismic regularities of the anthill and beehive. According to Wallace, a virtue of his definition is that it does not involve any essential reference to distinctly human properties (such as consciousness), enabling him to avoid what he sees as artificial anthropocentric restrictions on the subject matter of social science. His purely behavioral definition allows him to establish much closer links between social science and the rest of natural science, especially biological science.

Another significant difference is evident between the approaches of Gilbert and Wallace. Gilbert, like many other social theorists, comes very close to characterizing social phenomena in terms of those phenomena that require a social explanation (in terms of joint commitments, beliefs, projects, and the like). Wallace, in contrast, produces a purely descriptive definition of social phenomena that is quite neutral with respect to explanatory issues. Accordingly, for Wallace, it is an open question whether social phenomena have social explanations.

Paul F. Secord, in "The Mark of the Social in the Social Sciences," surveys a number of different approaches to social phenomena advanced by psychologists, symbolic interactionists, ethnomethodologists, anthropologists, and sociologists, discussing their strengths and weaknesses. He locates the mark of the social in the manner in which many interpersonal human actions and practices are constituted by shared forms of representations and relations: behaviors, practices, and enduring interpersonal regularities are socially constituted as social actions, social rituals, and social institutions by the networks of relations and representations within which they are embedded. Secord's analysis appears to mark a middle ground between the views of Gilbert and Wallace, by offering a richer characterization of social phenomena that does not appear, however, to presuppose that all social phenomena have social explanations.

Scott Gordon, in "How Many Kinds of Things Are There in the World? The Ontological Status of Societies," claims that social phenomena represent a distinct and emergent type of ontological entity. Among the natural kinds of things in the world, we may distinguish mechanisms, organized according to physical laws; organisms, organized by DNA instructions; and human societies, organized by customs, political systems, and market exchange processes. The form of organization of human societies is categorically distinct from (albeit parasitic on) familiar forms of material and biological organization. According to Gordon, the form of organization characteristic of human societies enables them to achieve ends unattainable by individual members alone.

Significantly, Gordon does not ground his distinction between organisms and societies in terms of any fundamental distinction between biological and human beings. Both biological and human beings (like the physical beings that constitute mechanisms) are nothing more or less than complexes of fundamental particles; the difference lies entirely in their different modes of organization. In this way Gordon is able to develop an entirely naturalistic account of human sociality that maintains its distinctive nature.

One might wonder whether human societies are quite so distinct. Some putative animal 'societies', such as those of ants and primates, seem to manifest elements of 'economic cooperation' and 'hierarchical ordering' characteristic of markets and political systems, yet they also appear to be maintained by chemical signals or inherited behavioral propensities. Nonetheless, it would be a mistake to assume that the recognition of levels of organization among animals analogous to those of humans shows that human sociality can be reductively explained in terms of chemical signals or inherited biological propensities. For, as Jonathan H. Turner originally and convincingly argues in "The Nature and Dynamics of 'The Social' among Humans," humans are the most social animals because they are innately low-sociality primates, in the sense of having few behavioral propensities for strong kinship ties and thus cohesive and continuous group structures.

According to Turner, the criterion for differentiating degrees of sociality among animal species is "the ratio of genetic to nongenetic coding in those communicative processes involved in interaction among the members of a species." The relations and structures organizing members of a species are more social the "more the communicative dynamics are learned, the more they are flexibly constructed in response to circumstances, and the more they reveal complexity in modalities and channels of communication used in interaction." The low sociality evident in existing ape societies and in humans' early hominid ancestors had to be overridden in humans by a wide array of learned interpersonal mechanisms. These were a product of alterations in the neuroanatomy of hominids—a neuroanatomy that evolved for reasons *other than* sociality but that provided the basic wiring for the learned interpersonal mechanisms that enable humans to manifest the highest degrees of sociality.

What Gordon and Turner demonstrate is that naturalism and evolutionary theory are consistent with a robust conception of the special nature of human sociality, but a conception that need not isolate human sociality from the realm of the biological and the physical sciences (as Wallace, for example, fears). However, as Lloyd E. Sandelands argues in "The Body and the Social," we do in practice tend to artifactually isolate the social. By overintellectualizing the social as a structured object of scientific inquiry, we miss the essential mark of the social, namely, our bodily based feelings of society. According to Sandelands, Durkheim was wrong to reject the intuitive, albeit confused, feelings of social actors in favor of the articulated conceptual analyses of social scientists. Theoretical description is not the royal road to the understanding of social phenomena: language "is unsuited to the task because its discursive form is incommensurate with the all-at-once dynamisms of society." Linguistic symbols "multiply unchecked by concerns for their tie to experience." In consequence, theoretical description in social science tends to "outrun its subject." For Sandelands, since our knowledge of society is grounded in bodily feelings, the challenge for social science is to take body as its focus of study. This approach may involve looking to art rather than systematic science as the source of our symbols: gestures, totems, logos, mascots, artworks, chants, song, and architecture may better convey the 'vital substance' of the social.

For Peter Manicas, in "Social Explanation," the important issue is not so much the demarcation of social phenomena but the proper understanding of the complexity and contingency of social explanation. Manicas characterizes the social in terms of those features of the human environment "other than the concrete acts of individuals," which, of course, suggests that what we call 'social mechanisms' may have little or nothing in common. Manicas dismisses attempts to discriminate correlations between macro- or microsocial variables, in order to identify the cause or causes of social behavior. According to Manicas, these misdirected inquiries are based on wildly misguided empiricist assumptions about causality and causal explanation, themselves based on the discredited principle of 'regularity determinism'. Manicas's own realist account of causality and social mechanisms emphasizes the complexity and interdependence of the varied elements comprising social mechanisms. This view allows Manicas to "make a place for genuine human agency," albeit enabled and constrained by the institutional forms and structures of the social world—forms and structures that promote and protect the interests of some and condemn others to poverty and crime.

For many, any appeal to social forms or structures marks an unwelcome return to the reification and mystification of Durkheim. Joseph Margolis's subtle analysis in "The Meaning of 'Social' " explains why a rejection of explanatory appeals to structured social entities need not lead one to embrace the equally doubtful virtues of 'methodological individualism' or 'methodological solipsism'. According to Margolis, social structure is not a property of populations that emerges when individuals are aggregated to form a new type of 'structured' entity. He denies that there are any social or collective entities that may be appealed to in putative causal explanations, but he insists that there are *collective properties*—language and other 'lingual' powers—attributable to persons who both comprise and constitute the social world.

Margolis argues that all those who postulate emergent collectivities (such as Durkheim, Gilbert, and perhaps Manicas) run foul of a version of the paradox exploited in Rousseau's social contract theory. The status assigned members of a structured collective is already presupposed by the notion of their being parties to its practices: "to form a social group is already to share the collective competence to do so." Ontological accounts of social collectivity thus offer impoverished conceptions of the social, by failing to recognize that the cultural competencies of persons standardly appealed to in explaining the formation of social collectives are themselves preformed as *collective* competencies of persons, through their internalization of "the natural language and associated practices of the society in which they mature from infancy." The true 'mark of the social' begins—and ends, according to Margolis—with these collective competencies.

Rom Harré, in "Crews, Clubs, Crowds, and Classes: 'The Social' as a Discursive Category," recognizes some intriguing and problematic differences among social phenomena but resists any attempt to formalize these differences into distinct ontological kinds. Harré argues that it is the discursive nature (broadly construed) of most human (and some animal) practices that leads us to suppose that there is a distinctive type of phenomena demarcable as social. Accordingly, he suggests that social phenomena are nothing more or less than an especially interesting variety of essentially discursive processes, of which human language is perhaps the most significant exemplar, and that these phenomena presuppose a radically different ontology, of positions in discursive space, that is only very loosely related to the material conditions that instantiate and sustain them. In a dramatic illustration of the essentially linguistic form of the discursive dynamics of modern social life, he imagines the social world devoid of language and writing:

> It is salutary to wander around downtown Washington and imagine the sound turned off, the marks on the trillions of pieces of paper fading into illegibility and so on. What would there then be? Some primates in a warren? Legislative acts, tax demands, investigations of savings and loan scams, the scams themselves, press conferences, debates, changes in the base rate, and so on, are through and through and exhaustively characterizable as discursive. They are one and all forms of conversation. (p. 204)

Margolis and Harré, in their own idiosyncratic ways, nevertheless maintain the distinctive nature of those phenomena conventionally characterized as social. Kenneth J. Gergen, with a touch of reflexive irony in this context, maintains his social constructionist credentials in "Social Theory in Context: Relational Humanism." Social constructionism denies that ordinary or theoretical language serves to represent reality or describe the essential properties of kinds of things. Rather, physical, biological, and psychological realities are socially constructed through the use of language, which serves to promote a variety of competing social, political, and moral positions. Consistently, but nevertheless problematically, Gergen maintains that social reality is itself a social construction through language, which does not describe social structures and processes but rather promotes various political and moral agendas.

Although this position appears to endorse a rampant relativism and undermine the most revered principles of liberal humanism, Gergen suggests that although we must abandon our cherished notions of intellectual privilege, the social-constructionist position illustrates the relational embeddedness of all significant human activities. Consequently, according to Gergen, it enables us to discriminate radically different but no less humane forms of action, engagement, and accounting.

For some this might seem perilously close (for a social constructionist) to an account of the essential dimension of the social (in terms of the relational embeddedness of significant human activity). That is, Gergen's avowedly social-constructionist analysis contains a residual dash of realism, insofar as it at least points to a distinct set of practices. Tim Ingold, in "Life beyond the Edge of Nature?, Or, The Mirage of Society," abandons even this tenuous hold. For Ingold, there is no defensible distinction between the world of nature and the social world: there are no grounds for supposing that those relations we characterize as social relations hold exclusively between human beings. Relations of production, history, socialization, language, and social interaction, which are normally held to be distinctive features of uniquely human sociality, are continuous with the relations of organic life and include relations between humans and animals, plants, and inanimate objects. Ingold does not, however, eliminate the social in any reductive fashion. Just as there is no region "beyond the edge of nature" in which humans lead distinctly social lives, there is no discrete world of nature "behind the domain of real, embodied relationships" between humans, animals, plants, and inanimate objects.

In the final contribution to the volume, "The Reversible Imaginary: Baudrillard and the End of the Social," Raymond L. M. Lee notes how our traditional conception of the social is rooted in the Enlightenment notion of a civil society, a conception that has been continuously threatened by the development of capitalism (which it enabled). The self-serving bourgeois reification of rights and roles in the social order has in postmodern times "been supplanted by its thinglike shadow in commodity structure." This has led some theorists, notably Baudrillard, to jettison the social and "all its conceptual inventions encapsulated within the power of linear time." Lee follows Baudrillard's poststructuralist journey from a philosophy of the subject to a philosophy of the object. He documents Baudrillard's initial deconstruction of civil society through a critique of commodity structure, and his subsequent focus on the dominance of "signs and simulacra"—the period in which Baudrillard established himself as the "incontrovertible theorist of hyperreality." In the final and most radical phase of Baudrillard's philosophy, the subject and social are obliterated, consumed by the "vertigo of serial signs" and "the cool universe of digitality." Baudrillard introduces us to a totally different world of

"nonrational causality in which the social is totally excommunicated"—the world of the "reversible imaginary."

Many theorists are likely to dismiss these explorations as poststructuralist indulgence. After all, liberalism and the notion of a civil society
seem to be enjoying a new renaissance, given the collapse of commu-
nism and the relentless pursuit of modernity by developing countries.
Yet Lee suggests this may be illusory: the advent of information
highways and cyperspace may have rendered the social superfluous,
and Baudrillard's vision a reality.

## III

The brief characterizations offered here do no justice to the subtleties
and complexities of the positions advanced by the contributors to this
volume. I have only tried to give the reader some indication of the
many differences between the approaches offered. These fundamental
differences demonstrate the essentially contested nature of our concept of the social and remind us that the sort of inquiry developed in
this volume is itself but a moment in the social process by which
concepts—including concepts of the social—are reformed and developed.

Like it or not, this dynamic feature seems itself to be an established
fact of social life. Rather than attempt to defend or deny it, commend
or bemoan it, I invite the reader to engage in the dialogue engendered
by the provocative contributions to this volume.

### Notes

1. Durkheim (1895/1982:59) also cites another common property of social
phenomena—namely, their 'generality'—but is careful to stress that this is not
a 'distinguishing feature' of social phenomena (since it is a property shared by
many psychological and biological phenomena).

2. "We do not say that social facts are material things, but that they are
things just as are material things" (Durkheim 1901/1982:35).

3. As is well known, Durkheim also to tried to characterize social phenomena or 'social facts' in terms of statistical facts about social groups, such as
statistical facts about differential rates of suicide among different age, gender,
and religious groups. However, this characterization of social phenomena
fares no better than his earlier one in terms of 'externality' and 'constraint',
for it also fails to delineate the 'distinct characteristics' of social phenomena.

Social facts do not appear to be social by virtue of their statistical nature. There would appear to be plenty of statistical facts about populations that are not themselves social facts, such as differential death rates for populations defined in terms of diet or geographic location. This suggests that certain statistical facts about populations are only social facts by virtue of their being facts about those populations that are social groups. That is, Durkheim's characterization of social facts as statistical facts does not explicate the social nature of such facts. It presupposes, but does not provide, some independent account of the social nature of some populations that enables us to characterize certain statistical facts about populations as statistical facts about social groups—that is, as social facts.

4. Such phenomena were, however, cited as examples of social phenomena in the 1935 edition of C. L. Murchison's *Handbook of Social Psychology*.

## References

Durkheim, Émile. 1895/1982. *The Rules of Sociological Method*, ed. Steven Lukes, trans. W. D. Halls. New York: Macmillan.

———. 1901/1982 "Preface to Second Edition." Pp. 34–47 of *The Rules of Sociological Method,* ed. Steven Lukes, trans. W. D. Halls. New York: Macmillan.

Gilbert, Margaret. 1991. *On Social Facts*. Princeton, N.J.: Princeton University Press.

Greenwood, John D. 1994. *Realism, Identity and Emotion*. London: Sage.

Murchison, Charles L. 1935. *Handbook of Social Psychology*. Worcester, Mass.: Clark University Press.

Weber, Max. 1922. *Economy and Society*, Vols. I and II, ed. Guenther Roth and Claus Wittich. Berkeley: University of California Press.

Wittgenstein, Ludwig. 1953. *Philosophical Investigations*. Oxford: Blackwell.

## Chapter 1

# Concerning Sociality: The Plural Subject as Paradigm

*Margaret Gilbert*

The adjective 'social' has been applied to a wide range of quite disparate phenomena.[1] So wide a range, indeed, that one may well wonder about the importance of sociality.[2] Is there a plausible way of characterizing—perhaps recharacterizing—sociality, such that it is without doubt something important?

In my book *On Social Facts* and elsewhere, I have argued that what I call *plural subjects* are central components of human life.[3] I have proposed that *social groups*—in a standard everyday sense—are plural subjects. I have also given plural subject accounts of, among other things: agreements, social rules and conventions, collective beliefs, group languages, and doing something together (for instance, working on a problem together, walking together, conversing). People form plural subjects when they are jointly committed to doing something as a body. The meaning of this brief characterization will be clarified later.[4]

In this chapter I present an argument for characterizing sociality in terms of plural subjecthood. The structure of my argument is as follows. The plural subject phenomena are the paradigmatic, or preeminent, social phenomena. They are also phenomena of great importance. They merit and repay serious study in their own right. If plural subjecthood is the mark of the social, the social is something worth marking. It would be a great loss to our self-understanding were the existence and consequential nature of plural subjects lost sight of through the blur of a broader notion of sociality. These points together

17

make a good case for characterizing—perhaps recharacterizing—social phenomena as plural subject phenomena.[5]

## The Broad Use of the Adjective 'Social'

The adjective 'social' has been applied to a wide variety of disparate phenomena. Thus, each of the following items would be judged to be 'social' phenomena according to some existing usage.

1. someone inadvertently dropping a morsel of food, which later is picked up by someone else
2. someone unintentionally imitating another's gait
3. someone searching for the perfect partner
4. someone dressing carefully in order to look good at an interview
5. someone pushing another person off a cliff
6. people entering an agreement
7. people conversing on a street corner
8. a committee in session
9. a coronation ceremony
10. two nations at war

One could add a flock of geese flying in formation and a dog barking at a cat.

Precisely why the listed items might be thought of as 'social' is not immediately obvious. Nor have philosophers or social scientists arrived at any one agreed-on account of what counts as a 'social' phenomenon, insofar as they have devoted any serious attention to this issue.[6]

## A Broad Account of Sociality

In earlier work I proposed a broad account of our everyday concept of sociality.[7] This was developed on the basis of a variety of actual uses of the adjective 'social' in relation to the human realm.[8] One or another person had apparently felt comfortable with each of these uses, which also seemed to have something to be said for them. My aim was to encompass these uses in a principled way. I made no attempt to weed out some uses as 'derivative', 'secondary', 'extended', and the like. Some of the phenomena in question, however, did seem to be more clearly 'social' than others. I therefore attempted also to capture the idea that there are degrees of socialness.

This account had two parts. The main part characterizes sociality:

1.  A phenomenon is a social phenomenon if and only if it involves one person's being connected either mentally or in some causal way with another person or persons.

A subsidiary part gave an account of degrees of sociality (or 'socialness'):

2.  The degree of 'socialness' of a phenomenon is in general directly correlated with the amount and degree of mental connectedness between persons that it involves, and with the amount and degree of causal connectedness between persons, where some mental connection always has priority over any causal connection.

A word should be said about what is meant here by 'mental connection'. Roughly, one person is mentally connected with another if the first person has the other in mind in some way. The relation of mental connectedness is thus not symmetrical: A can be mentally connected with B without B being mentally connected with A.[9]

The sociologist Max Weber defined a 'social action' as, roughly, one that takes account of another person and is thereby oriented in its course.[10] One who performs a 'social action' in Weber's stipulative sense would, clearly, count as mentally connected with another person. One can be mentally connected to another person in my sense, however, without performing a Weberian social action in regard to them. Thus, one might be thinking about a certain person while mowing the lawn. One's action of mowing the lawn would not count as a social action in Weber's sense, since one would not be 'orienting one's action' in relation to the other person. What Weber might judge to be 'subsocial', then, this account allows to be social.

This account correlates degrees of socialness with the amount and degree of mental connectedness in a situation. The idea that there are degrees of mental connectedness came from examples like the following. One who performs an action that is social in Weber's sense appears to be more closely mentally connected with another person than someone who is simply thinking about them. If Jim is walking to meet Mary, he is not only thinking about Mary but also doing something on account of her. She is, if you like, not only on his mind but affecting his will.

Let us consider some aspects of the aforementioned account of sociality. For present purposes we may call it, for short, 'the broad account'. It is, evidently, quite capacious, encompassing a wide range of actual uses of the term 'social'.[11]

Something about the broad account that may give one pause is that, given the account, the importance of sociality as such is not obvious. In particular, it is not obviously something worthy of study in its own right. If the broad account tells us what sociality is, we might well wonder why we should care about sociality. In this respect the account does not differ from a number of other broad accounts of sociality that have been proposed.[12]

A special feature of the broad account just presented is that it incorporates the notion of degrees of sociality. It thus suggests some new questions. Is there a kind of phenomenon that is apt to be judged the most highly social kind? If so, might sociality, or sociality proper, be defined in terms of this most highly social kind of thing? I now turn to these questions.


## Common Knowledge and Mutual Expectations

### Common Knowledge

In the light of the broad account, it might be proposed that the most highly social phenomenon is what has come to be called 'common knowledge'.[13]

Suppose that Jane has just fallen on the ice, right in front of Peter. In normal circumstances, it would then be common knowledge between Jane and Peter that Jane has just fallen on the ice.

The following is probably the standard definition in both philosophy and economics: The fact that $p$ is *common knowledge* between persons A and B if and only if (i) A knows that $p;$ (ii) B knows that $p$; (iii) A knows that B knows that $p$; (iv) B knows that A knows that $p$, and so on, ad infinitum.

It is not necessary to debate the realism of the notion of common knowledge so defined (people have queried the 'ad infinitum' in particular).[14] It is fairly clear that we sometimes go at least some way up the scale of *knowing about knowing*. In the previous example, assuming that Jane and Peter know each other, it will presumably be true at least that (1) Jane knows that she has just fallen on the ice, (2) Peter knows that Jane has just fallen on the ice, (3) Jane knows that Peter knows that she has just fallen on the ice, and (4) Peter knows that Jane knows that she has fallen on the ice. And it is not unreasonable to suppose that each one's knowledge of what the other knows will go further than this.

According to the broad account, a situation in which points (1) to (4) were true would itself appear to count as relatively highly social. Each of the parties is mentally connected to the other through their knowledge of them. Each level of 'knowing about knowing' makes for more mental connection.

Let us suppose for the sake of argument that there is common knowledge according to the standard definition. Would phenomena involving common knowledge be the most highly social phenomena? One might wonder how to go about answering this question. One way is to see whether one can find a phenomenon that seems to be more highly social from an intuitive point of view.

Charles Taylor has argued that when there is common knowledge of some fact something important may still be lacking.[15] Consider the following cases (derived from Taylor). First case: two strangers are walking along side by side in the heat. It is common knowledge between them that it is hot. Second case: the same as the first, but then one says to the other, glancing over at him, "Whew! It's hot!" The other replies "You bet!"

Taylor proposes that in the second case, and that alone, the fact that it is very hot is *'entre nous'*, or 'in public space'—after the words have been exchanged.

I shall not pursue Taylor's characterization of the difference between these cases in terms of something now being *'entre nous'* or 'in public space'. The examples suggest, however, that social, and indeed highly social, as common knowledge may be, there is something apt to be judged more 'social' than common knowledge. Perhaps it would not be going too far to say that any generic account of sociality that fails to indicate what this something is will have failed in some way. In any case, it appears that in our search for the most highly social phenomenon, we cannot stop with common knowledge or approximations to it.

## Mutual Expectations

A second suggestion about the acme of sociality in human relations, with a similar flavor, comes from a consideration of the type of situation studied in the mathematical theory of games.

Consider a typical coordination problem.[16] Harry is going to be at Grand Central Station around noon today and so is Sally. Each wants to meet the other. Neither one cares where they meet. All this is common knowledge. Where should each one go?

Suppose that last week they ran into one another by chance near the information kiosk. Each one remembers this and reasonably supposes that the other will also. For reasons we need not question, each now expects that the other will go to the kiosk today.[17] In addition, each expects the other to expect him or her to go to the kiosk. Such a set of mutual expectations can play an important role in the solution of a coordination problem. Given his personal preferences, and in the light of his expectations about Sally, reinforced by his expectations about her expectations about him, given his knowledge of her preferences, it will be reasonable for Harry to go to the kiosk. The same goes for Sally, *mutatis mutandis*.

Perhaps there can be higher and higher levels of expectation about expectation, as David Lewis has envisaged. Perhaps they can be imagined to go on ad infinitum. We would then have an 'expectations' analogue of common knowledge. Let us assume that we have this. Do we have a plausible candidate for the most highly social phenomenon?[18]

A problem here is this. As the example indicates, there can be a set of mutual expectations, helping to give rise to action, even though the parties use their expectations about others' actions and expectations purely as a predictive tool that will allow them to reach their own personal ends.

Those who, in relation to their fellows, operate purely in terms of their own personal preferences and their expectations of others (along with any relevant beliefs about the others' expectations and preferences) appear to be quite 'far apart' from one another, metaphorically speaking. Less metaphorically, each person views the relevant others in a way that could be characterized as completely detached and external.

Though 'mentally connected' in a way, these people are, one might say, in no way *unified*. Though everyone may end up better off, thanks to the actions of all, they are not partners in any meaningful sense; they partake of no real bond.[19]

It may well be that many of us often relate to one another in a detached, external way, a way that does not itself involve anything we would naturally refer to as a bond or a genuine unity of distinct persons. Is there not, however, another dimension to human life, a dimension involving much more saliently ties, links, bonds, connections? Both our everyday language (with such terms as 'bond' and so on) and our theoretical discourse (with such terms as a 'real unity') suggest that there is.[20]

I would now propose that, from the point of view of our unanalyzed everyday understanding, states of affairs in which it is clearly appropriate to speak of a 'real unity' between people, to speak of a 'bond' or 'tie' between them, have a higher degree of sociality than do mutual expectations or common knowledge or combinations of the two. One might conjecture that the clearest case of a real unity, or bond, or tie, will be the paradigmatically 'social' state of affairs.[21] Etymology supports this idea, given that our term 'social' comes from the Latin *socius*, associate or ally. It is plausible to suppose that Taylor's situation in which some fact is '*entre nous*' is of this type. The question, of course, is, What states of affairs are these? I shall shortly sketch an answer to this question.[22]

## The Plural Subject Concepts

How might human beings constitute a 'real unity'? Much as Hobbes and Rousseau, the classical contract theorists, proposed in discussing the 'social contract'. I draw here on my own understanding of the matter.

I believe that human beings standardly operate in terms of a family of concepts that I have called the 'plural subject' concepts.[23] These concepts involve a special unifying principle or mechanism, which I have labeled 'joint commitment'.[24]

### An Example: Walking Together

I shall introduce the plural subject concepts here by focusing briefly on the case of two people out on a walk together, or (as I shall put it) walking together.[25] The great German sociologist Georg Simmel wrote that "sociation ranges all the way from the momentary getting together for a walk to the founding of a family," acknowledging walking together as an example for sociology.[26]

As it turns out, it is not easy to say what it is for two people to be walking together. Presumably some behavioral condition must be fulfilled. For present purposes I shall take it that to walk together, two people must walk alongside each other.[27] Clearly, however, to be walking together in the sense in question here, it is not enough for two people simply to be walking along side by side. Something appropriate must be going on in their minds. What is hard is to say precisely what this something is.

It might be suggested that two people will be walking together if (roughly) each wants to walk along beside the other, and this is common knowledge. Or, bearing in mind Charles Taylor's remarks, it might be suggested that each person must tell the other of his desire so to walk. However, neither of these accounts is sufficient.[28] Here is one telling difference between a clear case of walking together and the conditions stipulated in these accounts.

Suppose you and I are walking together (by hypothesis). You begin to lag behind. Failing some special circumstance, both of us will understand that it is perfectly reasonable for me to rebuke you for this in some way. Thus, I might turn and say in a mildly rebuking tone, "Hey, it's hard for me to walk so slowly!"

In contrast, suppose that you and I are simply walking along side by side, both desiring to do so, and this is common knowledge. This could be true of two strangers, and let us suppose that we are indeed strangers. You begin to lag behind. I will presumably be disappointed. I may wonder why you have slowed down, given that you want to keep up with me. Meanwhile, it is by no means clear that we will both understand that my rebuking you would be in order. One might say that no clear basis has been established between us for my rebuking you. The same appears to be true in the case in which each of us has informed the other of his or her desire that we walk alongside each other. Unless more has been communicated than this, no basis for a rebuke has yet been established between us.[29]

If two people understand that they are walking together, they will automatically, for that reason, understand that it is appropriate for one to rebuke the other should the other make it hard for them to walk alongside each other. Such minute and humdrum observations as this point, I believe, to a profoundly important aspect of human relations. This cannot be captured by appeal to such things as similar goals and common knowledge of similar goals.

In this context it is natural to bring up the notion of a contract or (even more naturally) an agreement. People who are walking together, as so far described, certainly act *as if* they have agreed to walk along side by side for a while. Those who enter agreements understand that if one party defaults, the other has a basis for issuing a rebuke. Those who enter agreements are understood, more precisely, to take on obligations toward one another, obligations (among other things) to fulfill the terms of the agreement. If one fails to fulfill his obligation to another, the aggrieved party has a basis for rebuke.

Problems arise, however, in appealing specifically to agreements in order to explain what it is for people to be walking together. For one thing, it is not clear that an agreement is required to initiate the process of walking together. More significantly, however, the concept of an agreement itself stands in need of explication. We shall eventually need to ask what an agreement amounts to and how it obligates the parties to it.

In both the philosophical and legal literature, an agreement is standardly assumed to be an exchange of promises. As I have argued elsewhere, however, typical agreements do not seem to be promise exchanges. Rather, we need to appeal to the notion of a *joint commitment* in saying what an agreement is.[30]

In my view the notion of joint commitment, discussed later, is the key to understanding both agreements and many other phenomena such as walking together. In other words, the concept of an agreement (or of a contract) is not fundamental for our understanding of walking together and related concepts. The fundamental concept here is, rather, the concept of joint commitment.

I propose that what is crucial to walking together is this: the parties understand that they are jointly committed to espousing as a body the goal of their walking along side by side. Those who are jointly committed to doing A as a body, for any A, constitute (in my terminology) the *plural subject* of doing A.

### Joint Commitment

I must now at least roughly characterize the fundamental concept of joint commitment, as I understand it. I shall focus on the case of a joint commitment involving two individuals.

You and I enter a particular joint commitment by expressing to one another, in conditions of common knowledge, our individual readiness to enter the joint commitment. In effect, each of us expresses the following: I understand that just in case my expression of readiness is matched by one from you, each of us will be party to the relevant joint commitment. For example, I reach out my hand to shake yours; you put your hand out to meet mine. These gestures are common knowledge. We are now jointly committed to shaking hands.

But what is it for us to be jointly committed? A joint commitment is neither mine, nor yours, nor the simple conjunction of a commitment that is mine and a commitment that is yours. It is, rather, *our* commitment, the commitment of me and you. If you and I have a joint commitment, each of us is committed. So we can perhaps speak of our 'individual commitments' under the joint commitment. These individual commitments, however, are interdependent. If we are jointly committed, each one's individual commitment stands or falls with the individual commitment of the other. They cannot exist apart. Thus, you and I can only come by the relevant 'individual commitments' simultaneously. Nor can one of these commitments be sustained in the absence of the other.[31]

Consistent with the idea that our joint commitment is the commitment of me and you, it can only be abrogated or rescinded by both of us together. In this respect a joint commitment is like a locked door that needs two keys to open it: you (irrevocably) have one key and I (irrevocably) have the other, and both must be used in order that the door be unlocked. In contrast, a personal decision is like a locked door that needs only one key, and the person whose decision it is (irrevocably) has that key: a personal change of mind.[32]

In my view, the precise nature of a joint commitment is crucial for our understanding of such phenomena as walking together, with their attendant rebukes, apologies, and so on. Suppose that you and I have a joint commitment to uphold as a body the goal of walking alongside each other for some roughly specified period of time. As we both understand, that does not simply mean that I am committed to walking alongside you. It means that I am subject to a commitment that is under our joint control.

A natural way of putting things here is this: if I fail to do what I can to walk alongside you, I violate a right that you have to my walking alongside you, a right that our joint commitment provides. Alternatively, I fail in an *obligation* I have to you. Once the special nature of joint commitment is spelled out in these terms, the basis you have for rebuking me if I fail to do certain things becomes clear.[33]

So much, then, for joint commitment, and the way the hypothesis of an underlying joint commitment fits the phenomenon of walking together, complete with its apparent provision of a basis for rebukes. Similar things can be said with respect to 'shared actions' in general, to traveling together, working on a problem together, and so on.

## Plural Subjects in General

Though the term 'plural subject' is hardly an everyday one, plural subjects are, I take it, common or garden phenomena. I take it that a standard way of referring to a particular plural subject is by means of the first-person plural pronoun 'we'. Indeed, it can be argued that the use of 'we' to refer to a plural subject is a central and salient one.[34]

The interpretation of statements with premises about 'us' as statements about plural subjects in my technical sense helps explain the propriety of certain inferences first noted (to my knowledge) by Wilfrid Sellars. For example, it appears that from the premises "We are mounting an attack on the compound" and "I can best help our cause by keeping quiet and doing nothing," I can immediately infer that I have reason to keep quiet and do nothing, though "We are mounting an attack . . ." does not imply that I personally aim or intend to support our endeavor. If "We are mounting an attack . . ." is understood to imply the existence of a joint commitment in which I am a participant, then it becomes clear how I can infer that I have reason to keep quiet and do nothing without appealing to a personal intention to support our endeavor (or an independent personal commitment of some other kind).[35]

Plural subject formation creates a new motivational force, a singular type of force, in terms of which each of two or more people understand they must act, all else being equal, unless they concur in its dissolution. If they fail to act appropriately, they risk being approached in a corrective—indeed, a punitive—fashion by the other parties.

I take it that shared action is but one example of a context in which people form plural subjects or, in other words, jointly commit to doing something as a body.[36]

I have argued at length elsewhere that all of the following, among other things, are plural subject phenomena: everyday agreements, social rules,[37] social conventions,[38] group languages,[39] shared actions, the beliefs of groups,[40] and social groups themselves, at least in the sense that lies behind many of the lists of example groups given by sociologists and others, a sense I take to be a central one.[41] I shall not rehearse the arguments here. Suffice it to say that there is reason to believe that plural subjects are ubiquitous features of everyday human life.

## Sociality and the Plural Subject

Plural subjecthood involves a type of 'mental connection' between persons, the connection achieved by a joint commitment. According to the broad account of sociality previously considered, then, plural subject phenomena would certainly be social phenomena. Considering what might be judged the most highly social phenomena, we have seen reason to go beyond that account of sociality, in search of a particular type of mental connectedness.

I conjectured that the most highly social phenomenon from the point of view of our implicit everyday understanding will be the clearest case of a 'bond' or 'real unity' between persons. Plural subjecthood involves a salient and distinctive type of bond, a joint commitment that links people together and obligates them to each other. The commitment unites them precisely by virtue of its jointness. It is hard to see what closer general type of *association*—or at least mental association—there could be than participation in plural subjecthood. Given the underlying joint commitment, one could say that the parties have (in one respect) fused into a single entity, the plural subject.[42]

The existence and implicit knowledge of plural subjecthood would help explain, and indeed justify, the existence of a 'holist' position regarding social groups. The social whole (qua plural subject) may not be greater in value than the sum of the parts, but we can give a precise sense to the idea that the whole is distinct from the sum of the parts. This is the way to look at joint commitment itself: it is not the sum of two 'individual commitments', if such commitments are understood to be independent. And I propose that joint commitment is the foundation of paradigmatic social groups.[43]

If one were to ask for lists of paradigmatic social phenomena, before any analytic investigation into their nature, it would be plausible to cite agreements, social rules and conventions, the languages of groups, shared actions, social groups themselves, and so on. Insofar as all of these are plural subject phenomena, that supports the idea that plural subject phenomena are the most highly social ones from the point of view of our unanalyzed, implicit understanding of such matters. Assuming all this is right, is sociality, or sociality proper, to be understood in terms of the plural subject? Are things 'social' by virtue of being or involving plural subjects? Are broader uses of the predicate 'social' best seen as a matter of extending the notion to things that are related to plural subjects in some significant or even relatively tangential way?

It is possible that the breadth of actual uses could be explained by reference to connections, close or far, to plural subjecthood. To say any such thing is, of course, to speculate. This speculation has, I would think, some plausibility.

Suppose that we do not wish to be speculative, however, but are willing to be somewhat stipulative. The broad way in which the predicate 'social' has come to be used leads to accounts of sociality with great sweep, such that the importance of sociality as such is not obvious. If we want a notion of sociality that gives sociality as such an obvious importance, how might we best restrict our notion of sociality? If plural subject phenomena are, as I have suggested, the most highly social kind of phenomena, they would provide a plausible answer. Some brief words on the importance of plural subjects follow.

## The Importance of Plural Subjects

If I am right, humans act through much of their lives in terms of plural subjecthood. No possible explanation of the actual cognitive background of human behavior and practical reasoning could be complete, or even barely adequate, without appeal to plural subject concepts.

There is a good contrast here with Weber's technical concept of social action. It seems perfectly possible that most human beings never employ Weber's social action concept themselves. They never think ''I am taking account of the behavior of another animate being and orienting my behavior by reference to it.'' In contrast, anyone who ever thinks that 'we (collectively)' are doing something is employing the concept of a plural subject as is whoever thinks that 'we (collectively)' believe something, or 'we (collectively)' intend something, and so on.[44]

Not only is the concept of a plural subject ubiquitous in everyday human thought, but it affects the character of human life in a radical way. Were we to limit ourselves, conceptually, to the individual agent with its own independent preferences, beliefs, and commitments, we would overlook the possibility of joint commitment. Limited as described previously, we could contemplate a type of mutual dependence. You and I might depend on one another to meet our individual goals. I would, one might then say, need your cooperation to meet my goal. It is not clear how different each one's dependence here really is from a dependence on the natural world. The fact that there is a mutual dependence does not clearly affect either of us radically, though the relevance of mutual expectations may lead to complex situations involving numerous levels of expectations. Meanwhile, a newly formed joint commitment produces a radical change in each of us, for it involves a new and constraining motivational force: a force that ties people together, a bond.

Those who form a plural subject are linked in a unique and uniquely intimate way. In relation to some domain of activity, these people have, so to speak, "pooled their wills." They have, if you like, made "one will" out of disparate wills. By entering into a joint commitment, each now shares a power over a certain domain that was hitherto his own. Neither one can be said to be "in the other's hands," exactly. Rather, both are in the hands of both. Both are in the hands of the plural subject they form. If sociality is, in effect, plural subjecthood, sociality is, it must be acknowledged, a distinctive and consequential phenomenon, which helps structure the life of all actual human beings.[45]

As I have already indicated, there is reason to believe that an understanding of the structure of the plural subject concepts can help us understand some key normative concepts, including the concepts of an obligation and a right. The obligations of agreements and promises, in particular, appear to be understandable in terms of joint commitment. If this is right, an understanding of the plural subject concepts will be mandatory for those who are concerned with such matters, including moral, political, and legal theorists.[46] Those interested in the languages of groups, such as the English language, will usefully consider the structure of the plural subject concepts.[47] And so on.

Suppose we lost our ability to form plural subjects. For beings like ourselves, who operate to a large extent in terms of reasons for acting, our ability to form plural subjects may be crucial to our ability to coordinate dependably one person's actions with another's.[48] If we could survive as a species without being able to form plural subjects, we would still have lost a powerful tool, a tool whose utility can be indicated by asking what it would be like to be unable to enter agreements or make promises, or to go for a walk together, work on a problem together, and so on, relying on each other's understanding of the nature of joint commitment. Our lives would be severely impoverished and radically transformed.

In sum, if sociality is plural subjectivity, then sociality is of the utmost importance for the student of human life. Without the concept of a plural subject and a thorough understanding of plural subject phenomena, we must fail to understand the human world.

## Conclusion

The range of uses of the predicate 'social' that people find comfortable suggests that sociality is a very broad category. At the same time, there is reason to judge plural subjects to be the most highly social phenomena. They involve a strong, symmetrical type of mental connectedness, producing what one can see as a real unity between distinct persons. It is not implausible to conjecture that plural subjects are implicitly understood to be the social phenomena proper, while other so-called social things are so-called by virtue of their various relations—some quite distant—to plural subjects.

Given an understanding of sociality as plural subjecthood, sociality as such is worthy of study and investigation. However sociality in general is best understood, it is important to understand plural subjecthood. Without such scrutiny, we cannot come close to self-understanding.

## Notes

The original version of this essay, "Concerning Sociality," was an invited presentation at a one-day conference on "The Mark of the Social," held at the Graduate Center, City University of New York (CUNY), April 8, 1994, under the auspices of the CUNY Academy of Arts and Humanities. A later version with a different emphasis, "Is Sociality a Philosophically Significant Category?" appeared in the *Journal of Social Philosophy* (1994) 25:5–25. Material from that version is incorporated here by kind permission of the *Journal of Social Philosophy*. I should like to take this opportunity to thank John Greenwood, the conference organizer, for his enthusiastic support and encouragement of my work on sociality.

1. See the next section.

2. 'Sociality' is something of a technical term derived from the adjective 'social' along the lines of the derivation of 'mentality' from the adjective 'mental'. Instead of 'sociality', one might write 'the nature of social phenomena'. 'Sociality' has the virtue of brevity.

3. See Margaret Gilbert, *On Social Facts* (London: Routledge, 1989; Princeton, NJ: Princeton University Press, 1992) and a number of subsequent articles. Many of these are collected together, some in slightly amended form, in my book *Living Together: Rationality, Sociality, and Obligation* (Lanham, Md: Rowman & Littlefield, 1996).

4. See the later subsection Joint Commitment.

5. Cf. Émile Durkheim, *The Rules of Sociological Method*, trans. W. D.

Halls (New York: Free Press, 1982), Chapter 1. Durkheim argues that certain phenomena (those that have society as their 'substrate') are the phenomena most apt for the label 'social', which label should, then, be reserved for them. In both Durkheim's case and my own, I take it that the underlying concern is to focus the attention of theorists on a particular, important range of phenomena. For discussion of Durkheim's characterization of social phenomena and its relation to plural subject phenomena, see my article "Durkheim and Social Facts, in *Debating Durkheim*, ed. Herminio Martins and William Pickering (London: Routledge, 1994). See also *On Social Facts*, Chapter 5.

6. They have not devoted a great deal. Famous exceptions are Max Weber, Émile Durkheim, and Georg Simmel. For some discussion of the approaches of these authors, see *On Social Facts*, Chapter 2, and later portions of this essay (Weber); *On Social Facts*, Chapter 5, and "Durkheim and Social Facts" (Durkheim); *On Social Facts*, Chapter 4 (Simmel).

7. Margaret Gilbert (1978), doctoral dissertation, Bodleian Library Collection, Oxford University. This monograph has the same title as my book *On Social Facts*. Though these works are both concerned with the nature of social phenomena, and the second is an outgrowth of the first, they are very different in content. The 1989 book introduces *plural subjects* in the sense discussed later.

8. Cf. *On Social Facts*, Chapter 7, section 5.2, regarding my concentration in that book on the human case.

9. One could define a broader notion of mental connection according to which if A is mentally connected with B in the previously described sense, then B is mentally connected with A in this broader sense. (If A is thinking about B, then B is being thought about by A and is thus 'mentally connected' with A in a broad sense.) According to the narrow sense of 'mental connection' in the text, if my mind is empty of all thoughts of you, then I am not mentally connected with you, however much you focus on me.

10. Max Weber, *Economy and Society*, Vols. I and II, ed. Guenther Roth and Claus Wittich (Berkeley: University of California Press, 1978 [1922]) p. 4.

11. It may not be capacious enough to accommodate all of the uses anyone has ever—without obvious bizarreness—felt comfortable with, but given the project of this article that issue can be set aside here.

12. In *Principles of Scientific Sociology* (Chicago: Aldine, 1983) and elsewhere, the sociologist Walter Wallace, who has given the matter sustained attention, characterizes a social phenomenon as an "interorganismic behavior regularity." In *The Common Mind* (Oxford: Oxford University Press, 1993), pp. 119–20, Philip Pettit writes that a property is social just in case its realization requires that a number of individuals evince an intentional response. I question the importance of sociality as such according to these characterizations in "Sociality as a Philosophically Significant Category"; see pp. 6–9. On Wallace, see also my review of his book in *Ethics* (1987) 98:180–81. Max Weber's social action concept is another case in point. This is

not the place to compare and contrast the various broad accounts that have been proposed, but it is worth pointing out that those noted give different boundaries to the territory of sociality, nor is it clear that any one subsumes any other.

13. Following David Lewis, *Convention: A Philosophic Study*, (Cambridge, Mass: Harvard University Press,1969). In an independent discussion in *Meaning*, (Oxford: Oxford University Press, 1972), Stephen Schiffer wrote of 'mutual knowledge', indicating that he was not talking about 'common knowledge' in the everyday sense of the phrase. Also independently, game theorist Robert Aumann introduced what he too called 'common knowledge' into the literature of economics in "Agreeing to Disagree," *Annals of Statistics*, (1976), 4: 16–28.

14. Lewis and Schiffer both contemplate a rather different kind of definition in terms of the existence of a basis for an infinity of inferences. For some related discussion, see Jane Heal,"Common Knowledge," *Philosophical Quarterly* (1978), 28:116–31; Gilbert (1978) and (1989).

15. See, for instance, Taylor's example of the opera-goers in his review of Jonathan Bennett's *Linguistic Behavior* in *Dialogue* (1980) 19:210–18.

16. The term 'coordination problem' comes from David Lewis, 1969. Game theorists tend to talk, rather, of 'coordination games'. There is no need to decide on a precise definition of 'coordination problem' here. For discussion of some problems with Lewis's definition, see my "Game Theory and *Convention*," *Synthese* (1981) 46:41–94. reprinted in *Living Together*.

17. The qualification is suggested by considerations discussed in my articles "Rationality, Coordination, and Convention," *Synthese* (1990) 84:1–21, and "Rationality and Salience," *Philosophical Studies* (1989) 55:61–77 (both reprinted in *Living Together*). Among other things, I argue that a successful precedent does not in itself justify one's conforming to it, nor does the fact that one of the possible combinations of actions 'stands out' from the others.

18. David-Hillel Ruben connects sociality as such and 'nested expectations' in *The Metaphysics of the Social World* (London: Routledge & Kegan Paul, 1985): "a relation P is a social relation iff it follows from the fact that P obtains that a system of nested beliefs and expectations exists" (p.114). The thoughtful discussion of social relations of which this is a part is quite detailed.

19. See the discussion of the problem that may be posed by an 'absolute best point' for the rational agents of game theory in "Rationality, Coordination, and Convention."

20. A 'real Unity of them all': Thomas Hobbes, *Leviathan*, ed. C. B. MacPherson (London: Penguin Books, 1974 [1691]), Pt. 2., Chapter 17, p. 227.

21. There may be more and less clear cases with respect to our sense of a 'bond' between persons. Consider the way Frederick Schick defines the term 'social bond' in his book *Having Reasons: Essays on Rationality and Sociality* (Princeton: Princeton University Press, 1984). "Suppose now that Adam chooses somehow because of what he thinks the interests of Eve. I will say in

such a case that Adam is choosing *socially*"(p. 89). (Adam need not be *obliging*; he may be *spiting* Eve.) When, roughly, someone is disposed to choose socially in this sense, with respect to some person, Schick says "I shall say that a *social bond* holds between them" (p. 91). Note that there can be an asymmetry here between the parties. The social bond between Adam and Eve, in this definition, can be a function of Adam's being disposed socially toward Eve, while she does not reciprocate. I am therefore not clear whether Schick's use of the term 'social bond' here is particularly intuitive. However, an Adam who is responsive to the interests of others, however unpleasantly, would appear to be more closely *involved* with them than an Adam who is never so responsive. So one might feel that there is more of a bond, or something more like a bond, in the former than in the latter case.

22. The phenomena ranked for sociality in Gilbert (1978), including common knowledge phenomena, in devising the broad account did not include the phenomenon I now propose as the most highly social type. The broad account appears to allow for the correctness of the current proposal. It may even, as it happens, point toward it, but, if so, that is not a function of the data on which it was based.

23. See Gilbert, *On Social Facts*. See also *Living Together*.

24. Ibid.

25. For a more detailed discussion see Margaret Gilbert, "Walking Together: A Paradigmatic Social Phenomenon." Pp. 1–14 in *Midwest Studies in Philosophy*, Vol. 15, *The Philosophy of the Human Sciences,* ed. Peter A. French, Theodore E. Uehling, and Howard K. Wettstein (Notre Dame, Ind.: Notre Dame University Press, 1990) reprinted in *Living Together*.

26. G. Simmel, *On Individuality and Social Forms* (Chicago: University of Chicago Press, 1971), p. 24.

27. I here waive discussion of possible variants on this condition.

28. This can be shown without considering precisely what these conditions leave out (see what follows in the text). Criminals who are keeping an eye on each other (and hence wanting to walk side by side) need not be walking together in the sense intended here. They will not, one might say, be walking *together*. They may even communicate their intentions to one another without this being the case. (I thank Jonathan Vogel for the example, personal communication, May 1994.) Another example is someone who asks whether she may walk alongside another person because she is afraid to walk alone. The other person may reply, "That would suit me very well. I feel the same way." If the first person proceeds to walk alongside the other person, they may still not be walking together.

29. Similar things can be said regarding Michael Bratman's account of phenomena such as walking together in his "Shared Cooperative Activity," *Philosophical Review* (1992) 101:327–41.

30. For a lengthy discussion of this point see my article "Is an Agreement an Exchange of Promises?" *Journal of Philosophy* (1993) 90:627–49, reprinted in *Living Together*.

31. I should stress that here I am focusing on a two-person case. Other cases need an independent treatment. What one can say quite generally is that any given 'individual commitment' that exists through a joint commitment is not sustainable on its own.

32. Thanks, once again, to John Deigh for the metaphor of the lock with multiple keys.

33. For more on the nature of the obligations of joint commitment as compared with other types of obligation, including some paradigmatic cases of moral obligation, see Margaret Gilbert, "Agreements, Coercion, and Obligation," *Ethics* (1993) 103:679–706, reprinted in *Living Together*.

34. See *On Social Facts*, Chapter 4.

35. See *On Social Facts*, Chapter 7. See also "Agreements, Coercion, and Obligation" for some remarks on the reason-giving force of commitments both individual and joint.

36. The term 'doing something' is to be construed broadly here. Believing something will count as doing something in the relevant sense.

37. See Margaret Gilbert, "Hart on Social Rules: A Problem and Its Solution," unpublished manuscript. See also *On Social Facts*, Chapter 6.

38. Ibid., Chapter 6.

39. Ibid., Chapter 3.

40. See *On Social Facts*, Chapter 5, and my articles, "Modeling Collective Belief" *Synthese* (1987) 73:185–204, and "Remarks on Collective Belief," in *Socializing Epistemology: The Social Dimensions of Knowledge*, ed. Frederick Schmitt (Lanham, Md.: Rowman & Littlefield, 1994), both reprinted in *Living Together*.

41. See *On Social Facts*, Chapter 4.

42. Cf. my article "Fusion: Sketch of a Contractual Model" in *Perspectives on the Family*, ed. Robert C. L. Moffat, Joseph Grcic, and Michael Bayles (Lewiston: Mellen Press, 1990), and in *Living Together*.

43. See *On Social Facts* for further discussion of holism versus individualism in the context of the theory of plural subjects.

44. Here I distinguish what we (individually) are doing (i.e., what 'all of us' are doing) from what we (collectively) are doing, and so on.

45. Perhaps other beings also. On the question of nonhuman animals and plural subjecthood, see *On Social Facts*, Chapter 7.

46. See "Agreements, Coercion, and Obligation." See also my article "Group Membership and Political Obligation," *Monist* (1993) 76:119–31, reprinted in *Living Together*.

47. See *On Social Facts*, Chapter 3, sections on 'group languages', and *Living Together*, Chapter 11.

48. See "Rationality, Coordination, and Convention," where I argue that joint commitment to a principle produces a crucial stabilizing force not produced by concordant personal preferences or concordant personal principles of action.

## Chapter 2

# A Definition of Social Phenomena for the Social Sciences

*Walter L. Wallace*

After sketching the goal of the definition[1] of social phenomena to be proposed here for adoption by all the social sciences,[2] I present the definition itself, examine some of its implications for describing the various types of social phenomena and their hierarchical structuring, and discuss the guidance given by the definition to social science explanation and prediction.

### Goal of the Definition

The goal one seeks in formulating a particular definition of social phenomena (or of anything else, for that matter) is arbitrary—analyzable, of course, but arbitrary. As Max Weber puts it, "the ultimately possible attitudes toward life are irreconcilable, and hence their struggle can never be brought to a final conclusion" (1946:152), and "empirical data . . . can never become the foundation for the empirically impossible proof of the validity of evaluative ideas" (1949:111). It is precisely this arbitrariness, however, that compels me to heed Weber's cards-on-the-table injunction that "the maker of a judgment [should] clarify for others and for himself the nature of the ultimate subjective core of his judgments, to make clear the ideals on the basis of which he proceeds'' (1989:200, italics removed).

The reader should know, then, that I reject the idea (which, admittedly, many others cherish) of isolating social science from the rest of natural science by imposing anthropocentric or other such limitations on the former.[3] Instead, I believe social science should be coupled more closely to the rest of natural science both biological and physical, and further decoupled from the humanities (for discussion of this position, see Wallace 1988:23–30).[4]

## A Generic Definition of Social Phenomena

Pursuant to this goal, I propose that a social phenomenon should be defined generically, in all the social sciences, as an *interorganismic behavior regularity*—that is, as any set of nonrandom co-occurrences in time and/or space of two or more organisms' behaviors. Under this definition, in order to identify a social phenomenon empirically, we need to observe that if organism A manifests a behavior, then organism B regularly manifests a behavior—not necessarily the same behavior, not necessarily always or everywhere, and with no limits being placed on the spatial and/or temporal interval between the two manifestations. Note that it is the regularity between different organisms' behaviors, and not any regularity within the same organism's behavior, that constitutes a social phenomenon. Even if all the observed organisms' behaviors were shown to be irregular in themselves, the regular co-occurrence of their irregular behaviors would constitute an interorganism behavior regularity (the literature on crowds refers to ''milling'' and ''collective excitement'').

This definition is intended to subsume all existing social science definitions of social phenomena.[5] It is also intended to establish a strong and clear link between social science and the rest of natural science by adopting the latter's well-established format for defining almost any sort of phenomenon. The format I have in mind specifies that any phenomenon other than what many physicists refer to as structureless point particles—for example, electrons, neutrinos, quarks—is definable as a behavior regularity among more microphenomena that compose it (see, however, Capra 1975:243, 263, and Barrow 1988:219, for speculations about the possibility of a ''bottomless pit of complexity,'' the depths of which are permanently inaccessible to human observation).[6] Thus, organisms may be defined in terms of behavior regularities among organs; these, in terms of behavior regularities among cells; these, in terms of behavior regularities among cell membrane, cytoplasm, organelles, nucleoplasm; these, in terms of behavior regularities among molecules, and so on, with "emergent" properties at each higher level.

To define a social phenomenon as an interorganism behavior regularity, then, clearly implies an ongoing dependence of social science on the rest of natural science for information regarding the nature of the separate constituents of that definition—namely, organisms, behaviors, and regularities. It also implies a similarly ongoing dependence of the rest of natural science on social science for information regarding the social phenomena involved in the production, criticism, distribution, modification, and utilization of all scientific knowledge (see Zuckerman 1988).

Before examining each constituent of the definition more closely, note that the definition's *generic* character means it refers to only the most broadly inclusive category of phenomena that we may call "social," while permitting the specification of an unlimited number of varieties within that genus. Thus, while social scientists would be prohibited from removing any constituent of the generic definition (i.e., *non*organisms, *non*behaviors, and *non*regularities would not be constituents of social phenomena), they would remain free to limit their researches to certain organisms and not others, certain behaviors and not others, certain regularities and not others.

Regarding the term *organism*, its deliberate generality is meant to acknowledge that social phenomena are not limited to humans but are, to one degree or another and in one form or another, characteristic of all known life forms (see Wilson 1975). Such an acknowledgment would bring social science and biological science into closer contact by expanding the hitherto human focus of almost every social science discipline.[7] Moreover, the general principles that a social science whose subject matter extends to all species of life should eventually discover will probably make major contributions to natural science as a whole—by helping illuminate the processes of evolution, emergence, complexity, life, and intelligence wherever and whenever they may be found (see Boulding 1956; Davies 1988; Waldrop 1992).

By referring generically to *behavior*, the definition permits social scientists to pursue interests in the regular interorganism co-occurrence of literally *any* behaviors (and any combination of behaviors) of which their subject organisms are capable—whether these be regarded as physiological or psychological, conscious or unconscious, purposive or nonpurposive, voluntary or involuntary, learned or instinctual, motor, visceral, endocrinal, neurological, or whatever. Selection of the behaviors of interest would depend on disciplinary convention and on the particular interests of each investigator—provided only that the focal social phenomenon is described in terms of *some* designated behaviors that occur with *some* designated regularity between *some* designated organisms.

By referring generically to *regularity*, the definition requires, at minimum, only a nonzero probability of observing one organism's behavior, given that at least one other organism's behavior is also observed. Investigators are thereby free to specify *temporal* regularities of various kinds in social phenomena; free to specify *spatial* regularities of various kinds in those phenomena; and free, of course, to specify combined spatiotemporal regularities there.

Now consider the proposed definition's requirement of only a *regularity* in the co-occurrence between two or more organisms' behaviors. This purely descriptive, probabilistic term is meant to protect investigators against describing social phenomena according to some favorite explanation and thereby biasing their explanatory analyses by blocking out consideration of other possible explanations.

To illustrate: Weber defines a "social relationship" as "the behavior of a plurality of actors insofar as, in its meaningful content, the action of each takes account of that of the others and *is oriented in these terms*" (1978:26, italics added). This definition requires us to accept, a priori, that the actors' subjective orientations to each other are what explain (by orienting) those actors' actions, before we can say that the relationship is social and thus a legitimate subject for social scientific explanatory analysis in the first place. Unless this vicious circle is spotted and broken at the outset, it stacks the explanatory deck in favor of one particular kind of hypothesis—a stacking that comes out quite explicitly in Weber's dogma that "the *real* empirical sociological investigation begins with the question: What *motives* determine and lead the individual members and participants in [a] community to behave in such a way that the community came into being in the first place and that it continues to exist?" (1978:18, italics added). That "motive" is but one of many possible explanatory hypotheses, however, is implied by Weber himself when he adopts the principle of equifinality (see below), from which it follows that communities can be brought into being through causal influences other than their participants' motives—as when, for example, the participants are physically compelled to form communities by the natural environment (see Hawley 1950:12, 31, 296) or by deliberate architectural design (see Festinger et al. 1950:33–59; Sykes 1958).

Another unfortunately popular explanation-biasing definition views social phenomena as *interaction* among organisms (for example, "Society is merely the name for a number of individuals, connected by interaction" [Simmel 1950:10]). By requiring only "regularity," the definition proposed here prevents investigators from assuming, a priori, that in a given social phenomenon organism A acts on organism B and organism B acts on organism A; that is, they "interact" and thus jointly explain the social phenomenon in question—for this need not be the case. The regularity in the co-occurrence of A's and B's behaviors may result from other factors entirely, factors that act on A and on B separately from within and/or without. No generic definition of social phenomena should preempt the assessment of such factors. That is, the explanatory chips should be allowed to fall where they may.

## Principal Types of Social Phenomena

All social phenomena that have been studied so far by the social sciences seem divisible into broad types according to the following distinctions: (1) between human and nonhuman *organisms*, (2) between physiological (skeletal-muscular-visceral) and psychological (neuroendocrine) *behaviors*, and (3) between temporal and spatial *regularities*. Combining these, we have Figure 2.1.

Cells a, c, e, and g in this figure indicate what is (or rather, should be) customarily meant by "social structure"—human and nonhuman,

|  | Human Organisms | | Nonhuman Organisms | |
|---|---|---|---|---|
|  | Physical behavior | Psychical behavior | Physical behavior | Psychical behavior |
| Spatial regularity | a | b | e | f |
| Temporal regularity | c | d | g | h |

*Figure 2.1* Major Types of Social Phenomena

respectively—while cells b, d, f, and h indicate what should be customarily meant by "cultural structure" or "culture."[8] That is to say, the first set of cells refers to organisms *doing* things together regularly in space and/or time (interorganism physiological behavior regularities), and the second set refers to organisms *perceiving, thinking, and/ or experiencing emotions* together regularly in space and/or time (interorganism psychological behavior regularities).[9] Similarly, cells a, b, e, and f represent *spatial* regularities in social, and cultural, structure, while cells c, d, g, and h represent change, stability, and process (*temporal* regularities) in social structure and cultural structure.

More complicated subjects of social science research result from combining these cells in various ways. Thus, we have studies of social phenomena between human and nonhuman organisms—for example, between companion animals and their human owners. We also have studies of social phenomena in which correlated physiological and psychological behavior regularities (i.e., sociocultural structures) are of interest (e.g., schools, churches, legislative bodies, scientific laboratories). Finally, we have studies of social phenomena in which behavior regularities in both space and time (i.e., spatiotemporal regularities) are of interest (e.g., people hurrying to catch a scheduled train on a given track at Pennsylvania Station).

## Subtypes of Social Phenomena

Let us now look inside each type of social phenomenon shown in Figure 2.1, to assess further the extent to which the proposed generic definition subsumes the substantive interests of modern social science. With respect to social structure, Figure 2.2 represents a crude classification of kinds of physiological behaviors. Here we distinguish the object of the effect of any such behavior from what we may call the direction of that effect, cross-classify these two dimensions, and thereby derive six types of individual physiological behavior and six types of social structure in which these behaviors are distinctive.[10]

These include, first, an organism's self-nurturing behaviors—including self-constructive, self-transporting, and self-destructive varieties—and the social structures that are constituted by different organisms engaging in these behaviors together. Examples of the latter would be people taking food, or a walk, or poison, together. Second, are self-teaching behaviors and their related social structures—for example, people learning, translating, or forgetting something to-

| Object of effect | Direction of effect | | |
|---|---|---|---|
| | Construction | Transportation | Destruction |
| Self | | | |
|   Body | ——————————— Self-nurturing ——————— | | |
|   Mind | ——————————— Self-teaching ——————— | | |
| Other people | | | |
|   Body | ——————————— Social structuring ——————— | | |
|   Mind | ——————————— Cultural structuring ——————— | | |
| Things | | | |
|   Living | ——————— Domesticating, cultivating ——————— | | |
|   Nonliving | ——————— Extracting, fabricating ——————— | | |

*Figure 2.2* Typology of Individual Organism Physiological Behaviors

gether. The third group is social structuring behaviors and their related social structures—for example, people giving nutritional or medical care to other people, or imprisoning or killing them, or transporting them from place to place. Fourth are cultural structuring behaviors and the social structures that are constituted by different organisms engaging in these behaviors together—for example, people giving lectures or publishing books or performing music before audiences. The fifth classification is plant and animal domesticating and cultivating behaviors and their related social structures—for example, people growing, harvesting, distributing, or consuming agricultural produce. Sixth are extracting and fabricating behaviors and their related social structures—for example, people mining, hunting, fishing, logging, and manufacturing, and transporting, distributing, and/or consuming such products.

The next step in specifying types of social structure is to introduce a typology of ways that different individuals' physiological behaviors, each characterized according to Figure 2.2, can regularly co-occur. Figure 2.3 offers a classification of nine such ways—customarily called unison, competition, imitation, dominance, cooperation, conflict, administration, oppression, and segregation. For example, Figure 2.3 claims that when two organisms' physiological behaviors are the same (e.g., both are constructively self-nurturing) but incompatible (e.g., there is not enough food for both organisms to nurture themselves), and when they are of roughly equal strength, then we may call the social structure thus constituted "competition." If they are of grossly unequal strength, then we may call it "dominance"—and so on.

Turning to cultural structure, the same two-step procedure used earlier on social structure seems applicable. Figure 2.4 presents the first step. Here we have twelve types of individual psychological

| | A's and B's physical behaviors are: | | | |
| --- | --- | --- | --- | --- |
| | Same | | Different | |
| | Equal | Unequal | Equal | Unequal |
| Compatible | Unison | Imitation | Cooperation | Administration |
| Incompatible | Competition | Dominance | Conflict | Oppression |
| Isolated | | Segregation | | |

*Figure 2.3*  Typology of Interorganism Physiological Behavior Coincidences

behavior capabilities as characterized by their relationships to two dimensions: (1) mode of orientation—that is, cognitive, cathectic, and conative (otherwise called belief or knowledge, preference or value, and behavior-readiness—the latter exemplified by the dispositions of people in Western societies to shake hands with people they meet rather than, say, bow to them); and (2) referent of orientation. Note that such referents are classified here in the same way as the objects of effect shown in Figure 2.2, thereby reflecting the assumption that organisms can generally orient themselves psychologically toward the same types of phenomena on which they can act physiologically. And, as was the case with individual physiological behaviors, these individual psychological behaviors imply related types of cultural structure—for example, different people sharing similar cognitions (or cathexes, or conations) regarding the human mind and body, other living things, and nonliving things.

The second step here, again, is to consider the ways that different individuals' psychological behaviors (characterized according to Figure 2.4) may coincide. Figure 2.5 attempts such a typology, embracing the familiar concepts of consensus, complementarity, dissensus, and neutrality. For example, this figure suggests that when we say "consensus" exists between two organisms, we mean certain designated psychological behaviors are the same (e.g., one organism likes a given object and the second also likes that object). When we say "dissensus" exists between two organisms, we mean certain designated psychological behaviors are different and logically inconsistent (e.g., one organism likes, and the other dislikes, a given object)–and so on.

Next, we turn to the spatial and/or temporal regularity constituent of the generic definition proposed earlier. Here, it is essential to emphasize that the focus is not on space and/or time in themselves, nor is any challenge intended to the idea that all the events with which social scientists are concerned "actually" take place in space *and* time. Drawing a distinction between spatial and temporal regularities,

| Referent of orientation | Mode of orientation | | |
|---|---|---|---|
| | Cognitive | Cathectic | Conative |
| Self | | | |
|   Body | a | b | c |
|   Mind | d | e | f |
| Other people | | | |
|   Body | g | h | i |
|   Mind | j | k | l |
| Things | | | |
|   Living | m | n | o |
|   Nonliving | p | q | r |

*Figure 2.4*    Typology of Individual Organism Psychological Behaviors

| | A's and B's psychological behaviors are: | |
|---|---|---|
| | Same | Different |
| Consistent | Consensus | Complementarity |
| Inconsistent | [Empty cell] | Dissensus |
| Irrelevant | Neutrality | |

*Figure 2.5*    Typology of Interorganism Psychological Behavior Coincidences

however, allows one social science investigator to investigate, say, how different social or cultural structures are laid out on a given geographic terrain and another investigator to investigate how such structures change from day to night, summer to winter, or decade to decade. Still others may be interested in both kinds of regularities simultaneously. Figure 2.6 sets forth a typology of roughly parallel spatial regularity and temporal regularity features commonly used to describe interorganism behaviors, including extension and duration, pattern and rhythm, density and tempo, and uniformity and periodicity.

To this, we need to add consideration of how social phenomena, when described by any or all of the spatial and temporal regularity features shown in Figure 2.6, may vary regularly over space and may

| Definition | Spatial | Temporal |
|---|---|---|
| Extent of interorganism behavior | Extension | Duration |
| Recurrent set of interorganism behaviors | Pattern | Rhythm |
| Rate of interorganism behavior recurrence | Density | Tempo |
| Regularity of interorganism behavior recurrence | Uniformity | Periodicity |

*Figure 2.6*   Typology of Spatial and Temporal Regularities in Interorganism Behaviors

change regularly over time. Five types of such variation in space are: nearly random scatter, homogeneous plain, latitudinal (or longitudinal) strips or belts, grid (in which strips intersect), concentric, and radial. Similarly, seven types of change in time are: nearly random or chaotic, static, cyclical, evolutionary, devolutionary (the latter two marked by continuous increments or continuous decrements, respectively), revolutionary, and catastrophic (the latter two marked by one or more large positive, or large negative, discontinuities).

By combining the spatial and temporal patterns just discussed, we may construct descriptions of social phenomena as, say, "dispersing" or, alternatively, "concentrating" in space with the passage of time (see Durkheim 1965:245–6) and becoming, at least potentially, more "long-lived" in time when spatial extension is increased (see Spencer 1898, I:463–73).

## Hierarchic Structure in Social Phenomena

So far, we have concentrated on inter*organism* behavior regularities. Much social science research, however, concerns inter*group* behavior regularities. We now take this concern into account by applying the principle of hierarchic structure—specifically, the idea that certain aggregates of "micro" social phenomena may be regarded as constituting more "macro" social phenomena and that the latter may then be described, explained, and predicted from, on their own.

The idea of hierarchic structure may also be applied to each constituent of the generic definition separately, as follows. When social scientists speak of different social *collectivities*, we generally have in mind different rosters of participating organisms–and we may refer, hierarchically, to rosters of such rosters (e.g., the collectivity called the population of Chicago is part of the larger collectivity called the population of Illinois, and so on). When we speak of different social and/or cultural *systems*, we generally have in mind different sets of behaviors, and these, in turn, may be treated as constituents of still larger (societal and intersocietal) sets. When we speak of particular social *"locations"* (e.g., Roppongi Crossing) or particular historical *"periods"* (e.g., the eighties), we generally have in mind certain bounded regularities that characterize the collectivities and their behavior systems—and, again, we may refer to a location of locations (e.g., Tokyo) and a period of periods (e.g., the twentieth century). Thus, social collectivities, social and/or cultural systems, and social locations and periods may all be described as hierarchically structured.

To this, let us add that the three-part generic definition of social phenomena as interorganismic behavior regularities calls for identifying *associations* between a given level in one constituent and given levels in the others. That is, one of the most important things we want empirical *descriptive* research in the social sciences to tell us is which levels in the various hierarchies of aggregates, behavior patterns, and locations/periods are associated with each other—and to what degree (e.g., Georg Simmel claims three-participant groups can manifest behavior patterns that two-participant groups cannot [see 1950:145–69]). And then, of course, we want empirical *explanatory* research to tell us *why* and *how* they are associated in these ways.

This mention of why and how brings us to the final concern of this chapter—namely, the way the definition of social phenomena proposed here serves as a guide to social science explanation.[11]

## The Generic Definition as Guide to Social Science Explanation

The central point is the following: Imagine two organisms, each existing anywhere, anytime. One of the organisms may behave with any, or no, regularity whatever. The second organism, however, must behave regularly with respect to the first organism's behavior if they are to be considered members of the same social phenomenon (recall the earlier mention here of "milling" and "collective excitement"). It is therefore the constraining of the second organism's behavior into regularity with the first's—and/or vice versa–that we have to explain. To this explanatory focus on the individual social participant, we now add the principles called "equifinality" and "equi-initiality"—claiming that the explanation of (and prediction from) each organism's participation in a given social phenomenon may be different from that of every other organism's participation, as follows.

Equifinality means that any given phenomenon may be explained in two or more ways. We say, "There's more than one way to skin a cat"; "All rivers run to the sea"; "All roads lead to Rome"; "And how dieth the wise man? As the fool." Ludwig von Bertalanffy seems responsible for naming the principle: "the same final state may be reached from different initial conditions and in different ways. This is what is called equifinality" (1956:31; see also Simon 1965:66).[12] The physicist John Barrow's image is clear: "If you stir a barrel of thick oil it will rapidly settle down to the same placid state, no matter how it was first stirred" (1988:297). And Richard Feynman, inventor of a way to "calculate the probability of [a quantum] event that can happen in alternative ways" (1985:59, italics removed), says, "It is possible to start from many apparently different starting points, and yet come to the same thing" (1967:50). In the social sciences, Weber is a leading exponent of equifinality. We have already seen his claim "The same result may be reached from [different] starting-points," and he also says, "Processes of action which seem to an observer to be the same or similar may fit into exceedingly various complexes of motive in the case of the actual actor" (1978:10). Émile Durkheim has the same idea: "to arrive at the same goal, many different routes can be, and in reality are, followed" (1982:123; see also Wallace 1994:220–1).

The term *equi-initiality* is used here to designate the converse of equifinality; it means that more than one consequence may be predicted from any given ("initial") phenomenon. We speak of coming to a "turning point," a "crossroads," or a "crisis" from which alternative consequences may be expected to flow—depending, usually, on some ultimately infinitesimal factor (the "Butterfly Effect," "For want of a nail"). Equi-initiality is what Barrow has in mind when he argues for the "non-uniqueness of the future states of a system following the prescription of a definite starting state" (1988:284; see also Davies 1988:35–56; Gleick 1987:11–31). Weber, again, points out the bearing of equi-initiality on the study of social phenomena: "action that is 'identical' in its meaning relationship occasionally takes what is, in the final effect, a radically varying course" (1981:156), and on this, too, Durkheim agrees: "it is a proposition true in sociology as in biology, that the organ is independent of its function, i.e. while staying the same it can serve different ends" (1982:121).[13]

So the principles of equifinality and equi-initiality warn us (1) that each organism's participation in a given social phenomenon (even when that participation is, at any given level of analysis, descriptively indistinguishable from all the others') may have its own distinct explanation; and (2) that the predictable consequences of such participation may also be different for different participants. It follows that if we want to find variables that can explain, or predict from, a given social phenomenon we must, in principle, focus on each of its individual participants *one at a time* no matter how many they are—a principle that, of course, does not prohibit us from constructing *typical* explanations and predictions that we believe apply (with the error duly expected of any measurement of central tendency) across the relevant behaviors of all the participants.[14]

Figure 2.7 proposes a systematic and comprehensive matrix of such

*Origin of Causal Influence*

| *Location of Causal Influence* | Existentially Given (Not In Prior Social Phenomena) | Socially Generated (In Prior Social Phenomena) |
|---|---|---|
| In the participant's own: | | |
|    Mind | Instinct | Enculture |
|    Body | Physiology | Nurture |
| In the participant's environing people: | | |
|    Their minds | Psychical contagion | Cultural structure |
|    Their bodies | Demography | Social structure |
| In the participant's environing "things": | | |
|    Living | $Ecology_L$ | $Technology_L$ |
|    Nonliving | $Ecology_{NL}$ | $Technology_{NL}$ |

*Figure 2.7* Typology of Variables Explaining Social Phenomena and Predicting from Them

participant-focused variables. Here, as in the case of the generic definition of social phenomena set forth earlier as subsuming all existing social science descriptions of such phenomena, I claim that all the variables in existing social science explanations of, and predictions from, social phenomena are subsumed by this matrix. That is, they are all decomposable into various combinations of the twelve types of variables in this figure (plus combinations of twelve types of causal images, not discussed here, that serve to link such variables to each other and to whatever social phenomenon may be under investigation; see Wallace 1983:323–51; 1988:53–9).

The variables in this figure are partitioned into two broad categories: those located inside the individual social participant itself, and those located outside that participant—i.e., in its environment. That environment is then partitioned into two components: the conspecifics (in the human case, other humans) that may be found there, and the "things" (nonconspecific living things, and nonliving things) that may be found there.

Next, internal makeup is partitioned into two components—namely, features of the individual's neuroendocrine (mind) behavior, and features of the individual's skeletal-muscular-visceral (body) behavior. At this point, note the distinction that cuts across both mind and body variables as well as all the others shown in Figure 2.7. Each is regarded as having a "natural" component—one treated as given in the nature of existence independent of social phenomena—and a socially generated, "acquired" component.

Figure 2.7 also partitions each conspecific in the individual participant's environment into a mind component and a body component, and each of these is partitioned into an existentially given, and a socially generated, aspect. Finally, the rest of the individual's environment is divided into living (but nonconspecific) and nonliving components, and the existentially given versus socially generated distinction is also applied here.

There is not enough space here to explicate fully each of the twelve types of variables shown in Figure 2.7 and their combinations, to examine familiar subtypes subsumed under each, and to illustrate their roles in the existing social science (including sociobiological) literature, but perhaps the outlines of the argument can be grasped from the figure and these brief remarks (see Wallace 1983:187–322, 1988:39–53, for fuller expositions). It is essential to emphasize even in this small space, however, that neither the overall shape nor the specific details of this matrix should be regarded as fixed. In the long run they will almost surely change as social science, and natural science as a whole, changes.[15]

## Conclusion

Note that everything discussed here derives from a single point of origin—namely, the definition of social phenomena proposed here as "generic." If a social science convention regarding such a definition were to be established, it would therefore be likely to have wide ramifications that could drastically improve the quality of communication (including teaching) within and among the several social science disciplines, while strengthening basic substantive and methodological ties between those disciplines and the rest of natural science.

## Notes

1. By a "definition" I mean any description used as a criterion for naming other descriptions. For example, to define a "book" as "a collection of written, printed, or blank sheets fastened along one edge and usually trimmed at the other edges to form a single series of uniform leaves" allows one to decide whether a given description of an item justifies naming it a "book."

2. That different investigators adopt the same basic terminology, as an always modifiable cultural convention, is indispensable for communication in the sciences (and, indeed, everywhere else). Thus, Popper says science is "intersubjective" (see 1961: 44–45), and Rorty, calling science a kind of social "solidarity" (see 1991:5–45), says "What we cannot do is rise above all human communities, actual and possible. We cannot find a skyhook which lifts us out of mere coherence—mere agreement—to something like 'correspondence with reality as it is in itself' " (1991:38; see also Kaplan 1964:128).

3. See Weinberg's discussion of the "Copernican principle" in natural science (1992:254). This principle refers to the succession of changes in accepted scientific paradigms that have displaced the Earth away from what used to be thought of as its centrality in the solar system; displaced the solar system away from the center of our galaxy (and, recently, away from uniqueness in that galaxy); displaced our galaxy away from the center of the observable universe; displaced our era far away from both the beginning and the ending of that universe; and also displaced humans away from what used to be thought of as our absolute uniqueness among life on Earth.

4. Popper at first rejects the possibility of coupling the social sciences more closely to the other natural sciences on the ground that "objectivity in the social sciences is much more difficult to achieve (if it can be achieved at all) than in the natural sciences [because] only in the rarest of cases can the social scientist free himself from the value system of his own social class and so achieve even a limited degree of 'value freedom' and 'objectivity'." But Popper soon corrects this prejudice by noting that "it is just as impossible to eliminate [extra-scientific interests] from research in the natural sciences as from research in the social sciences" (1976:91, 96; see a similar prejudice, followed by a similar correction, in Mannheim 1955:79, 305–6).

5. Consider the following definitions: Auguste Comte says, "The exercise of a general and combined activity is the essence of society" (1975:20), thereby allowing the "regularity" component of the generic definition to remain implicit while making the "interorganism" and the "behavior" components explicit. Karl Marx and Friedrich Engels adopt a similar approach when they say, "By social we understand the co-operation of several individuals" (1969, I:31)—although "joint activity" seems a more faithful translation of their original "*Zusammenwirken*" than "co-operation" because it permits conflict (as in "class conflict") to be considered a social phenomenon as well. Weber is explicit about the "regularity" component: "Sociology seeks to formulate type concepts and generalized uniformities of empirical process" (1978:19), and his definition of a "social relationship" specifies "a plurality of actors" (i.e., the "interorganism" component) and their actions (the "behavior" component). Simmel underscores the "regularity" component when he says, "Sociation ranges all the way from the momentary getting together for a walk to the founding of a family . . . from the temporary aggregation of hotel guests to the intimate bonds of a medieval guild" (1971:24). Durkheim's treatment of "social facts" illuminates the generic definition in a special way. Durkheim offers two very different definitions back to back: (1) "A social fact is any way of acting *capable of exerting over the individual an external constraint*," and (2) "[a social fact is any way of acting] which is *general* over the whole of a given society whilst having an existence of its own, independent of individual manifestations" (1982:59, italics changed). Although Durkheim claims, "The second definition is simply another formulation of the first one" (1982:57), this assertion is clearly untenable: The "generality" stipulation is an arbitrary conceptual *definition* resting on the regularity with which a given observation is made (more exactly, the probability of finding a next instance of a particular way of acting, given that one or more other instances have already been found), whereas the "pressure-exerting" stipulation constitutes a hypothetical *explanation* that specifies the cause of the condition specified in that definition. We must therefore reject Durkheim's equivalence claim, reject his first definition on the ground that it is really an explanatory hypothesis (and would be a dogma if included in the definition), and accept only his second, "generality," definition—which reduces to a special (societal level) case of the generic definition proposed here.

6. Campbell says, "A hierarchy of levels of analysis exists in which the focus of differential description at one level becomes the assumed undifferentiated atoms of the next; this is the atom-molecule-cell-organ-organism-social group-etc. model" (1969:332). See also Simon (1965) and Davies (1988:142–6).

7. Alan Wolfe claims, "Social scientists ought to stop looking around them to decide how to carry out their work. Humans require a distinct science because they are a distinct subject" (1993:xv, 81). But Wolfe forgets that the essence of mind (which he regards as the principal "human difference," see 1993:27, 31, 51–54) is precisely to "look around" before deciding how to carry out a given work, and he also forgets that each individual human may be treated as a "distinct subject," but nobody (including Wolfe, one hopes) takes that as warranting 5.7 billion distinct sciences of the present human population.

8. To refer to social structure as simply "structure" and to cultural structure as simply "culture" is a grossly misleading (but all too frequent) error, for it implies that there is only one type of social phenomenon that is structured, and culture is not it. The position of modern natural science is that *all* types of phenomena (except the so-called structureless point particles mentioned earlier) are structured—including the *cultural* structures we call "beliefs," "norms," "values," "skills," "styles," and so on.

9. This distinction between social structure and cultural structure is controversial because, unfortunately, neither concept has yet been defined by social science convention. Thus, regarding the first concept Stanley Udy tells us (straightfacedly) that "the concept 'social structure' is so fundamental to social science as to render its uncontested definition virtually impossible" (1968:489). Charles Warriner follows with the claim that "Of all the problematic terms in the sociological lexicon, 'social structure' is perhaps the most troublesome. There is little agreement on its empirical referents" (1981:179); and Jonathan Turner says "despite sociologists' frequent use of the term social structure, its meaning remains unclear" (1986:407, italics removed). Steven Rytina, however, disagrees; his view is that "social structure is a general term for any collective social circumstance that is unalterable and given for the individual. Social structure is objective in the sense that it is the same for all and is beyond the capacity for alteration by any individual will" (1992:1970). But Rytina's view unaccountably ignores the well-documented generalizations that every participant necessarily alters (in however small a way) every social structure in which she or he participates and that a given social structure is not the same for those in its uppermost stratum and those in its bottom stratum—indeed, it is never absolutely the same for any two participants in it. Regarding the concept of cultural structure, Robert Wuthnow et al. note that the situation is similar to that of social structure: "Theorists of culture remain sorely divided on how best to define culture" (1984:3). Clifford Geertz, too, says, "Whether culture is patterned conduct or a frame of mind, or even the two somehow mixed together" (1973:10) is an unresolved question (note that the "interorganism" requirement discussed earlier is left implicit here). Sam-

uel Gilmore agrees: "there is no current, widely accepted, composite resolution of the definition of culture" (1992:409). Nevertheless, it seems to me that Robert Merton is on the right track when he says "cultural structure may be defined as [an] organized set of normative values [while] by social structure is meant [an] organized set of social relationships" (1957:162)—if we assume that by "relationships" Merton means interindividual *physiological* behavior regularities and that by "normative values" he means similarly interindividual *psychological* behavior regularities. A. L. Kroeber and Talcott Parsons also seem to be on the right track when they "define the concept culture [as referring to] transmitted content and patterns of values, ideas, and other symbolic-meaningful systems [but] suggest that the term society—or more generally, social system—be used to designate the specifically relational system of interaction between individuals and collectivities" (1958:583, italics removed; see also Parsons 1961:34). (Of course, we must substitute for Kroeber and Parsons' covertly explanatory term *interaction* the more purely descriptive *behavior regularity*.) For discussion of the distinction between the concepts "social structure" and "cultural structure" and their observable indicators see Wallace 1988:35–37.

10. Note that the individuals' subjective, or intended, object and direction of effect are not at stake here; such intentions come under the discussion of types of individual psychological behavior capabilities, and their related cultural structures (discussed later).

11. Hempel provides the basic justification for claiming the existence of such guidance: "requests for an explanation have a clear meaning only if it is understood what aspects of the phenomenon in question are to be explained." "No concrete event," Hempel says, "can be completely explained [because it has] infinitely many different aspects and these cannot be completely described, let alone be completely explained" (1965:34, 422; see also Wallace 1971:53–7). The definition of social phenomena proposed here, then, states in generic terms which aspects of the endless variety of concrete social phenomena are to be explained. Note, also, that by "prediction" I mean predicting *from* social phenomena; predicting *to* social phenomena from other phenomena is here regarded as basically synonymous with explaining social phenomena (see Hempel 1965:366–6), and is often used (on premises discussed in Wallace 1983:414) as a validation-falsification check on explanation.

12. The difference between equifinality and multiple causation can be put briefly: In the former, each cause (or causal complex) is an *alternative* to others; in the latter, each is a *supplement* to others. A similar difference prevails between equi-initiality and effect diffusion.

13. So-called "deterministic" explanations and predictions are special cases of equifinality and equi-initiality—cases in which the probability of a given alternative explanation or prediction is held to be either 1 or zero.

14. In fact, almost all explanatory empirical researches in social science involve the assessment of typicality rather than the pursuit of completeness

(see Weber 1978:26–7). That is, the principal aim of empirical research is to specify the relative typicalities of different equifinal explanations and different equi-initial predictions—that is, their empirical probabilities of being (or having been, or becoming) true.

15. In my judgment, given the many types of variables we need (both now and in the long run) to measure and model in the social sciences, it is large-scale computer simulation (plus disciplinary standardization of some of the basic concepts explicated here) that holds the key to dramatic progress in our explanations and predictions (see Collins 1994:170; Wallace 1995:317–18).

# References

Barrow, John D. 1988. *The World within the World*. New York: Oxford University Press.

Boulding, Kenneth. 1956. "General Systems Theory—The Skeleton of Science," *General Systems* 1:11–17.

Campbell, Donald T. 1969. "Ethnocentrism of Disciplines and the Fish-Scale Model of Omniscience." Pp. 328–48 in *Interdisciplinary Relationships in the Social Sciences*, ed. Muzafer Sherif and Carolyn Sherif. Chicago: Aldine.

Capra, Fritjof. 1975. *The Tao of Physics*. New York: Bantam.

Collins, Randall. 1994. "Why the Social Sciences Won't Become High-Consensus, Rapid-Discovery Science," *Sociological Forum* 9 (June):155–77.

Comte, Auguste. 1975. *Auguste Comte and Positivism*. New York: Harper & Row.

Davies, Paul. 1988. *The Cosmic Blueprint*. New York: Simon & Schuster.

Durkheim, Émile. 1965. *The Elementary Forms of the Religious Life*. New York: Free Press.

———. 1982. *The Rules of Sociological Method*. New York: Free Press.

Festinger, Leon, Stanley Schachter, and Kurt Back. 1950. *Social Pressure in Informal Groups*. New York: Harper.

Feynman, Richard. 1967. *The Character of Physical Law*. Cambridge, Mass.: MIT Press.

———. 1985. *QED: The Strange Theory of Light and Matter*. Princeton, N.J.: Princeton University Press.

Geertz, Clifford. 1973. *The Interpretation of Culture*. New York: Basic Books.

Gilmore, Samuel. 1992. "Culture." Pp. 404–11 in *Encyclopedia of Sociology*, Vol. 1, ed. Edgar F. Borgatta and Marie L. Borgatta. New York: Macmillan.

Gleick, James. 1987. *Chaos: Making a New Science*. New York: Viking.

Hawley, Amos. 1950. *Human Ecology*. New York: Ronald.

Hempel, Carl G. 1965. *Aspects of Scientific Explanation*. New York: Free Press.

Kaplan, Abraham. 1964. *The Conduct of Inquiry*. San Francisco: Chandler.

Kroeber, A. L., and Talcott Parsons. 1958. "The Concepts of Culture and of Social System." *American Sociological Review* 23 (October):582–3.

Mannheim, Karl. 1955. *Ideology and Utopia*. New York: Harcourt, Brace.

Marx, Karl, and Frederick Engels. 1969. *Selected Works*. 3 vols. Moscow: Progress.

Merton, Robert K. 1957. *Social Theory and Social Structure*. Glencoe, Ill.: FreePress.

Parsons, Talcott. 1961. "An Outline of the Social System." Pp. 30–79 in *Theories of Society,* ed. by Talcott Parsons, Edward Shils, Kaspar D. Naegele, and Jesse R. Pitts. New York: Free Press.

Popper, Karl R. 1961. *The Logic of Scientific Discovery*. New York: Science Editions.

Rorty, Richard. 1991. *Objectivity, Relativism, and Truth: Philosophical Papers, Vol. I*. New York: Cambridge University Press.

Rytina, Steven L. 1992. "Social Structure." Pp. 1970–6 in *Encyclopedia of Sociology*, Vol. 4, ed. by Edgar F. Borgatta and Marie L. Borgatta. New York: Macmillan.

Simmel, Georg. 1950. *The Sociology of Georg Simmel*. Glencoe, Ill.: Free Press.

———. 1971. *On Individuality and Social Forms*. Chicago: University of Chicago Press.

Simon, Herbert A. 1965. "The Architecture of Complexity." Pp. 63–76 in *General Systems: Yearbook of the Society for General Systems Research,* Vol. X.

Spencer, Herbert. 1898. *The Principles of Sociology*. 3 vols. New York: Appleton.

Sykes, Gresham M. 1958. *The Society of Captives*. Princeton N.J.: Princeton University Press.

Turner, Jonathan H. 1986. *The Structure of Sociological Theory*. Chicago: University of Chicago Press.

Udy, Stanley H., Jr. 1968. "Social Structure: Social Structural Analysis." In *International Encyclopedia of the Social Sciences*, Vol. 14, ed. by David L. Sills. New York: Free Press.

von Bertalanffy, Ludwig. 1956. "General Systems Theory." Pp. 1–10 in *General Systems Yearbook,* Vol. I.

Waldrop, M. Mitchell. 1992. *Complexity*. New York: Simon & Schuster.

Wallace, Walter L. 1971. *The Logic of Science in Sociology*. Chicago: Aldine-Atherton.

———. 1983. *Principles of Scientific Sociology*. Hawthorne, NY: Aldine.

———. 1988. "Toward a Disciplinary Matrix in Sociology." Pp. 23-76 in *Handbook of Sociology,* ed. Neil J. Smelser. Newbury Park, Calif.: Sage.

———. 1994. *A Weberian Theory of Human Society: Structure and Evolution*. New Brunswick, N.J.: Rutgers University Press.

———. 1995. " 'Why Sociology Doesn't Make Progress'." *Sociological Forum* 10 (June):313–8.

Warriner, Charles K. 1981. "Levels in the Study of Social Structure." Pp. 179–90 in *Continuities in Structural Inquiry*, ed. by Peter M. Blau and Robert K. Merton. Beverly Hills, Calif.: Sage.

Weber, Max. 1946. *From Max Weber: Essays in Sociology*. New York: Oxford University Press.

———. 1949. *The Methodology of the Social Sciences*. Glencoe, Ill.: Free Press.

———. 1978. *Economy and Society*. 2 vols. Berkeley and Los Angeles: University of California Press.

———. 1981. "Some Categories of Interpretive Sociology." *Sociological Quarterly* 22:151–60.

———. 1989. "The National State and National Economic Policy." Pp. 188–209 in *Reading Weber*, ed. by Keith Tribe. London: Routledge.

Weinberg, Stephen. 1992. *Dreams of a Final Theory*. New York: Knopf.

Wolfe, Alan. 1993. *The Human Difference: Animals, Computers, and the Necessity of Social Science*. Berkeley: University of California Press.

Wuthnow, Robert, James Davison Hunter, Albert Bergesen, and Edith Kurzweil. 1984. "Introduction." In *Cultural Analysis*, ed. Robert Wuthnow, James Davison Hunter, Albert Bergesen, and Edith Kurzweil. Boston: Routledge & Kegan Paul.

Zuckerman, Harriet. 1988. "The Sociology of Science." Pp. 511–74 in *Handbook of Sociology*, ed. Neil J. Smelser. Newbury Park, Calif.: Sage.

## Chapter 3

# The Mark of the Social in the Social Sciences

## Paul F. Secord

Although it may come as a surprise, what is meant by *social behavior* is far from obvious. Is the term synonymous with such terms as social conduct, social action, human action, and interaction? What specifically distinguishes *social* behavior from other kinds of behavior? Since social behavior presumably is the central subject matter of the social sciences, perhaps the answer lies in those disciplines? In fact, as will be shown, social scientists representing the various disciplines conceptualize it in vastly different ways. Many social scientists are at odds with one another, in that they think of the theory, methods, and findings of their own discipline as reasonable approximations to the truth but regard the approaches of other disciplines as misguided.

Several features of the social sciences markedly affect how behavior or conduct is conceptualized: (1) the methodology and theory used to observe, describe, and explain behavior, (2) the relative focus on the individual versus larger units of society and the relationship between them, (3) the degree of agency attributed to individuals versus an emphasis on individuals as organisms shaped by causal forces, and (4) the extent to which current behavior is related to past behavior and its history.

These features are not entirely independent; sometimes two or more work together to affect the conceptualization of behavior or conduct. The first of these features, methodology, is readily illustrated by psychological behaviorism, which limits its focus to behavior that can

59

be publicly and consensually observed and which explains largely in terms of empirical generalizations. Other psychological approaches use methodology for assessing the thoughts and feelings of the person, while sociology and anthropology place more emphasis on language, knowledge, and meaning systems.

The second feature, the relative emphasis on the individual versus societal structures, is an enduring, unresolved question that goes back to the contrasting views of two founding fathers of sociology: Émile Durkheim and Max Weber. Durkheim (1897/1951) often argued that *social facts* are beyond individual behavior or psychology and that they can be analyzed and understood in terms of structures or other societal properties, but Weber (1922/1968) maintained that sociology cannot ignore individual action.[1]

At one extreme in the various social science disciplines, the individual is characterized as an independent entity and, at the other, as a mere abstraction from what is actually an ongoing social process. From the individualist perspective, social behavior is merely the actions of individuals, and all social phenomena can be explained in their terms. From a more holistic view, these actions can only be adequately described and explained by taking into account the immediate situation and the surrounding social world, including ongoing relationships, relevant institutional structures, and the culture of the society where the actions are taking place.

The third feature, agency, implies that the individual originates actions, and the subdisciplines vary markedly in the degree of agency attributed to the individual. Perhaps this can be readily seen in the contrasting terms used in psychology and sociology. Psychologists refer to participants in experiments as *subjects* and consider the experiment a set of treatments intended to appraise their effects on the subjects. Sociologists refer to participants in their research studies as *actors*, clearly implying individuals behaving so as to produce an effect or consequence. Actors engage in intentional action, and they have knowledge, thoughts, and feelings about their actions and their effects. It is easy to see that, if one focuses on overt behavior to the exclusion of these properties, it becomes extremely difficult to deal with relationships and institutional structures.

Because of these widely varying perspectives, social science as currently practiced has no one mark of the social. What needs examination is how the various disciplines conceptualize the social, what criteria they use to define it, and what assumptions underlie their thinking. Disciplines looked at include psychological social psychology, two sociological social psychologies (symbolic interactionism and ethnomethodology), cultural anthropology, and sociology from the perspective of the micro-macro problem.[2] Such an analysis is difficult enough in itself, but it is further aggravated by the emergence in recent decades of critical movements that are challenging the fundamental assumptions of the social science disciplines; these movements include social constructionism and discourse analysis. A final question asks whether, despite disciplinary divergencies, it is possible to identify one generic sense of the social.

## Psychology and the Mark of the Social

Psychology as a science was profoundly marked by the fact that it developed during a period when the natural sciences were making impressive gains; psychologists strove to achieve status by following as closely as possible their methods. They took this to mean that studies of the mind and mental processes had to be abandoned in favor of studying behavior; moreover, they adopted the laboratory experiment as the prime method, which limited the study of *social* behavior mainly to individuals acting in relative isolation.

The first self-conscious step toward making psychology a science was made in 1879 by Wundt (Danziger 1990) in Leipzig, Germany, in his establishment of a laboratory for investigating private individual consciousness by adapting the experimental methods used in physiology. The second big step took place in the United States and is embodied in the classical behaviorism of John B. Watson (1924), who rejected consciousness as an appropriate object for scientific investigation and designated observable behavior as a replacement.

Watson thought of the movements that an individual made as constituting behavior, and his ideas ultimately led to an "atomistic" approach in which behavior was identified and described by breaking it down into stimuli and responses. The main idea was to avoid any reference to mental or subjective or semantic attributes. Although behaviorism became "liberalized" over the following decades of the twentieth century, the focus on behavior as a set of operations readily observable and easily describable is still reflected in much psychological research.

More recently, neobehaviorism has given way to cognitive psychology. It might seem paradoxical that cognitive psychology could become dominant, given the legacy of behaviorism. Yet in a sense this development could take place in psychology as long as the emphasis remained on the individual as an "information-processing machine" (by analogy to computer programs). This view seemingly avoids subjectivity, meaning, and interpretation.

Throughout most of psychology's history, experiments were not thought of as social situations involving a relation and interaction between two persons, the experimenter and the participant; instead, only the features of the interaction pertaining to the theoretical and procedural aspects as defined by the experimenter were considered. In striving to be "scientific," experimental psychologists adopted a rhetoric pertaining to subjects participating in experiments that models persons as isolated entities, as asocial and acultural—in essence, as organic machines. Participants were not regarded as persons in any sense of the word; they were completely interchangeable with one another; they had no biography or history, and they were not viewed as if they were members of a particular society or culture (Secord 1990).

This physicalistic or behavioristic perspective led psychologists to constrict severely the range of topics they investigated: they avoided subjective meaning and the social by focusing on the skills or capacities or powers that individuals had, accomplishing this by studying perception, memory, and learning, topics that were overwhelmingly dominant from about 1930 to 1960. Even *social* psychologists doing experiments strongly favored the study of capacities, especially cognitive ones; for example, social perception and attribution—a very substantial proportion of experimentation in social psychology is devoted to such topics.

Psychologists' views of how to make their discipline as scientific as possible may have worked reasonably well for psychobiological topics, but they have had a damping and distorting effect on psychological studies of the social, as Morawski (1986) has observed:

> Conventional social psychology has studied conduct through a conceptual lens that regards neither temporal dimensions (history) nor the nuances of language. Through such context stripping, social life has been decomposed into elementary components of behavior where person perception, self-perception, dyadic encounters, close relations, and the like have come to be taken as discrete and disparate events. Primarily through the ruse of metaphors the 'social' has been expurgated from the subject of inquiry, the social being. The nature of the social, sociality, has come to be conceptualized through mechanistic models of accounting, economic exchange, and physical machinery. (p. 47)

Given the emphasis by psychologists on the individual and on directly observable, measurable behavior, how was it possible to develop a *social* psychology? Social psychologists trained in psychology accomplished that by considering as social any behavior directed toward a social object—for example, another person, but also social symbols. Thus, not only interacting with other persons but also saluting one's national flag or praying to God would be social behavior. So the central subject matter of psychological social psychology is individuals acting toward social objects, sometimes in concert with other persons, or sometimes as members of small groups or larger organizations. The emphasis remains on individual behavior; the social is epitomized by *interpersonal behavior*, by actions directed toward and reciprocated by other persons.

Consistently such actions had to be directly observable and specifiable in objective terms. Even the study of behavior in groups or organizations is typically conceived in terms of interpersonal behaviors of the individual members. Methods for observing the actions of subjects most often take the form of ratings, scaled judgments, answers to questions, or simple behavioral acts. In the current cognitive era, these often represent social perceptions or attributions. Especially notable is that a human *observer* is rarely used to record or describe actions; instead, the investigator arranges for experimental participants to use paper-and-pencil instruments or, sometimes, apparatus with levers, dials, push buttons, or a computer keyboard.

Of course, in a sense a human observer *is* used; namely, the subject him- or herself. And the behavior is typically a judgment about a contrived situation or about the actions of a confederate of the experimenter. But notice the vast difference between having the subject as a self-observer and having an independent observer. Consider a psychological experiment in which the manipulation is intended to produce liking for a confederate: to test the result, subjects are asked to rate their degree of liking for the confederate, who often is only represented on paper or, at best, on a videotape. This contrasts with the observation of liking or attraction in a natural situation, in which liking is not a rational judgment and may involve warm facial expressions, standing closer, spending more time with that person, employing more warmth in one's speech and posture, and so forth.

A caveat is in order here, to avoid misunderstanding. My assertions pertain to a deeply rooted way of thinking that pervades mainstream psychological social psychology (PSP), thinking that has its origins in one's training as a psychologist.[3] It is largely implicit, an unconscious reference frame. In fact, many PSPs work in applied settings outside of the laboratory, such as with families, in hospitals or other medical settings, or in industrial settings, rather than in experimental laboratories. Obviously they are not working with individuals in isolation; nevertheless, their implicit reference frame is an individual one that deals only in the most limited ways with the structural or societal aspects of the settings in which they work. This may become more apparent when the sociological disciplines are discussed and contrasted with those of psychology.

## Symbolic Interactionism and the Mark of the Social

Symbolic interactionism (SI) has been with us throughout most of the twentieth century and, like most disciplines, has variants supported by competing proponents. The following quotation from Denzin (1992) reveals just how diverse it is:

> [Symbolic] interactionism (in its many forms) is anti-behaviorism, both pro- and anti-psychoanalysis, Marxism and utopianism, pro-democracy and social reform, pro-instrumental experimentalism, pro-ethnology, Durkheimian structuralism, dramaturgical frameworks, conversational studies, negotiated order theories, role-identity theories, formal theories of social processes, performance science, and interpretive, critical, contextual formulations. (p. 3)[4]

Most fruitful for our purposes, however, are earlier formulations of SI (roughly the period from about 1940 to 1960) when it was active in opposition to structural-functional sociology and to psychological social psychology. The label, symbolic interactionism, coined in 1937 by Herbert Blumer (1969), aptly identifies the emphases reflecting this approach. The term *symbolic* reflects the focus on the *meanings* that things in the world around us, including other persons, have for us, and our interactions are understood in terms of these meanings. In part this emphasis arose in opposition to the popularity of behaviorism during SI's formative years.

The other term, *interactionism*, brings out that, unlike PSPs, SIs focus not on individuals but on interactions between them. Meanings of encounters between persons are interpreted in terms of the interaction itself, including its context. Through interacting with other people, individuals learn to attach significance or meaning to their actions and those of others. In contrast to the direct observation of behavior favored by PSPs, most forms of action for SIs can only be characterized in language terms by a human observer: they go far beyond mere movements or physical activities; consider, instead, for example, participating in a church service, working at a job, or acting as a patient in a mental hospital. Only a member of society familiar with these activities and their setting can observe them or participate in them. Moreover, SIs think of individuals as "actors" rather than "subjects," and their actions are regarded as intended to produce an effect or project a meaning that is read by the other participant. The actor anticipates or imagines the effect that his or her actions will have on the other as well as the actions that the other is apt to take.

Until recent years, the prime method of investigation used by SIs was participant observation in life situations, in which a sociological observer becomes a pseudomember of a group over an extended period to become familiar with its interactions and the meanings that members attach to them. The aim was to keep the interaction as natural as possible, and it was believed that only by being in natural situations could observers put themselves in the place of members and become familiar with what their actions meant to them. But more recently, some SIs have been using video recording and interview techniques, and it remains to be ascertained whether these procedures continue to focus on paradigmatic symbolic interactions.

The interpretation of interaction as a process that varies from one time or situation to another, that changes from day to day or week to week, led SIs to derogate the experimental method, which requires stability and repetition. Interactionists believed that PSP experimenters gained stability at too great a price—by simply assuming little variation, by using variables that are so abstract that they have little relation to everyday action in the real world, or by reducing interaction to narrowly circumscribed behavior that can only be characterized as banal. For similar reasons, symbolic interactionists also derogated more abstract kinds of theory as developed by sociologists and PSPs. They felt that many of their theoretical concepts were so far removed from empirical reality that they were impossible to test. SIs believe in staying close to their observations of the real world.

Unlike PSPs, many SIs especially emphasized the interactive *situation*. Since their methodology involved observers in natural settings, their assessments of situations were largely qualitative and interpretative, and their antitheoretical bias kept them close to concrete situations and meant that they could not develop a taxonomy of situations. Although he never called himself a symbolic interactionist, Goffman's research fit the tradition; moreover, his treatise on frame analysis (1974) might be thought to be a theory of situations. Goffman, however, disclaimed any such interpretation, pointing out that he was not looking at situations or social structures out there but at the organization of individual experiences.

What, then, is *the social* for symbolic interactionists? Clearly it is the goings-on among people, as experienced and seen within the perspectives of the actors themselves. Moreover, these perspectives must anticipate or construct in imagination the perspectives of those with whom one is interacting. The meanings found in these multiple perspectives are the essence of the social. Whether the action is only in a friendship dyad or involves one's family or school, the essence of the action is grasped and understood in terms of the meanings attributed to it by the actors. If we ask what is a group or collectivity, the answer comes back only in terms of the meanings attributed by the actors to their ongoing action in the group or collectivity. For SIs, groups and collectivities are nothing more than that.

## Ethnomethodology and the Mark of the Social

Developed within sociology as a rebellion against mainstream sociology, ethnomethodology (EM) stresses the nontransparency of behavior and the importance of knowing how action is categorized. Moreover, ethnomethodologists stress the active, *rational* behavior of individuals; they believe that following social norms of conduct is not done blindly but involves an intelligent adaptation to one's own needs and circumstances. They also stress the identifiability of action:

> The identifiability of any action cannot be thought of as an exclusive function of the bodily (including vocal) articulations involved in its production; it is, rather, a complex function of the circumstances in which, and the assignable purposes for which, it is performed. Here, it is argued that this principle necessarily extends to "formulations" or specifications of the sense or meaning of an activity. (Coulter 1990, p. ix)

Harold Garfinkel, reacting to some of the ideas of his teacher, Harvey Sacks, is generally credited as the founder of ethnomethodology. Garfinkel (1958) recognized the centrality of action in human life and saw clearly that the sociology dominant shortly after midcentury, often referred to as structural-functional sociology, did not deal with action in any adequate way. He noted that any action can be accomplished in a myriad of different ways—different bodily movements and different language can produce the *same* action. He saw that since most actions are readily understood by individuals in our daily lives, there must be commonly accepted rules by which they are constituted. The question he asked was "How do actors make sense of their own and other's actions; how do they make them accountable?" Practical reasoning to accomplish this makes use of how the action was situated and employs the actor's cultural stock of knowledge.

The importance of commonsense knowledge for understanding social behavior had been recognized earlier in extensive classic works by Alfred Schutz (1967) and, also later, in a well-known work by Berger and Luckmann (1966). They argued that such knowledge was required for functioning in everyday life and that it should be a central focus of sociological study, however, they did not elaborate a research strategy; that remained for the EMs.

One parallel between symbolic interactionism and ethnomethodology is obvious; the meaning of the activity is salient. Yet the emphasis is quite different; for EMs, a prime factor in determining meaning is the circumstances or setting in which the action occurs. Another difference from SIs is that EMs emphasize that members of a society or subgroup must learn how to *produce* social actions, even those of the simplest, most elementary kind. Discovering *how* members manage to make actions intelligible—make themselves as well as other persons take the actions for what they intend them to be—is a necessary endeavor if social conduct is to be understood.

The principle applies not only to complex actions but also to the simplest, routine everyday accomplishments. Garfinkel paid attention to little-noticed features of human action that actually are so much a part of our conduct that we take them for granted. For example, when two people are in a relationship, how does one manage to end a verbal episode when they are temporarily parting? Research has revealed that participants typically feel a need to justify the ending and that certain routines for doing so occur repeatedly (Albert and Kessler 1976). Another example is gender role. Garfinkel rejects the idea that gender is "natural," arguing that we have to learn to conduct ourselves as boys or men or girls or women.

Stressing action as a situated accomplishment has important consequences, one of which is the denial of certain possibilities that social scientists often take for granted. Under this interpretation, research on behavior is denied the use of universal, abstract variables and categories unless consideration is given to how they are suited to and framed by the context, the situation, and the relations among actors. Of course, such considerations greatly reduce and sometimes destroy the universal and abstract character of the variables.

Ethnomethodologists have studied such social practices as telling stories, calling the police, making jury decisions, diagnosing patients' illnesses, teaching class, and insulting someone. An important difference between EMs and SIs is that the latter consistently pointed to interpretations and meanings as a property of individuals, although they acquire it from interacting with others and share it with them. To grasp such meanings as an observer, one had to "become the other." In contrast, EMs focus on meaning as a reflection of the situation, as a linguistic account of situated action.

Appreciation of the situated nature of human action is vital to understanding EM as well as social behavior itself. Ethnomethodologists argue that all behavior is situated or context bound, a condition that prevents scientists from formalizing it in too abstract a manner. Garfinkel (1958) refers to this problem as the *indexicality* of behavior. *Indexical* is a term from logic and linguistics and applies to such words as *I*, *you*, *that*, *soon*, and so forth. Such words resist formal analysis because the referents of the terms vary with the conditions under which they are used; for example, the meaning of "that" depends on what a speaker is looking at or pointing to, had previously spoken of, and so on.

Garfinkel extends this point further to show the difficulty of behavioral description. Shared agreements or conventions are not sufficient to convey lucid meanings in any verbal exchange because words do not have fixed referents; rather, the intelligibility of what is said depends on tacit use of commonsense knowledge and the social context. Moreover, not only is speaking itself a form of action, but nonverbal behavior itself is indexical; without context and background knowledge, its meanings are not understood. As Heritage (1984) notes, indexicality might be seen as a defect of natural language, but this is mistaken because in ordinary practices, indexical terms are always used with appropriate referents. The otherwise somewhat strange expression "I've just put the bird in the oven" is perfectly familiar if it is said on Thanksgiving morning (Heritage 1984).

Thus, social psychologists who, through an experimental research program, hope to develop general principles that apply to some behavior domain, such as *helping behavior*, are apt to be foiled by the indexical properties of such behavior. Like so many actions, helping behavior varies endlessly with different contexts, and the conclusions drawn concerning the instantiated actions studied in a research program may not apply to varieties of helping behavior having different referents. In drawing conclusions after completing his extensive review of research on helping behavior, Dovidio (1984) seems implicitly to grasp the point about indexicality when he concludes that such research has focused on the simple presence or absence of bystander intervention rather than on the nature of the helping behavior itself. He notes further that studying helping behavior in contrived situations tells us nothing about the rates and nature of helpfulness in life situations, that the dominance of the experimental paradigm has shaped the form of questions asked even in field studies thus greatly limiting their scope, and, finally, that among more than a thousand studies only a handful concern helping friends, family, or acquaintances, even though surely that is the form that occurs most commonly in our daily lives.

In sum, for ethnomethodologists, social behavior is a reproduction of a form represented in society or its subgroups, a form that is a representation or an improvisation of a social action that is consensually known to members of society and its subgroups. Ethnomethodologists emphasize actors' uses of reason, knowledge, and skill in enacting social behavior, and they note that many taken-for-granted aspects of social behavior nevertheless involve "how to do it" elements (e.g., behaving in a gender-appropriate fashion). In this thinking, EMs roughly parallel the emphasis by SIs on consensually known actions but differ in their stress on skills for constructing actions and successfully carrying them out. In contrast with both PSPs and SIs, however, EMs place the greatest emphasis on situated action. Social behavior is always situated, and elements of the situation convey much of the meaning.

## Anthropolology and the Mark of the Social

To conserve space, I shall barely touch upon anthropology, only to bring in the concept of culture, which relates closely to action and meaning. In midcentury anthropologists thought of culture as *patterns of behavior* (D'Andrade 1984). But as the computer and the cognitive paradigm came to the fore, anthropologists reinterpreted culture as *meaning systems* in terms of which members of society act. Anthropologists conceptualize culture in a variety of ways, as D'Andrade observes:

> [Culture consists] of learned systems of meaning, communicated by means of natural language and other symbol systems, having representational, directive, and affective functions, and [is] capable of creating cultural entities and particular senses of reality. Through these systems of meaning, groups of people adapt to their environment and structure interpersonal activities. (p. 116)

Some anthropologists emphasize the directive or normative aspects of culture; some, the representational or symbolic features, or the affective or emotional aspects, or the social world that culture creates, or some combination of these. Most salient from our perspective is the creation of social reality; this feature is virtually absent from our three social psychologies. However, in studying the interpersonal activities that make use of society's meaning systems, and in emphasizing an intersubjective world that can be understood only by its participating members, symbolic interactionism and ethnomethodology come somewhat closer than psychological social psychology to dealing with the social world. But a reading of almost any work in cultural anthropology immediately reveals the necessity for making the social world fully a part of social psychology. There are hopeful signs; for example, Denzin (1992) has recently developed a research agenda that integrates symbolic interactionism with cultural studies and takes into account poststructuralism and postmodernism.

## An Integrative View of Social Conduct

We have seen that there are many forms of the social, some relatively simple and some more complex—more structured—than others. It will be helpful in sorting these out if we first give some attention to the extensive philosophical literature on *human action*.

Psychologists overwhelmingly prefer the term *behavior* to other possible cognates, such as action or conduct. But because of its connotations, *behavior* is a term that strips away the personal and social qualities of an action; in defining the term in psychology, *response* is favored over *act* or *action*. Thinking in terms of responses has a tendency to fragment or atomize conduct. Because of this tendency, when the term *behavior* is combined with the adjective *social* to create the term *social behavior*, the expression does not adequately reflect the properties depicted by other terms like *social action* or *social conduct*. Contrast this usage with that of sociologists. They use the term *actor* instead of *subject*, implying a person engaging in deliberate acts, enacting a performance intended to convey some meaning or to have some effect; moreover, an audience of at least one other person is implied.

Suppose we think not of behavior but instead of social acts—for example, an insult. When we ask what constitutes a social act, the issue of social behavior becomes more complicated. Much social action has meaning in terms of the practices of a particular society, culture, or subgroup; one has to be a member to understand an act or even to perceive it for what it is, or, for that matter, even to carry it out. An act that is an insult in one society may not be an insult in another. Or consider the question of what constitutes an aggressive or hostile act. Recognizing or identifying behavior as hostile requires knowledge of the actor's intent to hurt or harm another. Unless that intent is present, a harmful action could be accidental and thus would not be hostile.

Although dozens of volumes have been written on human action, for our purposes we can follow Greenwood's (1991a) treatment of human action, which nicely cuts through much of the confusion and controversy over the topic and describes it in a way that makes it amenable to use in social science research. He notes that, to be sure, particular human actions are not definable in a physical sense but that this does not mean that they have to be treated subjectively. As we examine this philosophical position, we will be impressed with the extent to which its features parallel the ideas stressed in the previous discussion of symbolic interactionism, ethnomethodology, and cultural anthropology.

The conduct of humans is such that many of its forms are quite stable over time and place and are readily recognizable by members of the community or society. For Greenwood, many human actions are socially *constituted*; that is, they exist in a sense somewhat analogous to the manner in which a physical object exists; members of a subculture recognize and acknowledge the existence of many physical objects but also many human actions.

An action is constituted by some combination of the following three elements:

1. The *representations* that the agent associates with his or her action. Representations are thoughts, feelings, or intentions per-

taining to the relevant behavior. These may, under some circumstances, be salient to the actor, and, under other conditions, the
actor may only become aware of them through questioning or
other procedures or, in rare instances, may not ever be aware
of them.
2. The relationship of the actor to other relevant persons and to
   the social context, and the bearing of these relationships on
   the action.
3. The manner in which the act is collectively represented by
   members of the community, society, or culture.

Each of these elements needs some discussion. The idea of intentionality, generically connected with human action, is strongly associated with representation, the first of these elements. This does *not*
mean that the agent need *classify* or *categorize* his or her act but only
that in most human actions, the actor has certain thoughts, feelings, or
intentions concerning the act that are essential to constituting the act
as of a certain kind. For example, for an act to be an aggressive action,
the actor must have an intent to hurt or harm the victim; otherwise, it
could merely be an unintended incident—an accident. We need only
think of acts that involve jealousy, envy, revenge, love, sympathy, and
altruism to grasp the profound importance of this first element; such
acts can only be so constituted when they are accompanied by certain
agent representations.

The second element, the relation of the actor to relevant others or
to the social context, is easily understood. One's actions toward a
friend, parent, spouse, teacher, police officer, physician, or even a
stranger have certain qualities and take the forms that they do because
they are *actions toward those particular others*. The *identities* of the
acts are determined in part by the relationship and by the situation
encompassing the action.

Similarly, in laboratory situations, the actions of participants are
determined in part because of their knowledge that they are in an
experiment and by their attitude toward experiments and the experimenter, even though social psychologists do not routinely and system-
atically explore this condition in every experiment. Instead, for the
most part, they assume that the actions of the participants are those
that the experimenter has intended to build into the experiment.

The third element, *collective representations*, refers to the fact that
so many human actions are recognized by all competent members of a
collective (such as a community or society) as having a particular

identity. Part of being a person and a member of a particular culture or subculture is possessing shared knowledge concerning the human actions commonly occurring in that culture. Of course persons are biological organisms, but that statement, though true, does not describe the reality that is a person. One only need imagine what an individual growing up in total isolation from human company and human artifacts would be like to appreciate how different this individual would be from persons as we know them.

Given this understanding of human action, the best candidate for the most generic form of social behavior is quite simply stated. An action is social when it matches a *socially constituted* form recognized by members of society or some social subgroup. Most often this involves interacting with other persons, but that is not a necessary condition. Given that we all grow up in a civilizing society, most of our actions are apt to be social in this generic sense.

Few social scientists would be content with only this generic sense of the social. Collectively represented actions can take several easily identifiable forms that differ: the interpersonal, the group, and the institutional. For PSPs, SIs, and EMs, interpersonal action is a form of *elementary* social behavior, in the sense that it lacks institutional controls—participants are not acting as members of a social institution such as the family, the school, or the workplace. But in the present view, note that to be social, the actions must involve collective representations, and not all interpersonal *behavior* qualifies.

Interpersonal action involving collective representations may occur between strangers, acquaintances, or friends. Behavior is in part shaped by individual characteristics but also by social conventions that are widely accepted, by the circumstances of meeting, or, in the case of acquaintanceships or friendships, by the history of the relationship. Such interpersonal action is thought of as "subinstitutional," that is, not influenced by any particular social institution but by circumstances or the history of the relationship. Two or more individuals interact in socially constituted ways appropriate to their relationship; for example, friends or acquaintances might discuss politics or art, tell jokes, or go to a dance or a party.

Gilbert (1989) has made a helpful contribution to understanding social behavior at the interpersonal level or beyond. She distinguishes between *singular agency* and *plural agency*. Two or more individuals constitute a plural agent when they share a joint goal (e.g., two acquaintances engaging in conversation; or a sales clerk and a customer executing a purchase). Her idea characterizes an important kind of *social* conduct but does not exhaust the topic. As Greenwood (1991b) has shown, this is because some actions of singular agents are social—namely, when they are directed toward a social object and represent a socially constituted action.

When a number of individuals act as a plural agent, the interpersonal extends to the group (e.g., a fiscal committee recommending a budget or a sports team competing for a win). Plural agency is the essence of group action, although, of course, this does not mean that there are no dissenting members of the group—consider minority reports of committees, for example. In this example, despite the dissent, all parties are acting as a plural agent, in their capacity as members of the committee.

Psychologists traditionally have focused on understanding the individual within a narrow, contemporary time span, in relative isolation from other persons, from the a larger situation and social context; and they tend, in talking about interpersonal *behavior*, not to distinguish sharply between nonsocial and socially constituted behavior. Today's heavy emphasis on cognitive psychology accentuates this tendency. Most psychologists, even social psychologists, do individualistic analysis, taking the view that an understanding of individuals automatically provides an understanding of not only their behavior in isolation but also their behavior in relationships, groups, organizations, and society itself. This doubtful idea, still current, has been around for a long time. In contrast, as we have seen, symbolic interactionists emphasize interaction and its meaning rather than individual behavior, and thus they operate within the frame of socially constituted action. Ethnomethodologists and cultural anthropologists likewise operate within this frame.

*Institutional* action goes beyond the interpersonal and the group. If two persons are working jointly on a project for an employer, playing on a college football team, or having a family dinner, they are acting at the institutional level, although some of their actions may also be interpersonal. Institutional behavior can be seen in terms of an interlocking set of social roles that in part define the particular social institution, such as the workplace or the family, while the interpersonal level is more a function of circumstances, habit, and individual or joint motivation. Young children at play represent a paradigm case of interpersonal behavior; at later ages, some of their play takes a more structured, institutionalized form, as when they play baseball in Little League.

What of the conduct of a mother, senator, lawyer, judge, or police officer? These are not just any individuals; they are persons who occupy a certain social position in society or its subgroups. Their conduct is not merely a function of their individual character and personality; it also reflects the institutional role that they are enacting. Their participation as a member of the institution (e.g., the family, the courtroom) facilitates certain actions and constrains others. People act differently at work, inside the home, outdoors in the neighborhood, at school, or in the courtroom serving on a jury. Following up our earlier discussion, certain anthropologists and sociologists especially work at the institutional level. A disclaimer concerning the institutional level is important here. Both SIs and EMs have been strongly critical of social structural theory and analysis at that level. Their focus on the concrete interactions and on situated action, as well as the constructive, creative, adaptive activity of actors, leads them to reject social structures as relatively enduring entities and as social forces that place constraints on actors. Instead, they treat social structures as merely forms that multiple actors produce. The last section will move toward resolving this issue. Before moving to that, however, it is worth noting that certain contemporary movements relate to our discussion. A salient theme stressed so far has been that the social world differs markedly from the physical world of the natural sciences; it is an entity constructed out of human interactions taking place in a setting that is organized. Many factors contribute to this organization: society and its social institutions, the history of previous interactions, the local situation, and the relationships among the actors. Central here is the point that this setting and its structures cannot be described solely in physical terms but instead involves *meaning systems*.

This ties in closely with a powerful contemporary movement: *discursive psychology* (Potter and Wetherell 1987; Harré and Gillett 1994). Discursive psychology stresses the human capacity for language and its use. Many of the concepts used in this chapter pertain to complex ways in which humans use language. Human action itself, while it includes many nonverbal acts, is overwhelmingly linguistic in nature. Meaning systems can only be understood in language terms, and the social world itself is primarily a linguistic one. When psychological behaviorism was popular, one idea was that a perfect record of behavior could be obtained simply by filming it.

That this is an illusion generated by behaviorism is easy to see. For example, what would a Martian make of films of our earthly activities? The answer is, Not much. This is the case because all human action is heavily impregnated with meaning, meaning that can only be described in language terms. The more contemporary technology, videotape, with a clear record of the language used, is not complete either, in and of itself. In fact, what is occurring between the participants may be quite a mystery. Remember Garfinkel's indexicality and what lies behind it: situated action and social context. Beyond that are relationships, group and larger social structures, social institutions, and society itself. All of these entities generally involve collective representations, which are instantiated largely in language terms. So discursive psychology justifiably stresses the critical and pervasive role of language in human life, and it serves as a needed corrective to a traditional psychology that grew out of logical positivism and behaviorism. But one's enthusiasm for it should not be allowed to lead to a form of antirealism that argues that the only human reality is language activity and that that should be the sole focus of psychology. Even if language plays an important part in instantiating the theoretical entities discussed, these entities are more than just language activity; for example, the family, the justice system, or a particular science are more than mere talk.

A final topic that might help achieve a more integrative position is what sociologists have called the *micro-macro* polarity. This point returns us to our opening comment concerning Durkheim's emphasis on society and Weber's on the individual. Micro-macro is a continuum of exclusion and inclusion, of narrow focus versus wide-angle views, of individual acts versus group or societal actions. At the micro end, psychologists study individuals in relative isolation within a brief contemporary time span. At the macro extreme, many sociologists and anthropologists believe that social conduct cannot be described or explained without considering the contribution from institutional and other societal structures, while others believe that the micro level is irrelevant. Also toward the micro end, but to a less extreme extent, symbolic interactionists and ethnomethodologists focus on individuals not in isolation but in interaction, over a slightly longer time span than most psychologists cover. But to some extent they are like psychologists in tending to regard social conduct as primarily the actions of individuals and in considering institutional and other societal actions as not much more than the actions of many individuals.

Until about 1980, depending on individual sociologists' predilections, sociology went through a period of emphasizing either microsociology or macrosociology, as the way to understand and explain social conduct. But since that time, most sociologists have come to believe that adopting one or the other of these extremes is a mistake and that only explanations that link micro- and macrosociology will be fully adequate (Ritzer 1990). Ritzer points out that different forms of linkage are possible. Some sociologists are working toward integrating micro and macro *theories*, while others are trying to develop a "theory that deals with the linkage between micro and macro existential levels . . . of social analysis" (Ritzer 1990:152).

The micro-macro polarity is often identified with several others that resemble but are not identical with it: methodological individualism versus holism, and structure versus agency. Ritzer observes that most attempts to resolve the micro-macro problem start from one extreme or the other, essentially reducing the opposite extreme to the favored one. For example, microsociologists may try to explain or reduce macrostructural phenomena to the microstructural, and vice versa for macrosociologists. A more desirable approach, he says, is not to favor either extreme but to develop a theory that deals adequately with both micro and macro phenomena and their relations.

From my perspective, if one wishes to understand or explain *social* behavior, talk about individuals in isolation from the society of others and talk about society apart from its members are incomplete and misleading; this assumes an ontological dualism that renders asunder "individuals" and "society," and it becomes difficult or impossible to link them or integrate them. Individuals performing some socially constituted action would not be doing so were they not members of the society or a subgroup recognizing that action. Moreover, their membership connects their action to that of other members, and such connections or relations in the society or subgroup facilitate or constrain the action in various ways. Giddens (1984:2) recognizes this when he asserts that the basic domain of the social sciences "is neither the experience of the individual actor, nor the existence of any form of societal totality, but social practices ordered across time and space."

This avoids ontological dualism by doing away with both micro and macro: there is only socially constituted action, executed by individuals acting alone or in concert. Manicas (1993), following Bhaskar and Giddens, puts it this way:

"Society," or social structures, social relations, etc. do nothing. Society cannot make anything happen because, unlike a magnetic field, society has no independent existence . . . individuals . . . are not passive "role players," but . . . active agents using cultural materials which are available to them. (p. 223)

It would be a mistake to construe this position as using a micro approach to explain the macro; in Bhaskar's model, individuals do not create society, nor does society create individuals. Bhaskar (1989:37) says, "Human action always expresses and utilizes some or other social form." The *social* actions of individuals are executed in concert with others, and these actions are orchestrated and articulated to comprise various forms of life that have an ongoing existence that is rooted in the earlier history of these individuals, other members, and their ancestors. Individuals are not acting independently; these socially constituted forms provide a medium within which individuals act. Thus, the mark of the social is its socially constituted form.[5]

## Notes

1. Ritzer (1990) notes that although Durkheim and Weber were often seen as respectively favoring the social or the individual, they were in fact also concerned with linking these polarities.

2. These disciplines and topics are not exhaustive; for example, the psychology of personality, clinical psychology, political science, and economics, as well as some other domains, have some relevance to social behavior.

3. Of course, perspectives that diverge from the mainstream exist within PSP itself. One example is ecological psychology, initiated by Roger Barker (1968) and maintained by a few of his students and followers His approach places much more emphasis on the surrounding physical and social world, but, unfortunately, it does not receive much attention from mainstream PSPs.

4. About two dozen references have been omitted from this sentence.

5. Nothing said here is intended to argue that psychologists or micro- or macro sociologists cannot do their thing. Rather, it recognizes that research from those perspectives makes important contributions to understanding but asserts that, if the aim is understanding *social* action rather than individual behavior, such understanding is limited by those perspectives. Only a broader, more integrated perspective that looks at individuals acting as members of a social world can yield a more complete understanding.

## References

Albert, Stuart, & Suzanne Kessler. 1976. "Processes for Ending Social Encounters: The Conceptual Archaeology of a Temporal Place."*Journal for the Theory of Social Behavior* 6(2):147–170.

Barker, Roger. G. 1968. *Ecological Psychology: Concepts and Methods for*

*Studying the Environment of Human Behavior.* Stanford, Calif.: Stanford University Press.

Berger, Peter, and Thomas Luckmann. 1967. *The Social Construction of Reality.* London: Allen Lane.

Bhaskar, Roy. 1989. *The Possibility of Naturalism: A Philosophical Critique of the Contemporary Human Sciences.* New York: Harvester.

Blumer, Herbert. 1969. *Symbolic Interactions: Perspective and Method.* Englewood Cliffs, N.J.: Prentice-Hall.

Coulter, Jeff. 1990. *Ethnomethodological Sociology.* Brookfield, Vt.: Ashgate.

D'Andrade, Roy G. 1984. "Cultural Meaning Systems." Pp. 88–119 in *Culture Theory: Essays on Mind, Self, and Emotion,* ed. Richard A. Shweder and Robert A. LeVine. New York: Cambridge University Press.

Danziger, Kurt. 1990. *Constructing the Subject: Historical Origins of Psychological Research.* New York: Cambridge University Press.

Denzin, Norman. K. 1992. *Symbolic Interactionism and Cultural Studies: The Politics of Interpretation.* Oxford: Blackwell.

Dovidio, John F. 1984. "Helping Behavior and Altruism: An Empirical and Conceptual Overview." Pp. 362–427 in *Advances in Experimental Social Psychology,* Vol. 17, ed. Leon Berkowitz. New York: Academic Press.

Durkheim, Émil. 1897/1951. *Suicide.* New York: Free Press.

Garfinkel, Harold. 1958. *Studies in Ethnomethodology.* Englewood Cliffs, N.J.: Prentice Hall.

Giddens, Anthony. 1984. *The Constitution of Society: Outline of a Theory of Structuration.* Berkeley: University of California Press.

Gilbert, Margaret. 1989. *On Social Facts.* Princeton, N.J:. Princeton University Press.

Goffman, Erving. 1974. *Frame Analysis.* New York: Harper & Row.

Greenwood, John D. (1991a). *Relations and Representations: An Introduction to the Philosophy of Social Psychological Science.* London: Routledge.

———. (1991b). "The Mark of the Social" [Review of the book *On Social Facts*]. *Social Epistemology* 5:221–32.

Harré, Rom, and Grant Gillett. 1994. *The Discursive Mind.* Thousand Oaks, Calif: Sage.

Heritage, John. 1984. *Garfinkel and Ethnomethodology.* Cambridge: Polity.

Manicas, Peter.T. 1993. "The Absent Ontology of Society: Response to Juckes and Barresi." *Journal for the Theory of Social Behavior* 23(2):217–28.

Morawski, Jill G. 1986. "Contextual Discipline: The Unmaking and Remaking of Sociality." Pp. 47–66 in *Contextualism in Understanding in Behavioral Science: Implications for Research and Theory,* ed. Ralph L. Rosnow and Marianthl Georgoudi. New York: Praeger.

Potter, Jonathan and Margaret Wetherell. 1987. *Discourse and Social Psychology.* London: Sage.

Ritzer, George. 1990. "Micro-Macro Linkage in Sociological Theory." Pp. 347–70 in *Frontiers of Social Theory: The New Syntheses,* ed. George Ritzer. New York: Columbia University Press.

Schutz, Alfred. 1967. *Collected Papers. I. The Problem of Social Reality*. The Hague: Nijhoff.

Secord, Paul F. 1990. " 'Subjects' versus 'Persons' in Social Psychological Research." Pp. 165–88 in *Harré and His Critics: Essays in Honour of Rom Harré with his Commentary on Them*. Oxford: Blackwell.

Watson, John B. 1924. *Behaviorism*. Chicago: University of Chicago Press.

Weber, Max. 1922/1968. *Economy and Society*. New York: Bedminster.

## Chapter 4

# How Many Kinds of Things Are There in the World? The Ontological Status of Societies

### Scott Gordon

The first step of science is to know one thing from another. This knowledge consists of their specific distinction; but in order that it may be fixed and permanent, distinct names must be given to different things.

—*Linnaeus*

At the risk of appearing pretentious, I would describe this chapter as an essay in "ontological systematics," since what I want to do is construct a classification of the fundamental types of entities that exist or, at least, those of them that are objects of empirical experience. Since I am a social scientist, my main interest lies in trying to understand human sociality, and the primary object of this chapter is to elucidate the nature of the enterprise that social scientists are engaged in. To achieve this goal, the domain of the social has to be located in a classification that distinguishes it from the territories of other disciplines, so I shall be discussing some matters that lie outside my own field of expertise.

Every scheme of classification must rest on a taxonomic principle. The principle I adopt is that the things that constitute the world of our empirical experience are most fundamentally differentiated from one another as reflecting the operation of different *processes of organization*. Typically, I think, the literature of "ontological systematics" has focused on the fact either that things have different *properties* or that they are composed of different (or, for hard-line monists, the same) *basic constituents*. These taxonomic principles simply do not work. My argument is that one should instead direct attention to whether things are simple or complex and, among the latter, on how the complexes are organized into integrated wholes. If one pursues this notion, it will appear that there are only a small number of different kinds of things in the world, and one of them, deserving a class by itself, is the kind of thing that social scientists attempt to study.

The tension between *monism* and *pluralism* has punctuated the history of Western thought, and it continues to do so. Ontological monists claim that there is only one "fundamental" kind of thing in the world, the diversity of experience evincing merely the "secondary" properties of a basically homogeneous substrate. Pluralists, on the other hand, have argued that diversity is itself a basic property of existence. This tension is strongly manifest in the literatures of ethics and political philosophy, which are of special concern to the social scientist, but in this chapter I want to address the metaphysical and epistemological bearings of the issue in the study of human social phenomena.

To a lay observer such as myself, it seems that the strong thrust in the natural sciences at the present time is monistic. Biology is really chemistry, chemistry is really physics, and physics is in hot pursuit of the great undifferentiated One that composes all existents. Stephen Hawking (1988:10) tells us that "the eventual goal of science is to provide a single theory that describes the whole universe," and, if I understand him correctly, he does not mean to exclude human social phenomena from "the whole universe."[1] Biology was, at one time, *the* natural science of diversity, strongly reinforced in this by the focus on organic divergence in Darwin's theory of evolution. But modern molecular biology stresses the unity of organic phenomena rather than their diversity, and "sociobiologists" have contended that, in due course, the sorts of things that sociologists and economists have concerned themselves with will be explained in terms of the chemistry of the human genome—which, in turn will be explained by what physicists call a GUT, a Grand Unified Theory that embraces everything there is.

One should not depreciate the power of reduction in scientific investigation. My own methodological predilection is to explain the large in terms of the small, to search for the microdeterminants of macrophenomena. But this can be carried too far. Without a doubt, societies are composed of human organisms, which are composed of cells constructed from chemical molecules that, ultimately, consist of "quarks" and "leptons," or "strings," or "fields," or whatever it is that physicists will ultimately use as the constituents of a Grand Unified Theory. But I am skeptical that the GUT equations will be able to explain phenomena such as inflation, juvenile delinquency, or the sudden downfall of communist regimes in Eastern Europe. To investigate social phenomena effectively, it is necessary to appreciate the special nature of the domain of the social.

How many kinds of things are there in the world? The pre-Socratics contended that there are four kinds of things, which derived their different properties respectively from earth, water, air, or fire, a notion that Aristotle employed in his attempt to explain observed phenomena in terms of the "essences" of things. The Greeks were, in my view, on the right track in trying to establish a pluralistic schema of basic ontological categories, and they did get the number right. There *are* four such categories. But that is all they can be given credit for. The fourfold classification that I will propose consists of (1) undifferentiated elementary particles, (2) mechanisms, (3) organisms, and (4) human societies. The first three of these will come as no surprise. My main object is to defend the award of a special ontological status to the fourth. To do so, I will show that it is the necessary consequence of the taxonomic principle employed in establishing the categorical distinctiveness of the first three, and especially the distinction between mechanisms and organisms.

Before I proceed to develop this argument, a word or two is necessary concerning whether I am taking a "realistic" or "nominalistic" stance. One could claim that the four categories I will be talking about correspond to "natural kinds," that is, that all the many specific things there are in the world fall "naturally" into the four categories. Or, one could take the view that this classification is an artifact constructed by the human intellect and that the four "kinds" are merely names that we have invented and use as epistemic heuristics.

I find both of these stances rather unpalatable. I do not see how one can possibly know what natural kinds there are without the use of a great deal of theorizing, as well as manipulating, counting, measuring, and other procedures that involve much human artifice. But, on the other hand, there can be no scientific value in constructing theoretical classifications, models, and so forth, that are devoid of reference to the real world. The procedures of science, it seems to me, consist of using theories and empirical facts as complementary instruments of cognition. We, as humans, make and use the instruments; to that extent, science is "nominalist." But our instruments will not work (that is, they will not yield knowledge about the real world) unless they "model" it in some fashion; in that way science is unavoidably "realist."[2]

The relation between the "real" and the "nominal" or, more generally, between the domain of "matter" and that of "mind" is more complex for the social sciences than for the natural sciences. Social phenomena reflect the operation of material factors, to be sure, but they also reflect mentational factors: beliefs, desires, expectations, and so forth. Such things as these have no role in the play of natural phenomena, but, for the social scientist, mental entities are "facts" no less than material entities are. The statement "The sun revolves around the earth" is false, and astronomers need pay no attention to it. But the statement "Pope Urban VIII believed that the sun revolves around the Earth" is true; that is, it is a true fact about Urban VIII. Such mentational facts do not concern the astronomer, but only the naive materialist would argue that they can be excluded from the scientific study of social phenomena.

## The Organization of Mechanisms

Physicists tell us that the world was very simple at the time of the Big Bang and remained so for only a small fraction of a second thereafter. Since then it has been becoming increasingly complex, but, nonetheless, complex entities are combinations of simple ones.[3] It would be, I understand, a bit old-fashioned to regard these simple entities as being like tiny hard homogeneous billiard balls, one exactly like another. For one thing, numerous different types of fundamental entities seem to exist; physicists now speak of three "families" of them, and their language decidedly does not suggest billiard balls or, indeed, any other guileless material entity. Fortunately, we need not concern ourselves with this. Let us simply say that there is a category of very small things that is the domain of study of subatomic physics. If it is a bit unsophisticated to refer to these things as "homogeneous particles," it will not matter for the purpose of this chapter, and we can move on without further ado to the second kind of thing, "mechanisms."

By "mechanisms" I mean all those complex things whose structural configuration and behavior can be ascribed to the operation of one or more of the four basic physical forces. The term, then, embraces a very wide range of material entities, both natural and human-made.

According to the taxonomic criterion I am using, mountains, rivers, planets, sand dunes, cathedrals, and umbrellas all belong to the same category. Their *organization* is mediated by the operation of physical forces.

Now, one might ask, is this not true of *everything* that exists? Most assuredly it is, so why have I not mentioned elephants, or sycamore trees, or any other organic entity among these "mechanisms"? Because, I would contend, in the case of organic entities the processes of organization involve more than the blunt operation of physical forces. The organism-mechanism distinction will concern us in a moment. Before considering it, I want to say a word or two more about the taxonomic criterion I am using.

It seems to have become customary to refer to the empirical differences between complex things and the simpler things of which they are composed as reflecting the "emergence" of novel properties when certain combinations are made. Thus, hardness is said to be an "emergent property" of bronze, a property not displayed by its component copper and tin taken separately. And, similarly, liquidity is an emergent property when hydrogen and oxygen are combined, saltiness to the taste is an emergent property of the combination of sodium and chlorine, and so on.

I see no harm in such locutions unless they are construed to mean that when, say, sodium and chlorine are put together, some new entity, saltiness, devoid of all physical properties such as mass and location in space-time but an entity nonetheless, has come into existence. Mysticism of this sort is, I think, often smuggled into ontological debate when it is asserted that "the whole is greater than the sum of its parts." Of course, water is different from the two gases that compose it, and table salt is different from sodium and chlorine, but the "emergent properties" that manifest themselves in such cases can, it seems to me, be construed as properties that devolve from their *organization*, without any need to flirt with the notion that some ineffable new entity springs into existence when a complex is formed from simples. In the literature of Western thought, the temptation to regard emergent properties as bespeaking the creation of such mysterious entities has not been much evident in the discussion of chemical or metallurgical properties, but it has been prominent in the consideration of organic phenomena, and the notion is not without practical import even today, in the domain of human biology. Thus, for example, the doctrine that when a human sperm and egg come together to form a zygote, a new and precious thing called "life" emerges, is the focal point of a continuing acrimonious dispute over public policy. Similar notions about emergent properties punctuate the long literature on the relation between human individuals and the social "wholes" that result from their combination: "cultures," "nations," and so forth. More on this point later.

## Mechanisms and Organisms

Anthropologists tell us that it is a common belief among "primitive" peoples that entities such as mountains, rivers, trees, and so on, are endowed with life spirits that do not differ fundamentally from that which is known directly to self-conscious humans. This notion— "animism" or "panpsychism"—is also to be found in the ancient literatures of our own culture. It suffered a steady decline, however, in Western thought and received its death blow from the formulation of the laws of mechanics in the seventeenth century.[4] The creation of the "mechanistic philosophy" as a general ontological outlook is one of the main reasons that the time of Galileo, Kepler, and Newton is called the era of the "Scientific Revolution." In the wave of enthusiasm for Newtonian mechanics that dominated European thought for the next two centuries, the notion that the world is a mechanism, and nothing but a mechanism, was prominently expressed, even though it was considered an "atheistic" doctrine and was strongly opposed not just by one church but by all. The great French mathematician and astronomer Pierre Simon de Laplace (1749–1827) epitomized the mechanistic view in his famous contention that if an intelligence sufficiently powerful to make the calculations were provided with the positions and velocities of all the material constituents of the universe at any moment of time, and knew the laws of physics, he (she? it?) could predict the entire future and reconstruct the entire past, since the calculations would be comprehensive, excluding nothing that really exists.[5]

In the early twentieth century the same view was expressed by the distinguished French biologist Jacques Loeb, especially in his lecture on "The Mechanistic Conception of Life" (1912/1964), which was delivered to the First International Congress of Monists at Hamburg in 1911.[6] Loeb's thesis was that there is no important difference between organic and inorganic phenomena. They are both governed by the laws of physics and chemistry.[7] The main object of his paper was to urge his fellow biologists to search for the physicochemical factors that govern organic processes. Unless this is done, Loeb declared, biology will not achieve the status of a true science, and organic phenomena will remain inexplicable. On the other hand, he contended, if biology were to become scientific (i.e., mechanistic) it would conquer not only the domain of the organic but that of the social and the ethical as well.[8] The economist-philosopher Frank Knight was fond of remarking that the Western intellect, having struggled for centuries to free itself from the notion that stones are like people, was busily engaged in promoting the view that people are like stones.

Jacques Loeb may have been, at least partly, reacting against a notion that was becoming very prominent and popular in the early decades of the twentieth century. This was the doctrine of "vitalism." One of its most prominent proponents was Loeb's countryman and contemporary, the philosopher Henri Bergson. His book *Creative Evolution*, first published in 1907, was a great popular success and was largely responsible for the award to him of the Nobel Prize in Literature in 1927. On the scientific side, the doctrine was ardently embraced by the German biologist Hans Driesch.[9] The argument of vitalism was that the difference between organisms and mechanisms is that there is present in organisms a special thing or property, which Bergson called the *élan vital*.

At this distance from the heyday of vitalism, it is difficult to credit the enthusiasm with which it was embraced, for indeed it explains absolutely nothing. Noting that organisms can do things that mechanisms cannot, and attributing this to the existence of an *élan vital*, is like the Molière character who "explained" that opium makes one drowsy because it possesses a "dormative property." Bergson, Driesch, and the other proponents of vitalism were unable to show how the vital force works. Without doing that, one may as well say that mechanisms differ from organisms in that the former are governed by physical forces while the latter are governed by fairies.

It would lead us very far afield to discuss the many attempts that have been made to delineate the differences between mechanisms and organisms, some of which are quite bizarre.[10] But one of them deserves a moment's attention here: Erwin Schrödinger's (1943) celebrated essay *What Is Life?* According to Schrödinger, organisms are special because they are able to counteract a basic law of physics, the second law of thermodynamics, which states that in the universe as a whole, there is a persistent increase in "entropy." Following Ludwig Boltzmann's definition, an increase in entropy is a decrease in the degree of orderliness of a system, such as, for example, that which occurs when one shuffles a new pack of playing cards, initially arranged in perfect order of suits and values. Schrödinger contended that the "decay" in physical systems due to the second law is counteracted by organic processes. The special property of organisms is that processes such as photosynthesis and metabolism can increase orderliness, or decrease entropy. Therefore, says Schrödinger, the "ordinary" laws of physics do not apply to organisms; they work by "a new type of physical law" (1956/1967:81, 86).

According to Schrödinger's biographer, Walter Moore, *What Is Life?* was "a major contribution to the history of biological thought" and had "an enormous influence" in the development of physics-oriented and chemistry-oriented biological research (1989:394, 403). Undoubtedly, Schrödinger's essay was much discussed, perhaps more than any other modern paper on the theme of the special properties of organisms, and it has been enthusiastically hailed by some scientists (more by physicists and chemists, it appears, than by biologists), but a little reflection is sufficient to convince one that Schrödinger was altogether on the wrong track. He did not really intend to claim that organisms are capable of setting the second law of thermodynamics aside, that is, that they are capable of producing a net decrease in the entropy of the universe as a whole. Organisms are construed as being able to accomplish a purely *local* (and temporary) increase in orderliness. But this is also the result of many nonorganic phenomena as well—for example, the uplift of a new mountain range, or the scouring of a river channel. Human-made nonorganic artifacts, such as houses, roads, and umbrellas, are deliberately designed to achieve a local decrease in entropy. In short, Schrödinger's taxonomic principle does not work. *What Is Life?* stands as yet another failure to differentiate organisms from mechanisms by focusing on *properties*.[11]

Before I go on to describe the right way to distinguish between organisms and mechanisms, let us take a moment to note a matter that has been lying just under the surface of the discussion thus far. In most of the literature of the organism-mechanism debate, the real point at issue has not been whether organisms in general deserve a special ontological status but whether a particular organism, *Homo sapiens*, does. Many writers on this question are quite convinced that man has properties that distinguish him "fundamentally" from other members of the animal kingdom. Some have focused on the capacity for articulate speech, others on the power of abstract thought, or the invention of the means to store and transmit ideas in writing, or the ability to use tools, or to *make* tools, or humans' consciousness of their selves, or of their history, or the future that awaits them. James Boswell observed that man is the *cooking* animal. The Dutch philosopher Johan Huizinga finds significance in the fact that humans are the animal that engages in *play*. Mark Twain once remarked that humans are the only animal that blushes or has cause to. So, there is a rich menu of humans' special properties that one can call on if one wishes to proceed in that direction.

The really important debate on the issue of the ontological status of humans was initiated in the seventeenth century by René Descartes, who divided the world into two exclusive categories, one consisting of entities that are governed entirely by physical laws, the other of entities endowed with the possession of "soul" or "mind." Everything in the world, including all organisms except humans, is contained in the first category, the domain of *res extensa*; humans alone inhabit the second, the domain of *res cogitans*. One is tempted to dismiss Descartes's dualism as a particularly gross display of *amour-propre*, a property that is more clearly unique to humankind than the possession of "soul." But, in fact, Descartes built a philosophical system on his ontological notion that revealed fundamental problems that philosophers, and indeed scientists, have had to contend with, unresolved, down to the present day. The relation between the scientist and the domain of investigation, between the knower and the thing that is known, raises some profound issues for all sciences, and perhaps especially for the social sciences. A century after Descartes, another Frenchman, Julian Offray de La Mettrie (1748) published his famous (or infamous) *Man a Machine* in which he tried to dispose of all the problems Descartes had raised in one fell swoop, by simply declaring that humans, like everything else in the universe, are automatons, governed entirely by physical forces, without freedom of choice and action. Presumably La Mettrie exempted himself and the readers he was trying to persuade; otherwise, he had just been making scratches with an inked goose quill on paper, like the goose itself scratching the dirt of the barnyard, devoid of any meaning beyond what the laws of physics can explain.

The question of the status of man was, of course, central to the debate over the Darwinian theory of evolution that took place in the next century. Many of those who were deeply offended by Darwin would have been quite content if he had said that all species had developed by evolution from more primitive forms except *Homo sapiens*. Indeed, most would, I think, have been satisfied, or even gratified, if he had said that his theory applied to all organisms except

*European* humans. Darwin himself was convinced, however, that the races of humans are not very different from each other and, moreover, that *Homo sapiens* differs greatly in degree, but not categorically, from other higher mammals.[12] Among the many, including scientists, who rejected this view, Alfred Russel Wallace, the independent codiscoverer of the "Darwinian" theory of evolution, is especially worth noting. The species *Homo sapiens*, said Wallace, had evolved by the mechanism of natural selection like other members of the branching tree of life, but with the emergence of this species, something categorically new had come into being, a spiritual something, that transcends the constraints of material existence: *mind* independent of *brain*. This did not lead Wallace to embrace one of the established religions but to develop a deep interest in spiritualism. He became an enthusiastic devotee of seances, at which table rappings, the voices of the dead, and other metaphysical wonders were displayed.

It is easy to feel superior to Darwin and Wallace, but the problem that they addressed remains. Are humans categorically different from other entities? Do they deserve a special place in our ontological taxonomy? In terms of the taxonomic principle I have adopted, my answer to this is an unqualified no. As an organism, there is no ground for drawing a categorical distinction between *Homo sapiens* and other species. But a special category is required for *human societies*. To advance toward this thesis, I must first explain why organisms deserve a separate ontological category. The resolution of the long debate on mechanism and organisms is easy, but not because we are smarter than Descartes or LaMettrie, or Wallace, or the many others who have engaged in it. The solution could not have been found before the development of our understanding of the operation of the organic genome following the discovery in 1953 of the structure of the DNA molecule by James Watson and Francis Crick. As Newton once noted, standing on the shoulders of giants enables one to see farther than they, even though one's own stature may be small.

## The Organization of Organisms[13]

So far as I know, the first person to explain clearly that the fundamental difference between mechanisms and organisms lies in their processes of organization was the Harvard biologist Ernst Mayr.[14] I will state his essential argument in my own words.

The DNA molecule is like any other material entity in being subject to the ordinary laws of physics. But, in the cells of an organism, it plays a special role. It contains an implicit "blueprint" of the morphological structure of the organism and "instructions" for its construction and physiological functioning. In the cell, segments of DNA transmit their instructions to the RNA "messengers," which carry them to the ribosomes where proteins are constructed, or "synthesized," by assembling amino acids in the prescribed fashion. These proteins are the basic materials out of which the somatic structure of the organism is made, and they also constitute the enzymes that command its dynamic processes. When for example, a human egg and sperm combine under appropriate conditions, a single cell, a zygote, is formed that contains a double set of DNA molecules, the human genome. The zygote divides and two cells are formed, then four, and so on, each one containing a complete genome. At a particular stage, the bundle of cells folds in upon itself to form a tube, which becomes the gastrointestinal tract of the finished organism. Heart, lungs, eyes, bones, nerves, and so on, are produced. The heart begins to beat, circulating blood to the tissues. After a time, the new organism is ejected from the womb, the lungs begin to expand rhythmically, further somatic growth takes place, and additional physiological functions commence. After a time, these functions become impaired and eventually the organism "dies"; that is, it becomes *disorganized*, and its somatic material decomposes into the original chemical constituents. All these processes, except the last, are governed by commands contained in the genome.

A bumpkin, when told that a thermos bottle will keep hot things hot and cold things cold, asked, "How does it know which is which?" This is the wrong question to ask about mechanisms such as thermos bottles, but it is not off the mark for organisms. In a metaphorical, but not inappropriate, sense, the embryonic cells "know" how, and when, and where, to form a tube, a liver, an eye; how and when to pulsate, secrete, and so forth. The genome contains all the necessary information and commands.[15]

The difference, then, between mechanisms and organisms is plain. The organization of a mechanistic complex is solely due to the operation of physical imperatives: the two nuclear forces, the electromagnetic force, and gravitational attraction. Organisms are organized by a different kind of imperative, the information-command system of the genome. Organisms do not differ *materially* from mechanisms, and both are integrated systems of differentiated parts, but they are organized through the operation of different *processes*. This is what justi-

fies the separation of mechanisms and organisms into distinctive ontological categories.

This argument leads immediately to a further question. The notion
that organic complexes may validly be distinguished from mechanical
complexes in the way I have described is based on the acceptance of
organizational processes as a fundamental taxonomic principle. If, on
this principle, organisms and mechanisms must be recognized as
categorically distinct "things," yet other different things may exist in
the world as well, if there are other processes of organization at work
that cannot be reduced either to the information-command procedures
carried out by DNA molecules or the four primary forces of physics.
My contention is that there is (at least) one more kind of thing in the
world—*social* complexes. I go on now to support this contention. For
convenience I shall speak simply of "societies," but the processes of
organization on which I will focus are most distinctive of and, in some
cases, unique to *human* societies, so the social complexes for which I
claim special ontological status are the ones to which we ourselves
belong.[16]

## The Organization of Societies

The great French sociologist Émile Durkheim was insistent that social
phenomena are "things." Unfortunately, he did not recognize their
distinctiveness from other things and, in effect, tended to claim that
societies are like organisms. He advanced the notion that every society
has a *conscience collective,* a collective consciousness and/or conscience,[17] which operates as a controlling and integrating force on
the individuals who compose it, producing the "solidarity" that he
considered the property essential to a viable society. If he did not do
so altogether, he came very close to embracing the mystical notion
that there is a "collective mind."[18]

Durkheim was not the first, or the last, to advance the notion that
societies are organisms or, at least, that they are sufficiently like
organisms that the findings of biology can be validly extended by
analogy to societies. Numerous writers on social questions, from Plato
through Saint Paul to the present day, have adopted such a line of
attack, with little success in producing a scientific analysis.[19] Durkheim's English contemporary Herbert Spencer is, justifiably, regarded
by historians as having pursued the organism-society analogy with
exceptional tenacity, but, in speaking of societies as "superorganic,"

Spencer made it plain that he did not mean to say that societies are a superior kind of organism but that they represent a level of organization above that of the individual human being.[20] In this he was on the right track but unfortunately, he did not follow where it leads.

Many devotees of the notion that human societies are like organisms have, like Spencer, been persuaded by the existence of apparently analogous properties. Societies are composed of individuals who differ in their roles and occupations. That is, within a social complex there is "division of labor," like that which characterizes the functions of the liver, heart, and other specialized organs of an organic complex.[21] In addition, societies can be said to "reproduce" themselves, as organisms do; both may "grow," both may "die," both may be regarded as the product of an "evolutionary process," and so on.[22] Beyond such notions, the society-organism analogy has been prominent in Western political philosophy, especially since the rise of nationalism as a dominating political ideology.[23] This prominence is exceptionally evident in political romanticism, but even pedestrian utilitarians have sometimes been prone to argue as if the nation-state has a life of its own, with its own values and aims, to which the welfare of the individual must be, or "naturally" is, subservient.[24]

In claiming that the special ontological status of human social complexes derives from the fact that they are organized by unique processes, what do I mean by a "social complex" or, for brevity, a "society"? We use this term in ordinary speech in a variety of ways. If it is to carry the freight I wish to load on it, a clear definition is necessary. Let me first give some illustrations. Geographically bounded nation-states such as France and the United States are indeed societies, but so are, for example, the English-Speaking Union, the AFL-CIO, Indiana University, the Modern Languages Association, General Motors, the Gordon family, the Baseball Writers Association, the American Association of Retired Persons, the stock market, and the market for pork bellies. What is common to such a diverse collection of entities? They are complexes that enable their members to achieve certain purposes. Humans may be gregarious "by nature," but the significant feature of the societies they form is that they are utilitarian artifacts. So, my definition of a society is *an association of individual persons that permits the achievement of ends that cannot be achieved by the individuals separately*. That is, societies enable their members to cooperate effectively for a variety of purposes: defense, the construction of roads, the nurture and education of the young, the acquisition and transmittal of knowledge, the production and exchange of goods and services, the exercise of political power, and others too numerous, and too fluid, to list. I make no moral judgment in this definition. Cooperation may enable individuals to do evil as well as good: to defend themselves from attack, or to attack others; to produce goods, or to steal them; to educate the youth, or to indoctrinate them with myths, or Platonic "noble lies" that facilitate the exercise of arbitrary power by some persons over others.

An important feature of this definition is that the individual may simultaneously be a member of more than one society. He may be employed in one business firm and be a shareholder of others, while also being a member of a tennis club, a militia, a church, a nation, and a political party, and a participant in the social processes of buying and selling, to name only a few. The whole human macrosocial system is an elaborate network or ensemble of these particular social complexes that, with modern communication and transportation, has become worldwide.[25]

What, then, are the organizational processes that permit humans to cooperate through the formation of societies? This can be best explained by focusing first on *economic* cooperation, which is exceptionally comprehensive in its scope. I sit in a chair made in Grand Rapids, wear a jacket made in Hong Kong of wool grown in Australia, listen to Leonard Bernstein conduct the Vienna Philharmonic, on a record player made in Japan. These things have not been furnished to me because the people who made them desire to serve my needs or pleasures; they demand something for themselves in return for their efforts. What have I provided in exchange? I have provided lectures in the history of economic theory for the youth of Indiana that, through the social complex that economists call "the mechanism of markets," enables people in far-off places, who I have never seen or talked with, to acquire some of the things that they want. Through this process I, and others, can produce far more and a much greater variety of things than if each of us had to provide everything for him- or herself. The mechanism of markets then is a mode of social organization, enabling people to cooperate to achieve ends that are beyond the reach of isolated individuals.[26] Clearly, this is not explicable by the processes that are at work in the organization of a biological entity or a physical mechanism. That I have a liking for New Zealand lamb may be encoded in my genome, but the process whereby I can trade a lecture for it is assuredly not. Nor can any analogy be reasonably drawn. Even the most determined devotee of analogical reasoning would hesitate to suggest that the liver, kidneys, bones, and other organs of the body, or the gears and levers of a clock, function together like a multilateral trading system. Is it not just as fanciful to say that trading systems are like organisms as to say that organisms are like trading systems?

Markets, however, constitute only one of the modes of social organization. Another, no less important, is epitomized by an army. This is a hierarchical ordering of individuals, each level of which has defined powers and duties. Decisions flow down the hierarchy as commands, supported by threat of enforcing sanctions, which integrate the actions of the members into a cooperative enterprise. A small number of persons organized as an army can easily overwhelm a much larger number who are not organized, even if they are equally well armed. We might call this mode of social organization, the DCE mode— designating that it is a process that works by means of decisions, commands, and enforcement. The internal administrative structure of most social institutions, business firms, churches, universities, and so on, is characterized by the DCE mode. The most notable of these is the nation-state since it is the repository of "sovereign" power in a geographic domain. Some states are indistinguishable from armies, but one of the most significant social developments of modern times has been the construction of political systems, called "constitutional democracies," which have modified the hierarchical ordering into a much more complex "pluralist" structure of organization, without impairing the ability of the DCE mode to achieve the benefits of cooperation. Indeed, the weight of empirical evidence is that constitutional democracies do better than simple hierarchies not only in dispersing political power and in the degree of individual freedom they permit but also in achieving economic ends in producing "collective goods" such as roads, judicial systems, flood control systems, waste disposal, and a host of other things that are beyond the capacities of unorganized individuals. One should note also that the efficient production of collective goods is not achievable by the market mode of social organization, so the DCE mode is an essential component of a well-functioning social ensemble.[27]

This does not exhaust our subject. So far I have spoken only of the modes of social organization studied by economists and political scientists. Sociologists, anthropologists, and social psychologists might be quick to point out that individuals are also bound together into societies by established customs, traditions, and conventions, commonly shared ethical and metaphysical beliefs, and so forth. These control individual behavior over a wide range. Such things as the rules of personal deportment, the use of language, marriage practices, styles of cooking, and innumerable others, integrate individuals into a social unit that facilitates their cooperation with one another. Neither the market mechanism nor the hierarchical DCE system are at work here. So, we must recognize the existence of a third mode of social organization. For lack of any better term, it may be called the "cultural" mode.[28]

One of the most notable features of the human species is the exceptionally long period of time between birth and maturity. A human is, to borrow a term from ornithology, an exceedingly "altricial" animal. During this period, not only are biological growth and development taking place, but the young are being "enculturated" into a particular set of social complexes. The education of the young is not solely an "investment" process that can be discussed in economic terms; it also plays a vital part in the functioning of the cultural mode of social organization.

Obviously, a great deal more needs to be said about the role of culture as, indeed, about the other modes of social organization as well. But perhaps these terse remarks are sufficient to convey what I have in mind when referring to these various processes.

## Conclusion

The central object of the social sciences is the examination of the processes of social organization that, I have argued, are unlike the processes by which biological and mechanical complexes are organized. This does not mean that the social sciences should not be viewed as oriented to the study of social *problems* (inflation, pollution, drug addiction, bureaucracy, etc.). On the contrary, most of these problems are due to the fact that the processes of social organization are imperfect, and the amelioration of them requires the invention and implementation of improvements in one or more of the three modes of organization I have described. The distribution of the tasks of social organization among these three modes is also a matter of great importance. At the present time, in Eastern Europe, the failure of the social system to serve the wants and needs of the populace is widely attributed (rightly, in my view) to an excessive use of the DCE mode, and it is contended that the market mode should be allowed to take over more of the functions of social organization. There is, however, another theme that punctuates the history of social thought, from ancient times to the present. This is the notion that social problems are due to defects in the biological and/or psychological characteristics of human beings, and the solution of them requires changes in humans' "fundamental nature," to create individuals more suitable for a social existence than we now seem to be. Virtually all of the long stream of utopian literature focuses on this perceived need. The eugenics movement, the first instance in which it was claimed that the natural sciences held the key to the solution of social problems, was based on the same notion. In Pol Pot's Cambodia, a primitive sociological doctrine served as the foundation for efforts to create a "new man" through the wholesale slaughter of all those contaminated by "bourgeois" culture. I could go on to recite a long litany of theories, and actual attempts, to solve social problems by means of the modification of *Homo sapiens*, from the Greek notion that a well-functioning *polis* requires people endowed with the quality of "civic virtue," to the idea that the crime problems associated with the trade in drugs can be solved by inducing the users of them to desist and "just say no." All of these have been failures, some of them disasters. I would not argue that humans are perfect, but, in setting social policy, it is better to accept them as they are, warts and all. Attacking social problems by improving the processes of social organization holds much greater prospect of success than trying to attain the ideal of a perfectly "socialized" human being.

## Notes

This chapter is a revised version of a "Distinguished Faculty Research Lecture" delivered at Indiana University in 1990. Some of the ideas were advanced earlier (see Gordon 1989).

1. Albert Einstein would apparently have agreed with this, since he argued that from the general laws of physics *everything* could, in principle, be deduced, the only barrier in practice being the limited capacity of the human brain to perform such a deduction (Holton 1988:395).

2. This is argued more fully in the final chapter of my book on the history and philosophy of social science (Gordon 1991).

3. A century ago, in the flush of zeal for evolution that followed the publication of Darwin's *Origin*, Herbert Spencer postulated a "law of increasing differentiation," which he viewed as the necessary result of the fact that the whole cosmos was evolving. A modern physicist, Paul Davies, in his recent book, *The Cosmic Blueprint* (1988), expresses a similar view with nearly Spencerian conviction.

4. Perhaps "death blow" is too strong. The notion is occasionally ex-

pressed today, even by scientists. Paul Davies (1988:190) notes that the physicist Freeman Dyson has embraced panpsychism and quotes him as having declared that mindlike forces really sit in governance over material events since "mind is inherent in every electron." Davies does not accept this, but his own notion that scientists should recognize "nature's creative ability to order the universe" induces him to flirt, at least, with a similar mysticism.

The so-called "deep ecologists" seem to embrace an animistic view. It is difficult to see why trees, rivers, and so on, have "rights" without ascribing to them something akin to consciousness.

5. The desire for a Grand Unified Theory would seem to be based on the same mechanistic monism as Laplace entertained, but, since the advent of quantum theory, of course, physicists are disinclined to speak in such deterministic terms.

6. The German "Monist League" was founded in 1906 by the eminent zoologist Ernst Haeckel. One of its main objects was the promotion of "eugenic" policies aimed at achieving "racial improvement." The eugenic movement, the first major introduction of biology into the domain of public policy debate, was at the zenith of its influence in this period.

7. In Loeb's (1912/1964:4) opinion, "Scientific biology begins with the attempt made by Lavoisier and Laplace (1780) to show that the quantity of heat which is formed in the body of a warm-blooded animal is equal to that formed in a candle, provided that the quantities of carbon-dioxide formed in both cases are identical. This was the first attempt to reduce life phenomena completely to physico-chemical terms." Loeb spent a good deal of time in his lecture showing how organic processes, previously thought to be beyond the domains of physics and chemistry, had been successfully investigated by them. Loeb had a great deal of influence in persuading biologists to study chemistry, but not until the 1950s did the chemistry requirements in the training of biologists become more than trivial, and some historians attribute this to the influence of Erwin Schrödinger's 1943 lecture *What is Life?* which will be noted later.

8. If, says Loeb (1912/1964:5; see also 32–3), a physicochemical explanation of organic phenomena can be achieved, then "our social and ethical life will have to be put on a scientific basis and our rules of conduct must be brought into harmony with the results of scientific biology."

9. Driesch performed an experiment, in the 1890s, in which an early-stage sea urchin embryo was cut into fragments, and these fragments were cultured into complete, viable, sea urchins. This was a striking experiment; biologists, at this time, did not know that every cell of an organism contains full plans and instructions for the somatic development and physiological functioning of the organism. Driesch's inference from his experiment was that it showed that embryological development is controlled by some nonmaterial agent, a vital force or "entelechy." This experiment only worked because Driesch sliced

the embryos along their vertical axis. If they are sliced horizontally, the fragments disintegrate (Waddington, 1961:55). Driesch would have had to argue that the nonmaterial entelechy is impervious to some types of physical trauma and not others. For a recent, more sympathetic appraisal of Driesch, see Freyhofer (1982).

10. For example, Ernst Haeckel postulated the existence of special molecules, called "plastidules," that account for life phenomena. In the course of embryonic development these plastidules undulate, said Haeckel, creating "waves" that differentiate one organism from another. The plastidules are themselves composed of special atoms, which have mindlike properties; human emotions such as love, hate, and fear are due to them.

11. We might note in passing John von Neumann's notion that if a machine could be programmed to assemble a functioning replica of itself from a warehouse of parts, it would be a "living" entity. The initial plausibility of this idea derives from defining entities in terms of properties. In this case, the property of self-reproduction is singled out as the crucial one, and von Neumann is able to make the contention that, at least in principle, mechanisms do not differ from organisms in this respect.

12. In *The Descent of Man* (1874), Darwin sought to contradict many of the notions then current about humans' distinctiveness. Other animals, he argued (and tried to document), display at least incipient capacities for language communication, abstract thinking, and even the aesthetic appreciation of beauty, the metaphysical notion that there are transcendental powers, and the moral sense of right and wrong. Humans differ most from the other animals, he contended, in having a much deeper sense of regret and remorse.

13. Etymologically, *organism* and *organization* come from the same stem, the Greek *organon*, which in turn derives from *ergon*, meaning "work."

14. C. H. Waddington (1961) argues that the crucial property of living entities is that they are "organized," but this will not serve since *all* complex entities, including such things as crystals, rivers, and galaxies, are organized systems. Paul Davies (1988) distinguishes between "order" and "organization," the former characterizing nonliving complexes, and the latter living ones. This approach, it seems to me, merely supplies additional *names* for the distinction between mechanisms and organisms without explaining why the distinction is justified. Ernst Mayr's argument is most conveniently ascertained from the papers in Section I of his *Toward a New Philosophy of Biology* (1988).

15. It is difficult to avoid anthropomorphic language in speaking of organismic development and functioning. Since biologists regularly talk this way, I may consider myself licensed to do so as well. But, of course, the word *know* does not refer here to a mentational process. It is a convenient metaphorical locution, not to be construed as literal.

One should also eschew any suggestion that the development of the organism is controlled by anything akin to Aristotle's "final causes." Language referring to end states is permissible as long as one recognizes that organismic development is, so to say, "pushed", not "pulled." Causes must, necessarily, be temporally antecedent to effects. Organic processes are remarkable, but not miraculous. Mayr uses the term *teleonomy* (first apparently suggested by Claude Bernard) to distinguish the phenomenon of end-achieving organic development from Aristotle's end-controlling "teleology."

16. Some would claim that insect societies, such as those formed by bees and ants, are more highly organized than human societies, and the colonial invertebrates are perhaps even more highly organized still. But these complexes seem to achieve their sociality solely by genetic processes, so they belong to the category of "organisms" according to the taxonomic principle I am using.

17. The French word *conscience* does double duty for the two distinct notions expressed in English by *consciousness* and *conscience*. Since Durkheim seems to have meant to refer to both of these, English commentators on him usually use the French term.

18. Durkheim's philosophical ideas are most easily obtained from his *The Division of Labor in Society* (1893/1964) and *The Rules of Sociological Method* (1895/1964).

19. Among recent writers who have employed the organism-society analogy, one might note the work of physicist Charles Lumsden and entomologist E. O. Wilson (1981) and that of Carl Swanson (1983), a botanist. Lumsden and Wilson postulate the existence of "culturgens" and "epigenetic rules," embodied by evolution in the human genome, which control human behavior and, therefore, account for at least a substantial part of social phenomena. Swanson contends that social phenomena are the product of "sociogenes" that operate as commanding forces, like "biogenes" do in organisms. For example, he construes religion as due to a sociogene that generates mythological beliefs; particular religions, such as Christianity, are "socioalleles" of this sociogene.

It is easy to postulate unperceived entities and give them impressive names, but demonstrating that they exist is a different matter. At present, the only way in which one can even begin to locate the gene that produces a specific phenotypic phenomenon is to ascertain the protein that is involved in the phenomenon. Then, one can search the genome for the DNA segment that contains the code for the production of this protein. To explain a social phenomenon such as, say, religion or war, one would first have to show how it devolves from a specific sort of behavior on the part of individual human organisms, and then trace this to a particular protein. In effect, we would have to know the behavioral causes of religious faith or war before we could do its genetics. Sociology would have to precede biology!

20. See, for example, the beginning pages of Spencer's (1876) *Principles of Sociology* and the first chapter of Part II.

21. The notion of division of labor has a long history, going back at least to the political and social theories of Plato and Aristotle. It was introduced as a

key concept in economic theory by Adam Smith (1776/1937) in the opening chapters of the *Wealth of Nations*. In the nineteenth century, its significance for biology was emphatically argued by the distinguished biologists Henri Milne-Edwards and Karl E. von Baer. Spencer seems to have derived his view of its sociological significance from von Baer rather than Adam Smith.

22. Gerald Holton, a philosopher, avers that *science*—that is scientific knowledge—is "a growing organism analogous to a biological species, for the growth in both cases depends to a large extent on the operation of four quite analogous mechanisms [continuity, mutation, multiplicity of effort, selection]." Holton says that he finds it "helpful" to construe the history of science in such terms (1988:410–1; see also Richards 1987:451). I fail to appreciate this notion. What aspect of the history of science is captured by the analogy that would not be just as clear without it?

23. The idea that the nation-state is coextensive with "society," or "culture," each with its special *Volksgeist*, was given its most distinctive formulation by G. W. F. Hegel (see Manicas 1987, Chapter 5). Some historians would trace a connection between Hegel's philosophy and the modern political notion of a "totalitarian" state.

24. With only a modicum of inventiveness, the analogy may be made to serve any partisan political purpose. For example, during the English Civil War of the seventeenth century, some Royalists contended that the king should rule the nation, just as the head rules the body, both relationships having been ordained by God; while some of the Parliamentary party, no less assured that God was on their side, declared, as John Pym put it in his celebrated speech to the Short Parliament, that "the powers of Parliament are to the body politic as the rational faculties of the soul [are] to man" (Fraser: 1975:82–3).

25. In answer to a philosophical question that might be raised at this point, I might say that social complexes and networks of them are "real" but not "material." They do not have specific locations in space-time as do, say, leopards or overcoats, but they do, nonetheless, have real existence, that is, they are "things." The issue I want to address is whether they are things of a unique *kind*.

26. Economists emphasize the role of "competition" in a well-functioning market process. In common speech, *competition* is usually construed as the antithesis of cooperation. But, as the term is used in economics, competition facilitates *cooperation*.

27. Some "libertarian" followers of Ludwig von Mises claim that the DCE mode could be dispensed with altogether since its functions can be carried out as well by the market mechanism. This has never been tested in practice, but it seems highly unlikely. Some others, who claim to have derived their inspiration from Karl Marx (who, in fact, said almost nothing on this question), contend that the market mode could be dispensed with and its functions performed by the DCE mode, which Lenin thought would require merely a handful of accountants and clerks. This notion *was* tested (or tested as well as

can be in the domain of social phenomena) in the former Soviet Union, and in China and the countries of Eastern Europe after World War II. The verdict on this, the largest and costliest social experiment ever made, now seems to have been rendered, since the populations experimented on appear to have concluded that the attempt to organize the economy by means of centralized "planning" was a failure.

28. "Culture" is a notoriously vague term, suffering from what appear to be irremediable difficulties of definition (see Hallowell 1956), but the phenomena it seeks to capture do not disappear because this is so. I am using the term in the same sense as does Clifford Geertz (1966) to refer to a "control mechanism," or "a set of symbolic devices for controlling behavior." Geertz makes the same argument as I do, but somewhat stronger: "Undirected by cultural patterns man's behavior would be . . . a chaos of pointless acts and exploding emotions, his experience virtually shapeless." (p. 7)

# References

Darwin, Charles. 1874. *The Descent of Man, and Selection in Relation to Sex.* Rev. ed. New York: Merrill & Baker.

Davies, Paul. 1988. *The Cosmic Blueprint.* New York: Simon & Schuster.

Durkheim, Émile. 1893/1964. *The Division of Labor in Society.* Glencoe, Ill.: FreePress.

―――. 1895/1964. *The Rules of Sociological Method.* New York: Free Press.

Freyhofer, Horst H. 1982. *The Vitalism of Hans Driesch: The Success and Decline of a Scientific Theory.* Frankfurt: Lang.

Geertz, Clifford. 1966. "The Impact of the Concept of Culture on the Concept of Man". *Bulletin of Atomic Scientists*, pp. 2–8.

Gordon, Scott. 1989. "Why Does *Homo sapiens* Differ?" *Journal of Social and Biological Structures* 11:427–41.

―――. 1991. *The History and Philosophy of Social Science.* London: Routledge.

Hallowell, A. Irving. 1956. "The Structural and Functional Dimensions of a Human Existence." *Quarterly Review of Biology* 31:88–101.

Hawking, Stephen W. 1988. *A Brief History of Time.* New York: Bantam.

Holton, Gerald. 1988. *Thematic Origins of Scientific Thought: Kepler to Einstein.* Cambridge: Cambridge University Press.

La Mettrie, Julien Offray de. 1748. *Man a Machine.* Chicago: Open Court.

Loeb, Jacques. 1912/1964. *The Mechanistic Conception of Life.* Chicago: University of Chicago Press.

Lumsden, Charles J., and Edward O. Wilson. 1981. *Genes, Mind and Culture: The Coevolutionary Process.* Cambridge, Mass.: Harvard University Press.

Manicas, Peter. 1987. *A History and Philosophy of the Social Sciences.* Oxford: Blackwell.

Mayr, Ernst. 1988. *Toward a New Philosophy of Biology: Observations of an Evolutionist.* Cambridge, Mass.: Harvard University Press.

Moore, Walter. 1989. *Schrödinger, Life and Thought.* Cambridge: Cambridge University Press.

Richards, Robert J. 1987. *Darwin and the Emergence of Evolutionary Theories of Mind and Behavior.* Chicago: University of Chicago Press.

Schrödinger, Erwin. 1943. *What Is Life?* Cambridge: Cambridge University Press.

————. 1956/1967. *Mind and Matter.* Cambridge: Cambridge University Press.

Smith, Adam. 1776/1937. *An Inquiry into the Nature and Causes of the Wealth of Nations.* New York: Random House.

Spencer, Herbert. 1975. *Principles of Sociology,* 1876–1897. Westport, Conn.: Greenwood.

Swanson, Carl P. 1983. *Ever-Expanding Horizons: The Dual Informational Sources of Human Evolution.* Amherst: University of Massachusetts Press.

Waddington, Conrad. H. 1961. *The Nature of Life.* London: Scientific Book Club.

## Chapter 5

# The Nature and Dynamics of 'The Social' among Humans

*Jonathan H. Turner*

To conceptualize the fundamental properties of 'the social' requires a criterion to differentiate the *degree of sociality* among various species of organized animals. With such a criterion, we should be able to distinguish among the so-called social insects, the diverse species of herding and pack animals, and, in particular, the various species of primates. In my view, this criterion is the ratio of genetic to nongenetic coding in those communicative processes involved in interaction among the members of a species. The more the communicative dynamics among conspecifics are learned, the more they are flexibly constructed in response to circumstances, and the more they reveal complexity in modalities and channels of communication used in interaction, then the more *social* are the relations and structures organizing members of a species.

When the social is viewed in this manner, two related questions emerge. First, what evolutionary forces caused humans to become the most social species of all in the terms enumerated here? Second, what properties of sociality are critical for understanding behavior, interaction, and organization among humans? Sociological analysis has tended to concentrate on the second question, but as I will argue in this chapter, answers to the first question are critical to unraveling the second.

## The Biology of Human Sociality

Humans are evolved apes, having once shared a common ancestor with all living apes (Maryanski 1993, 1992). Hominoidea (apes and humans) and Cercopithecoidea (Old World monkeys) diverged at least twenty-five million years ago. After their separation, apes seemingly had the initial competitive edge over monkeys, but then, as the fossil record documents, species of monkeys proliferated and moved into the former ape niches, while species of apes dramatically declined and relocated to peripheral arboreal niches, such as extremities and undersides of branches, where monkeys could not easily step (Andrews 1981; Tattersall et al. 1988). The extinction of ape species during the Miocene and the relocation of remaining apes to marginal habitats were to have profound consequences on hominoid anatomy, neurology, and, most significantly, on *behavioral* and organizational propensities. In particular, ape behavior propensities differ from those of monkeys, primarily because apes had to survive in marginal arboreal habitats that could not support the larger, well-organized troops typical of monkeys. For monkeys live in relatively discrete social groups that are organized around strong kinship ties, with males dispersing at puberty (often to another group) and with females remaining in their natal group creating "matrifocal" kinship cliques (Fedigan 1982; Jolly 1985; Napier and Napier 1985; Cheney et al. 1986; Wrangham 1980). In contrast, apes are organized around mostly weak ties, with females (and in most cases males as well) dispersing from mother at puberty. Such female dispersal at puberty is a rare trait among primate species (and mammals generally), but it is characteristic of all apes and prevents the formation of matrifocal kinship networks and group continuity over generational time (Moore 1984; Greenwood 1980; Pusey and Packer 1987; Maryanski 1992). The end result was, and is today among all apes, a network of social relations revealing only a few strong ties (e.g., a mother and her dependent offspring), no tight-knit "female bonds" as is the case with monkeys (Wrangham 1980), no powerful sense of groupness (save for the diffuse sense of being part of a loose-knit regional, community population), and few encumbering ties or structures limiting autonomy and freedom of movement. There is some hierarchy in ape societies between the sexes, as when a leader silverback gorilla dictates daily foraging patterns (although in gibbons males and females are codominant), but dominance behavior is rather relaxed because adult male and female apes are relatively free agents who part company at will depending on their own predilections (see Maryanski 1993, 1992).

As the earth grew colder and the forests began to recede during the Miocene, some hominoid species left the relative safety of the forest and moved onto the predator-ridden woodlands and savanna (see Malone 1987). What did these hominoid pioneers bring with them from their original African forest adaptation? They brought a large hemispheric brain with neocortical control over visual and haptic (touch) responses; they brought a vocal-auditory channel still directly wired to the older, emotionally-based limbic cortex in the brain; they brought a dramatically diminished sense of smell (the major sense modality among most terrestrial mammals); they brought neurological wiring with vision the paramount sensory organ followed respectively by the tactile and auditory senses, with a truncated olfactory somewhat isolated from visual control; they brought a basic ape morphology with a short and wide trunk, limbs of unequal length, no tail, mobile and specialized shoulders with specialized wrists and hands (Hunt 1991; Swartz 1989); and, most important, they brought few behavioral propensities for strong ties and, hence, cohesive and continuous group structures. Indeed, they brought to the savanna and canopy woodlands propensities for weak ties, mobility, and autonomy. Selection pressures would have to work, therefore, on what these hominoid pioneers carried with them from the forest niche.

## Selection for Anatomical Changes and Human Sociality

Bipedalism was the first adaptation because it enabled hominids to see above the tall grasses, a critical but easy adaptation for apes with a poor sense of smell (White and Suwa 1987; Latimer and Lovejoy 1990). The emergence of bipedalism was to have profound consequences for social relations among humans. First, early hominids and later those closer to *Homo sapiens* can stand and face each other, with full bodies exposed and with prehensile hands freed for general body contact or complex gesturing. Thus, as hominids developed symbolic capacities for communication, these would involve a great deal of "body language" revolving around (1) posturing of hands, head, hips, and chest; (2) relative place and location of bodies; and (3) movement of bodies. Additionally, facial displays revolving around movement of lips, jaws, and cheeks could be used to enhance and promote communication. Such body language would be a focal point for a primate with binocular, color vision and a dominant visual modality, making visual signals more significant in face-to-face interaction than auditory, tactile, or olfactory cues. Moreover, such visual sophistication can pick up texture and nuances in the cues of conspecifics and, hence, could give later hominids the capacity for extremely fine-tuned and subtle interactions. Thus, human sociality would be circumscribed by body and vision; and whereas linguistic-based communication would dramatically increase sociality, visually based body language is still the principal communicator and the channel through which most of the texture and subtlety of human communication passes (see Napier and Napier 1985; Preuschoft and Preuschoft, 1994).

### Selection for Closer Social Ties and Human Sociality

How are fifteen to twenty million years of selection favoring behavioral propensities toward weak ties, mobility, and autonomy suddenly reversed when early protohominids left the forest and moved on to the savanna where stronger ties, continuity, and coherence of social structure would surely be advantageous in such an open and predator-ridden habitat?[1] One answer resides in alterations to the structure and functioning of the neocortex and in the relationship between the neocortex and the older limbic cortex of the brain. These changes enabled those hominids on the direct line to humans to use learned interpersonal and emotional responses for bonding. Indeed, the reason that symbolically mediated interaction is so complex in humans, and hence "social" in terms of my earlier definition, is that the relatively low sociality evident in existing ape species and evident, no doubt, in humans' early hominid ancestors had to be overridden by a wide array of learned interpersonal mechanisms.

### Selection for Structural Changes in the Brain and Human Sociality

The cognitive capacity for language was not a dramatic neurological breakthrough; rather, it was an extension of capacities already developed under selection forces having little to do with communication.[2] And it is for this reason that chimpanzees and gorillas who are closest to humans can learn and use grammar-based symbolic codes at a rudimentary level when channeled through their visual-tactile modalities and, in the case of bonabo chimpanzees (*Pan panicus*), can spontaneously learn to comprehend speech sounds at the level of a normal three-year-old child (Gardner et al. 1989).[3] What were these earlier cognitive changes in the brain that enabled our hominid ancestors, and humans' contemporary ape cousins, to interact symbolically? The most crucial changes revolved around the integration of the sense modalities, with vision being dominant, and the voluntary control by the neocortex of emotional centers in the older limbic system. Let me examine each of these changes in turn.

## Integration of Sense Modalities

Among all higher primates (i.e., monkeys, apes, and humans), vision is the dominant sensory modality and is located primarily in the occipital lobule of the neocortex. In hominoid (ape and human) evolution, association areas in the neocortex underwent extensive elaboration, in particular in the inferior parietal lobule, which appears to serve as a superamodal area for sensory convergence (see Andersen et al. 1990; Horel 1988) and for integrating other sense impressions under visual dominance. Additionally, regions in the temporal lobule underwent expansion, which seemingly led to a capacity to think more abstractly and, given the necessity, to symbolize. For example, auditory association tissues homologous to humans have been identified in chimpanzees (Newman 1988). Thus, the initial hominoid wiring for symbolic representation seemingly occurred with elaborations of association cortex, and it is intriguing that extant apes have left-hemisphere asymmetries similar to humans along the Sylvian fissure near Broca's and Wernicke's areas that function as core language regions in humans (Sherman, et al. 1982). Indeed, Geschwind (1985:272) was so intrigued with this finding that he remarked that "if the [cognitive] abilities possessed by the chimpanzee were in fact earlier stages of linguistic ability, then it would be reasonable to expect them to have an anatomical localization similar to that of human language." Seemingly it is this initial elaboration of neural circuitry in parietal and temporal regions that laid the foundation for abstract thinking and eventually propositional speech. Several implications follow from these changes in the brain: (1) thinking is primarily visual and organized as gestalts by the neurochemistry of the neocortex (it is not covert speech that is lineal and slow); and so, when humans vocalize, the brain translates (in Broca's, Wernicke's, and related cortical areas) visually-based thought into spoken language; (2) interaction is visually dominant because what humans hear, touch, and see are first cortically processed and usually integrated under the dominant visual modality, thereby making sociality primarily a visual process of seeing body movements, body positioning, body countenance, gestural sequences, and verbal utterances as perceptual fields organized by the association cortexes of the brain.

*Cortical Control of the Limbic System*

In the initial radiation of Old World monkeys and apes in an arboreal niche, selection favored an expansion of the visual cortex and a reduction in the olfactory that signaled "an increased emphasis on vision and a decreased emphasis on smell" (Radinsky 1975:156). This shift in dominance reflected much more than a simple modality change: it radically altered primate perceptual processes from an information system (smell) that usually projects to the limbic system, which is concerned mostly with an organism's preservation and emotionally-based responses, to one (vision) that projects to the neocortex, which is concerned mostly with rational thought and intentionally-based responses to meet the challenges of a complex and changing environment (MacLean 1990:17; Isaacson 1982). The primate neocortex also contains the tactile and auditory modalities; and, although vision and touch for higher primates are under full voluntary control for learned and purposeful responses, nonhuman primate acoustic responses— that is communication through the vocal-auditory channel—are largely limbic-controlled vocalizations. Only in humans does the vocal-auditory system have a true faculty for voluntary and semantic vocalizations.[4] Thus, there must have been intense selection pressures for "rewiring" the hominid brain for humans' ancestors to gain neocortical control over acoustic sounds. One effect, I hypothesize, of this rewiring was to elaborate association areas and to create more complex integrative connections between the neocortex and various limbic system structures that, in turn, were to influence the expression of emotion. For an increase in cortical size was seemingly accompanied by an increased diversity of emotions in later hominids and, eventually, in humans.

In my view, then, the nature of human sociality—especially its complexity of interpersonal mechanisms, its visual basis, and its emotional tones—can only be understood by tracing how an ancestral hominoid evolved into the hominid line leading to *Homo sapiens*. Visual dominance, bipedalism (which I should note, also facilitated alterations in the hominid vocal tract apparatus so that speech became possible [see Hill 1972], given the necessary neurological changes and selection for better communication), sensory integration, visually dominant thought, and cortical control of emotions emanating from limbic structures all help explain why a low-sociality primate became among the most social of Earth's mammals. These evolutionary forces also help to explain just how human sociality operates, as is examined next.

## The Processes of Human Sociality

A large-brained primate who must rely upon learned communication to organize itself and who has genetically driven propensities for relatively low sociality must, as I have emphasized, depend on multiple channels and mechanisms for interaction and, ultimately, for its patterns of social organization. These channels and mechanisms overlap considerably, giving human interaction a kind of seamless quality. Yet, if we are to ascertain the mark of human sociality, these must be separated with the proviso, of course, that they overlap and blend into each other.

In a number of places (e.g., Turner, 1992, 1989, 1988a, 1988b, 1987a, 1987b, 1986), I have sought to conceptualize the essential properties of social interaction; here, I will draw on these earlier efforts to address questions about the mark of the social in more general and perhaps even philosophical terms. I will begin by dividing the nature of human sociality into three general topics: (1) the basic capacities behind human sociality, (2) the basic channels through which social communication occurs, and (3) the basic interpersonal mechanisms by which social activity is constructed among humans.

### The Capacities behind the Social

Humans are capable of high degrees of sociability because of the size and organization of their brain. In particular, the human neocortex has greater neocortical autonomy than is found in most mammals, in part because it relies on a highly elaborated visual modality for most spatial information and because it has specialized association cortices, which make up 95 percent of human neocortex (McGeer et al. 1987:586). Since association tissue is known to regulate higher cognitive functions and can even exert control over the expression of emotion from subcortical connections, the human neocortex can be viewed as a structure "that speaks primarily with itself" (Braitenberg 1977), although neocortical and limbic systems are highly integrated and give the human brain the following capacities.

### *The Capacity for Symbolization*

This capacity is possessed by most large-brained mammals, especially higher primates, and revolves around the ability to denote objects in the environment, to assign "meaning to them," and to respond to these meanings. When this capacity is great, the processes of denotation and assignment of meanings, and responses to such meanings, can involve the use of arbitrary signs and symbols organized into syntactical constructions that are not directly wired into the neurochemistry of the brain.

### The Capacity for Cognitive Storage and Retrieval

Symbolization depends on the ability to store information and retrieve it, an ability that all mammals possess to comparatively high degrees (at least when compared to reptiles and birds). Because humans have such large brains relative to other primates, and because so much of the human neocortex is devoted to association areas, human capacities for storage and retrieval are truly vast. Large amounts of information can be stored, and this information can be retrieved rapidly in ways that are still not well understood. The processes involved are chemical, mechanical, and neurological, but just what occurs is one of the great frontiers of brain research. Alfred Schutz's 1932/1967 metaphor on "stocks of knowledge at hand" is a useful conceptualization, although he tended to overemphasize the verbal nature of these stocks. Storage is, for the most part, done in the language of the brain, which is a mechanical, neurochemical process seemingly directed by visual dominance. It is thus a process of storing by gestalts, configurations, and patterns, thereby making the initial cognitive retrieval more visual than verbal and requiring translation into linguistic symbols when needed (by Broca's and Wernicke's areas). Thus, contrary to much sociology that has implicitly conceptualized the operation of the brain in linguistic metaphors, culturally-defined language is probably the last step in retrieval, with most information being stored and retrieved through visually dominant processes lodged in the neurochemistry and mechanics of neuronets and association cortices among brain cells.

### The Capacity for Emotional Storage and Retrieval

Mammals with a small neocortex, but even ones with a large one, such as the Great Apes, can stimulate their emotion centers and bypass regulation by the neocortex. The more social an animal, the more is emotional stimulation of the limbic centers mediated and controlled by the neocortex. Repression is perhaps the extreme case of such control, in which unpleasant emotions are pushed from consciousness and made difficult to retrieve. More typically, cognitive storage of information is laced with different emotions; in fact, the emotional content of information and the intensity of the emotions involved are probably one basis for cognitive storage as memory and subsequent retrieval. This process involves a complex and elusive interplay between the neocortex and limbic system, but I would venture at least this much as a hypothesis: primary emotions arise in the limbic system and are the ultimate fuel behind all emotions (indeed, cognitions may be channeled through limbic zones to "influence" them affectively if they become too "cerebral"); the capacities for symbolization and cognition inhering in the human neocortex allow for, and actively construct, variants of all primary emotions and, then, first-order combinations of emotions that can be attached to memories, current events, and states of active cognitive and physical mobilization. Table 5.1 illustrates one way to visualize these emotional capacities of cortical control of the limbic system by positing a list of primary emotions (from Kemper 1987; Ekman 1982), a number of variants, and then, in the right column, some first-order combinations among different primary emotions. As another working hypothesis, I would assert that all of the first-order combinations must be learned.

### The Capacity for Self-Awareness

Large-brained animals can all see themselves, to varying degrees, as objects in social contexts. Humans have this capacity to a high degree, revealing complex sets of cognitions and emotions about themselves in varying situations that are implicitly lodged in the neurochemistry of the brain's modes of thinking and that, on occasion but only imperfectly, can be retrieved and translated into culturally-defined language (Rosenberg 1979). In both cases, the cognitions and emotions of "self" in a situation greatly influence the organization of other cognitions and emotions actuated within the brain and the ways that these are manifested outside the brain in social behavior and interaction (Heisse 1979; Shott 1979; Epstein 1980; Gecas 1991, 1982).

### The Capacity for Reflective Thought

The large neocortex of all higher mammals and, in particular, humans allows for what George H. Mead (1938, 1934) and John Dewey (1922) termed "mind" or the ability to retrieve memories, assess situations, see oneself in a situation, visualize goals, ponder alternative

**TABLE 5.1**
**Primary Emotions and Their First-order Combinations**

| (1) Primary Emotions | (2) Range Of Variation | (3) First-Order Combinations* |
|---|---|---|
| Happiness | satisfaction<br>pride<br>love | gratitude, hope, wonder (fear)<br>vengeance (anger)<br>nostalgia (sadness)<br>joy (surprise) |
| Fear | anxiety<br>apprehensiveness<br>aversiveness | awe (happiness)<br>guilt, envy (anger)<br>worry (sadness)<br>panic (surprise) |
| Anger | contempt<br>distaste<br>aggressiveness | snobbing (happiness)<br>shame, hate, jealousy (fear)<br>depression (sadness)<br>rage (surprise) |
| Sadness | resignation<br>ennui<br>sorrow | yearning (happiness)<br>hopefulness (fear)<br>grief, boredom (anger)<br>crestfallen (surprise) |
| Surprise | startlement<br>amazement<br>astonishment: | delight (happiness)<br>shock (fear)<br>disgust (anger)<br>disappointment (sadness) |

*In this column, each of the primary emotions in column (1) is paired with another primary emotion, which appears in parentheses. For example, for the top line in column (3), gratitude, hope, and wonder are a combination of happiness and (fear).*

lines of conduct, anticipate the consequences of these alternatives, and select those alternatives most likely to realize goals and to foster adaptation to a situation. The more an organism possesses this behavioral capacity, the greater its potential sociality. This capacity became particularly evolved in later hominids to provide alternative mechanisms for social cooperation and, eventually, to accommodate speech, and, more fundamentally, to expand the underlying capacity of hominids and eventually humans for symbolization and rational thought (again in the brain's visually-based modes of thought, rather than speech). For once the basic neurological structures were in place under selection pressures for integration of the sense modalities and control of limbic responses, selection could work to expand reflective thought and symbolization as means for increasing the adaptation of an innately low-sociality primate to ever more organized group activity.

**The Channels for the Social**

Social activity is produced through specific channels dictated by the phenotype and by the cognitive capacities of an organism. As a bipedal, visually dominant primate with a large cerebral cortex and with the capacities just described, the channels for the production of "the social" would be primarily verbal and visual, involving complex abilities to generate signification with respect to (1) vocalizations, (2) face, (3) body, (4) demography of bodies, and (5) touch.

*Vocalization*

The ability to symbolize in terms of a verbal language is usually considered the most distinctive feature of humans and their social conduct. However, chimpanzees (*Pan panicus*) can also reveal a responsive auditory system that can organize significant sounds into phonemes and then effectively combine them into words and sentences for speech comprehension (Savage-Rumbaugh et al. 1993). Yet, only humans possess the capacity for both speech comprehension and *production* through complex speech acts. The substance of such speech acts in the vocal channel is only part of the story because alongside the use of words in accordance with a learned syntax is the use of inflection and rhythm to add additional layers of meaning and signification to vocalization. Thus, the auditory-vocal apparatus is a multidimensional channel, carrying very complex sets of messages operating at many different levels. Indeed, the substance of what speech acts signify is often far less important than the way speech is inflected and the pace, pauses, turn taking, and other rhythmic dimensions of speech. For inflection and rhythm reveal emotions in ways that allow vocalizations to carry the additional force necessary for organizing social ties and bonds among low-sociality primates. Without the supplementation of speech with inflection and rhythm, humans would not be as social because they could not effectively sustain attention or activate the emotions so necessary for sociality.

*Face*

Erving Goffman (1967, 1959) made the term "face" famous. Because humans stand and sit upright, and organize their thoughts in terms of a visually dominant integration of the brain, the expressive qualities of the face are as crucial to human sociality as the vocal channel—if not more so. "Brain language," as I argued earlier, is seemingly visually organized and executed by the mechanical association of brain cells, the movement of chemicals, and the activation of electrical currents; hence, the way the brain "thinks" is not sequential or syntactical. If it were, we would think very slowly and ponderously. By reading facial gestures, an enormous amount of information on mood, emotion, and intent can be communicated rapidly as a gestalt in ways that bypass the slow auditory channel and feed directly into the neurochemical and visually organized language of the brain. Because the face reveals so much across many different dimensions— skin tones, eyes, mouth, skin movement, head movement, and the like—a great deal of information can be transmitted and received (both consciously and subconsciously) in ways that dramatically increase human sociality. Again, this channel is used by other primates; indeed, it is much more important than the vocal channel for social interaction, and so it should not be surprising that this information mode would be so fundamental in the construction of social relations among humans.

### Body

There has been a renewed sociological interest in "the body" (Featherstone et al. 1991; Shilling 1993), but I am not sure that this work fully captures the importance of the body as a channel of social production. Dress and other adornments of the body carry signification, as does sex and other biologically structured and culturally embellished differences among humans. More fundamental is body countenance with respect to posture and hand movements that, like face, communicate gestalts of visually processed information and, as such, provide yet another means for generating social understandings about intent, mood, and emotions so essential to producing and reproducing "the social" among humans.

### Demography

The number of bodies present, their juxtaposition in space, and their movements are all important paths of social production. They provide information and activate memories that enable humans to construct the social. And in a primate with a long phylogenetic legacy for weak-tie formation, mobility, and autonomy, the demography of bodies takes on even more importance for interpreting and responding in situations. This is why, for example, formal situations of culturally defined importance (such as inequality) involve so much concern about where individuals are positioned and how they move; and what is so obvious in these formal situations is equally true of more informal ones, where demography adds yet more information in constructing the social.

## Touch

The most underutilized sense modality in humans, especially in constructing the social, is the haptic capacity or active touch (i.e., reaching out and touching or exploring using the highly sophisticated prehensile hands). As a legacy of their distant ancestors' evolution in the trees, humans have a very sensitive and fine-tuned sense of touch; yet, because humans are visually dominant, this sense is not used as much as are visual cues in interaction. But, this fact does not mean that touch goes completely unused. Just the simple act of touching, or not touching, others is itself a marker for sociality. And then, within those relations where active touching occurs, the nature of the touching—from a kiss to a pat on the back—becomes an important channel for constructing the social. The rituals of greeting and partings are often punctuated by touch—handshakes and kisses on regions of face, for example—because this highly sensitive modality activates and mobilizes the cognitions and sentiments so essential to the social. And the more social are relations among humans, the more they employ touch as a channel for sustaining this sociality.

## The Mechanisms of the Social

Through these different channels—from vocal to haptic—an incredibly robust and complex array of signification passes. This large bulk of information is, however, organized and focused by what I have termed the "mechanisms" of social interaction (Turner 1988b). The master mechanism of interaction is the reciprocal emission and interpretation of gestures through the various channels enumerated above. Gestures are mutually presented, read for their meaning, and interpreted in order for the individuals involved to interact. As noted earlier, this fundamental process is incredibly complex in human interaction, operating along numerous dimensions and levels. Among the most important of these are several interrelated clusters of processes that I will term (1) orienting mechanisms, (2) ordering mechanisms, and (3) orchestrating mechanisms.

## Orienting Mechanisms

Social interaction among humans always involves a process of mutual orientation in which individuals emit and interpret gestures to

provide a common perspective for the duration of the interaction. I see
two such orienting processes as critical: framing and categorizing.

**Framing.** Goffman (1974) was, of course, the sociologist who made the
notion of "frame" popular. At the same time, computer science was
also employing this term, and more recent efforts to apply computer
science ideas to the analysis of the brain have relied on the concept of
framing. My use of the concept will blend these traditions and, as
such, stress that framing involves the use of gestures to demark
simultaneously what is to be excluded and included in an interaction
(Turner 1995, 1988a). Figure. 5.1 summarizes my views on the dimensions along which framing occurs.

**Categorizing.** As frames are being established, categorization within a
frame is occurring. Following Goffman (1967) and Collins (1988, 1975),
one dimension of categorization is in terms of the ratios of work/
practical (i.e., instrumental), ceremonial, and social content of the
interaction. Another dimension is the level of intimacy, ranging from

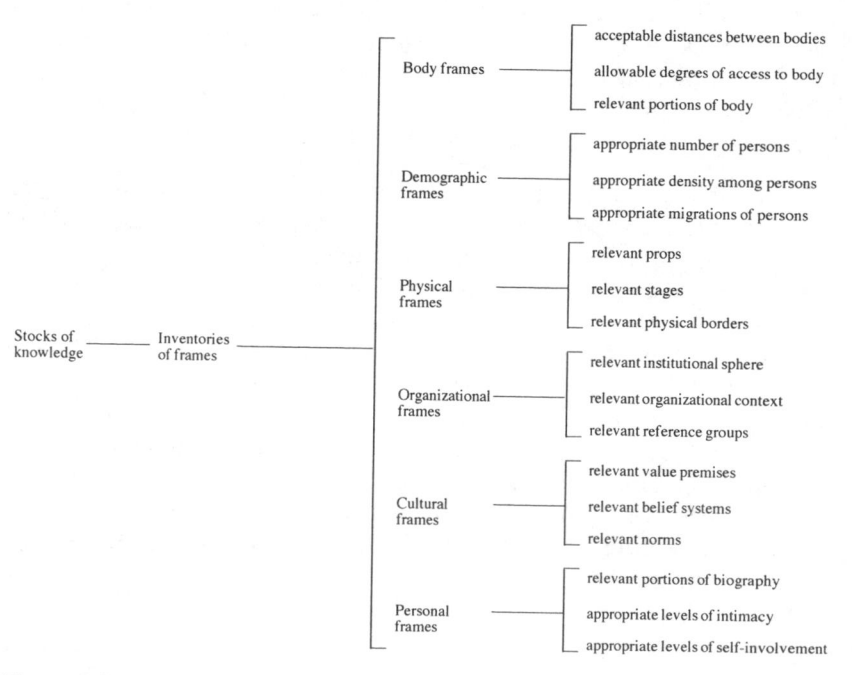

*Figure 5.1*   The Dynamics of Framing

the treatment of others as categories to ever more personal contact. Table 5.2 roughly summarizes my views of the basic types of categorization that occur within frames (Turner 1988a).

If frames are altered, or "rekeyed," then categorization will also change, and vice versa. Indeed, some of the most visible gestures in an interaction revolve around reframing and recategorizing the situation and others. Often this is done with what I will term "ordering mechanisms."

### Ordering mechanisms

An interaction occurs in space and unfolds over time. Those gestures that sequence the interaction across time, specify the expectations on individuals, and organize the interaction in space are what I mean by ordering mechanisms; and they involve the use of gestures with respect to ritualizing, normatizing, and regionalizing.

**Ritualizing.** Stereotyped sequences of gestures structuring the flow of interaction constitute rituals, and as such, they are crucial to all interactions. Figure 5.2 delineates what I see as the important classes of ritual activity (Turner 1988a): bracketing rituals that open, close, and key initial frames; forming rituals that sequence and resequence the verbal flow, while rekeying frames; totemizing rituals that reify and imbue with special significance (as an object of secular "reverence") the persons, the encounter itself, and lamentations and embellishments of frames; and repairing rituals that denote breaches, appropriate compensation, and repairs to disrupted interactions. Rituals are also a mechanism in the activation of emotions, thereby giving interaction an emotional force.

**Normatizing.** Much of what occurs in an interaction is mutual signaling over the rules of the situation. Because of humans' large cerebral cortex, they can carry large inventories of normative rules, while being able to retrieve and assemble these sets of expectations in ways that give order to the interaction. This capacity or what I term "normatizing" is virtually unique to humans, although higher mammals can perhaps normatize to a small degree; and so, constructing rules to guide conduct is a clear marker of the social. Figure 5.3 summarizes what I visualize as the most important inventories of rules that humans carry and use when producing social interaction.

# TABLE 5.2
## A Provisional Typology of How Humans Categorize

### TYPES OF SITUATIONS

| | Work/practical | Ceremonial | Social |
|---|---|---|---|
| Categories | Others as functionaries whose behaviors are relevant to achieving a specific task or goal and who, for the purposes at hand, can be treated as strangers | Others as representatives of a larger collective enterprise toward whom highly stylized responses owed as a means of expressing their joint activity | Others as strangers toward whom superficially informal, polite, and responsive gestures are owed |
| Persons | Others as functionaries whose behaviors are relevant to achieving a specific task or goal but who, at the same time, must be treated as unique individuals in their own right | Others as fellow participants of a larger collective enterprise toward whom stylized responses are owed as a means of expressing their joint activity and recognition of each other as individuals in their own right | Others as familiar individuals toward whom informal, polite, and responsive gestures are owed |
| Intimates | Others as close friends whose behaviors are relevant to achieving a specific task or goal and toward whom emotional and responsiveness is owed | Others as close friends who are fellow participants in a collective enterprise and toward whom a combination of stylized and personalized responses are owed as a means of expressing their joint activity and sense of mutual understanding | Others as close friends toward whom informal and emotionally responsive gestures are owed |

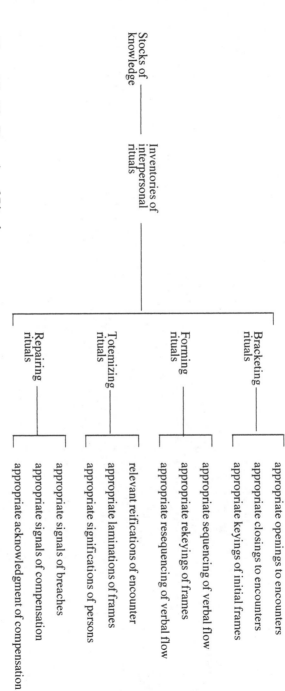

*Figure 5.2*   The Dynamics of Rituals

Stocks of
knowledge ——— Inventories of
interpersonal
rituals

Bracketing ———
rituals
    appropriate openings to encounters
    appropriate closings to encounters
    appropriate keyings of initial frames

Forming ———
rituals
    appropriate sequencing of verbal flow
    appropriate rekeyings of frames
    appropriate resequencing of verbal flow

Totemizing ———
rituals
    appropriate significations of persons
    appropriate laminations of frames
    relevant reifications of encounter

Repairing ———
rituals
    appropriate signals of breaches
    appropriate signals of compensation
    appropriate acknowledgment of compensation

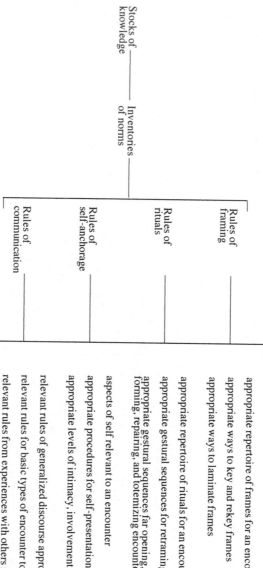

*Figure 5.3*   The Dynamics of Normatizing

Stocks of knowledge ——— Inventories of norms

Rules of framing
- appropriate repertoire of frames for an encounter
- appropriate ways to key and rekey frames
- appropriate ways to laminate frames

Rules of rituals
- appropriate repertoire of rituals for an encounter
- appropriate gestural sequences for reframing encounters
- appropriate gestural sequences for opening, closing, forming, repairing, and totemizing encounters

Rules of self-anchorage
- aspects of self relevant to an encounter
- appropriate procedures for self-presentation
- appropriate levels of intimacy, involvement, and emotion

Rules of communication
- relevant rules of generalized discourse appropriate to an encounter
- relevant rules for basic types of encounter to be invoked in talk
- relevant rules from experiences with others in past encounters

**Regionalization.** Humans do not naturally order interaction in space; they must learn and store cognitions about the meaning of particular types of space, the objects and props in this space, the partition of space, the number of people in space, and the movement of people in space. Without these understandings, humans would bump into each other in public places, while having difficulty in aligning their bodies in more focused encounters (Goffman 1967, 1963). The general categories of regionalizing behavior are delineated in Figure 5.4.

### Orchestrating Mechanisms

Not only is the social marked by interpersonal mechanisms that orient and order interaction, it also involves orchestrations by individuals with respect to conceptions of self, emotions, roles, and claims. These presentations also order and orient the flow of interaction, but they do so from the point of view of the individual who orchestrates, both consciously and unconsciously, the emission of gestures to present self, emotions, roles, and claims to others.

**Conceptions of Self.** Interaction among social beings always involves mutual presentations of oneself as a particular type of individual with attributes and qualities that are deserving of certain responses from others. Indeed, as a large literature documents (e.g., Gecas 1991, 1989, 1986, 1985), there is always an implicit, and frequently an explicit, manipulation of gestures to inform others about the relevant attributes of an individual, the degree of self-anchorage (e.g., role embracement, role distance) in the situation, and the expectations for how others should respond to an individual.

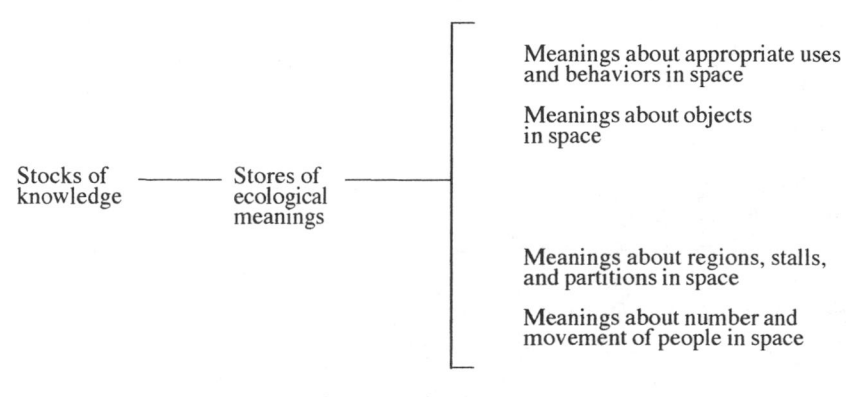

*Figure 5.4* The Dynamics of Regionalization

**Emotions.** All social interaction is embellished by emotions, emitted and interpreted both unconsciously and consciously. As Table 5.1 summarizes, humans are capable of communicating a subtle and complex array of emotional states, and in doing so, they can dramatically increase the level of attunement to each other as well as adding significance to other interpersonal mechanisms, such as the degree of self-involvement, the salience of norms, the boundaries of frames, or the power of rituals (Franks and Gecas 1992). Thus, emotions add punch, texture, and significance to all other interpersonal processes; and because they are communicated through all channels and read visually as gestalts, they are presented in the "brain's language" and, hence, are capable of being read instantaneously. They are, perhaps, the single most important mechanism for creating social bonds among a low-sociality primate.

**Roles.** Humans carry prepackaged syndromes of behavioral sequences in their stocks of knowledge. These stocks are used by individuals in what Ralph Turner (1974, 1962) has termed "role-making" to assert and orchestrate roles, or the specific line of behavior to be pursued by an individual in a situation. These stocks of roles are also used to interpret the roles asserted by others. And, when this mutual process is operating smoothly, individuals can relax and go on "automatic pilot" because they can anticipate the likely sequences of behavior without intensive efforts at what George Herbert Mead termed "role-taking" or the mutual reading and interpreting of gestures to ascertain how people are likely to behave. By being capable of storing large inventories of roles that can be assembled and retrieved for interpretation and implementation, the storage and retrieval capacities of the human neocortex can be used to "program" the flow of interaction without instinctual programmers, with this learned programming revealing flexibility and capacities for reprogramming as might be required.

**Claims.** In any interaction, individuals implicitly, and if necessary, explicitly, assert that they are sincere, competent, and behaving appropriately with respect to orienting, ordering, and presentational processes (Turner 1988a). Reciprocally, those responding to these assertions interpret these claims and implicitly validate them with their own gestures. If claims are made and not validated, however, an interaction will stall; and there will be a new round of claim making and validating until the individuals involved can agree (for example, if someone asserts that another is being "insincere" or "dishonest," the interaction will be interrupted by renewed efforts at asserting sincerity and having others accept this assertion). This process only becomes evident when interactions stall because of a refusal to validate a claim, but it is always occurring across all channels of communication because it is essential for generating trust, predictability, and security in social relations among low-sociality primates.

In sum, all of these orienting, ordering, and orchestrating mechanisms, and perhaps others that I have failed to visualize, are possible because of the enabling capacities of the human neocortex and the diverse channels of communication available to humans. They are the most visible manifestation of the social because they must be learned and because they provide considerable flexibility to social relations. They are complex because humans' primate legacy toward low sociality requires as many "hooks" for sociality as the neuroanatomy and physiology of a big-brained, bipedal primate can allow. Too often, the social is defined in terms of only one or two of these mechanisms, but, from the perspective that I advocate, it is time to see human sociality as incredibly complex for reasons explained by the evolution of apes and hominids.

## Conclusion

Drawing upon the pioneering work of Maryanski (1994, 1993, 1992, 1987), I have challenged some of social philosophy's and many of sociology's sacred assertions about the innate sociality of humans. If such were the case, why would humans have to work so hard at getting along, and why would social interaction be so complex? Sociologists have often tended to gloss over important leads that can answer these questions by glibly talking about big brains, deep structures, culture, and the like, without really knowing a lot about primate evolution or brain neuroanatomy. Once these latter fields are more carefully reviewed, an entirely different picture of humans emerges: we are innately low-sociality primates, and evolution worked to compensate for this deficiency (in an environment that demanded a quiet, bipedal primate with more cohesive patterns of social organization) by altering the neuroanatomy of the brain—a neuroanatomy that, I should emphasize again, evolved for reasons other than sociality but that nonetheless provided the basic "wiring" on which selection could work when selection for greater sociality accelerated.

It is these evolutionary events that make humans the quintessential mark of the social, because human sociality involves (1) learned programming made possible by the capacities of the large neocortex, (2) constructed and flexible social relations, and (3) use of a full array of communicative channels and a complex set of dynamic interpersonal mechanisms.

By my definition, therefore, the "social insects" are not very social; they are organized, to be sure, but this organization does not meet these three points that mark the social.

## Notes

1. For the hominoid neuroanatomy and accompanying behavioral propensities for loose ties and individual autonomy could not easily revert back to a monkey-like pattern because selection forces are typically conservative and because large mutations are usually harmful (Fisher 1930). Moreover, as Stebbins (1969:103) has emphasized, highly complex animals have an equally complex and precisely programmed pattern of gene (and gene products) that must be integrated with any new adaptive responses. Thus, it is reasonable to assume that early hominids were greatly circumscribed by the neuroanalogical (and anatomical) legacy of their hominoid ancestors.

2. However, let me emphasize that as protohominids moved onto the African savanna, the neurological and anatomical bases for language, symbol use, and higher reflective thought were laid under selection forces relatively unrelated to their eventual consequences for social communication (Maryanski and Turner 1992). Indeed, it would be difficult, if not impossible, for the selective advantages of symbolic communication to suddenly and dramatically rewire the ape brain without prior selection doing much of the necessary groundwork. Imagine, for example, a random mutation creating a capacity for language: if one member of a species developed this capacity, but conspecifics did not, what selective advantage would it convey? Or, consider the opposite scenario as Geschwind (1985:272) put the matter: it would be difficult to even envision how "simultaneous mutations would take place in many individuals so that communication could take place between them." Thus, we must seek the origin of language in other selection pressures producing smaller changes that would culminate in a basic capacity for symbolization that, if selection so favored, could take the last and small increment step to propositional speech (Maryanski and Turner 1992).

3. As long as vocalizations remained under limbic control, hominid auditory sounds had to be restricted to mostly emotionally based responses. Recent findings on the auditory capacities of bonobo chimpanzees (*Pan panicus*) who are able to employ grammatical rules for perceiving speech sounds suggest that

the placement of the vocal channel under cortical control for the production of voluntary sounds would not involve a major neurological overhaul since the neocortex already houses much of the auditory modality (see Savage-Rumbaugh et al. 1993).

4. Recently, some Old World monkeys have shown some capacity for voluntary vocalizations that include encoded semantic qualities. For example, vervets (*Cercopithecus aethiops*) are able to vocally distinguish between friend and foe, and can even warn conspecies of danger. There is a "leopard" alarm call that seemingly means to flee to the top of the canopy and a "snake" alarm call to warn conspecifics to keep away from thickets (Cheney 1984). While these signals are clearly learned, the anterior cingulate gyrus within the limbic system retains control of most nonhuman primate vocalizations (see Snowdon 1990; Steklis 1985).

# References

Andersen, R. A., C. Asanuma, G. Essick, and R. M. Siegel. 1990. "Cortico-cortical Connections of Anatomically and Physiologically Defined Subdivisions Within the Interior Parietal Lobule." *Journal of Comparative Neurology* 296:65–113.

Andrews, Peter. 1981. "Species Diversity and Diet in Monkeys and Apes During the Miocene." In *Aspects of Human Evolution*, ed. C. B. Stringer. London: Taylor & Francis.

Braitenberg, Valentino. 1977. *On the Texture of Brains*. Berlin: Springer.

Cheney, Dorothy. 1984. "Category Formation in Vervet Monkeys." Pp. 58–74 in *The Meaning of Primate Signals*, edited by Rom Harré and Vernon Reynolds. Cambridge: Cambridge University Press.

Cheney, Dorothy, Robert Seyfarth, and Barbara Smuts. 1986. "Social Relationships and Social Cognition in Non-Human Primates." *Science* 234:1361–6.

Collins, Randall. 1975. *Conflict Sociology: Toward an Explanatory Science*. New York: Academic Press.

———. 1988. *Theoretical Sociology*. San Diego: Harcourt, Brace, Jovanovich.

Dewey, John. 1922. *Human Nature and Conduct*. New York: Holt.

Durham, William H. 1991. *Coevolution: Genes, Culture, and Human Diversity*. Stanford, Calif: Stanford University Press.

Ekman, Paul. 1982. *Emotions in the Human Face*. Cambridge: Cambridge University Press.

Epstein, Seymour. 1980. "The Self-Concept: A Review and the Proposal for an Integrated Theory of Personality." Pp. 27–39 in *Personality: Basic Issues and Current Research*, ed. E. Staub. Englewood Cliffs, N.J.: Prentice-Hall.

Featherstone, Mike, Mike Hepworth, and Bryan S. Turner, eds. 1991. *The Body: Social Processes and Cultural Theory*. Newbury Park, Calif.: Sage.

Fedigan, Linda M. 1982. *Primate Paradigms: Sex Roles and Social Bonds.* St. Albans, Vt.: Eden Press Women's Publications.

Fisher, Ronald A. 1930. *The Genetical Theory of Natural Selection.* Oxford: Clarendon.

Franks, David D., and Viktor Gecas, eds. 1992. *Social Perspectives on Emotion,* Vol. 1. Greenwich, Conn.: JAI.

Gardner, R. Allan., Beatrix Gardner, and Thomas E. Cantfort. 1989. *Teaching Sign Language to Chimpanzees.* Albany: State University of New York Press.

Gecas, Viktor. 1982. "The Self-Concept." *Annual Review of Sociology* 8:1–33.

———. 1985. "Self-Concept." Pp. 739–741 in *The Social Science Encyclopedia,* ed. A. Kuper and J. Kuper. London: Routledge & Kegan Paul.

———. 1986. "The Motivational Significance of Self-Concept for Socialization Theory." *Advances in Group Processes* 3:131–56.

———. 1989. "The Social Psychology of Self-Efficacy." *Annual Reviews of Sociology* 15:291–316.

———. 1991. "The Self-Concept as a Basis for a Theory of Motivation." Pp. 171–87 in *The Self-Society Dynamic: Cognition, Emotion and Action,* ed. Judith A. Howard and Peter L. Callero. Cambridge: Cambridge University Press.

Geschwind, Norman. 1985. "Implications for Evolution, Genetics and Clinical Syndromes." In *Cerebral Lateralization in Non-Human Species,* ed. Stanley Click. New York: Academic Press.

Goffman, Erving. 1959. *The Presentation of Self in Everyday Life.* Garden City, N.Y.: Doubleday.

———. 1967. *Interaction Ritual: Essays on Face-to-Face Behavior.* Garden City, N.Y.: Anchor Books.

———. 1963. *Behavior in Public Places.* New York: FreePress.

———. 1974. *Frame Analysis.* New York: Harper & Row.

Greenwood, Paul. J. 1980. "Mating Systems, Philopatry, and Dispersal in Birds and Mammals." *Animal Behaviour* 28:1140–62.

Heisse, David R. 1979. *Understanding Events: Affect and the Construction of Social Action.* New York: Cambridge University Press.

Hill, Jane. 1972. "On the Evolutionary Foundations of Language." *American Anthropologist* 74:308–15.

Horel, James. 1988. "Limbic Neocortical Interrelations." In *Neurosciences,* Vol. 4, ed. Horst Steklis and J. Erwin. New York: Liss.

Hunt, Kevin. 1991. "Positional Behavior in the Hominoidea." *International Journal of Primatology* 12:95–118.

Isaacson, Robert. 1982. *The Limbic System.* New York: Plenum.

Jolly, Alison. 1985. *The Evolution of Primate Behavior.* New York: Macmillan.

Kemper, Theodore. 1987. "How Many Emotions Are There? Wedding the Social and the Autonomic Components." *American Journal of Sociology* 93:263–89.

Latimer, Bruce, and C. Owen Lovejoy. 1990. "Metatarsophalangeal Joints of *Australopithecus afarensis.*" *American Journal of Physical Anthropology* 83:12–23.

MacLean, Paul. 1990. *The Triune Brain in Evolution.* New York: Plenum.

Malone, David. 1987. "Mechanisms of Hominoid Dispersal in Miocene West Africa." *Journal of Human Evolution* 16: 469–81.

Maryanski, Alexandra. 1987. "African Ape Social Structure: Is There Strength in Weak Ties." *Social Networks* 9:191–215.

———. 1992. "The Last Ancestor: An Ecological-Network Model on the Origins of Human Society." *Advances in Human Ecology* 2:1–32.

———. 1993. "The Elementary Forms of the First Proto-Human Society: An Ecological/Social Network Approach." *Advances in Human Ecology* 2:215–41.

———. 1994. "The Pursuit of Human Nature in Sociobiology and Evolutionary Sociology." *Sociological Pespectives* 37:375–89.

Maryanski, Alexandra and Turner, Jonathan H. 1992. *The Social Cage: Human Nature and the Evolution of Society.* Stanford, Calif.: Stanford University Press.

McGeer, Patrick, Sir John Eccles, and Edith McGeer. 1987. *Molecular Neorobiology of the Mammalian Brain.* New York: Plenum.

Mead, George Herbert. 1934. *Mind, Self, and Society.* Chicago: University of Chicago Press.

———. 1938. *Philosophy of the Act.* Chicago: University of Chicago Press.

Moore, Jim. 1984. "Female Transfer in Primates." *International Journal of Primatology* 5:537–89.

Napier, John R., and Prue H. Napier. 1985. *The Natural History of the Primates.* Cambridge, Mass.: MIT Press.

Newman, John. 1988. "Primate Hearing Mechanisms." Pp. 469–99 in *Neurosciences,* Vol. 4, ed. by Horst Steklis and J. Erwin. New York: Liss.

Preuschoft, Sabina, and Halgh Preuschoft. 1994. "Primate Nonverbal Communication: Our Communication Heritage." In *Origins of Semiosis,* ed. Winfeid Noth. New York: Mouton de Gruyter.

Pusey, Anne., and Craig Packer. 1987. "Dispersal and Philopatry." Pp. 250–66 in *Primate Societies,* ed. B. Smuts, D. Cheney, R. Seyfarth, R. Wrangham, and T. Struhsaker. Chicago: University of Chicago Press.

Radinsky, Leonard B. 1975. "Primate Brain Evolution." *American Scientist* 63:656–63.

Rosenberg, Morris. 1979. *Conceiving Self.* New York: Basic Books.

Savage-Rumbaugh, Sue, Jeannine Murphy, Rose Seveik, Daren Brakke, Shelly Williams, and Duane Rumbaugh. 1993. *Language Comprehension in the Ape and Child,* Vol. 58. Monographs of the Society for Research in Child Development. Chicago: University of Chicago Press.

Schutz, Alfred. 1932/1967. *The Phenomenology of the Social World.* Evanston, Ill.: Northwestern University Press.

Sherman, Gordon, Albert Galaburda, and Norman Geschwind. 1982. "Neuro-anatomical Asymmetries in Non-Human Species." *Trends in Neurosciences* 5: 429–31.

Shilling, Chris. 1993. *The Body and Social Theory*. Newbury Park, Calif.: Sage.

Shott, Susan. 1979. "Emotion and Social Life: A Symbolic Interactionist Analysis." *American Journal of Sociology* 84: 317–34.

Snowdon, Charles. 1990. "Language Capacities of Non-Human Animals." *Yearbook of Physical Anthropology* 33: 215–43.

Stebbins, G. Ledyard. 1969. *The Basis of Progressive Evolution*. Chapel Hill: University of North Carolina Press.

Steklis, Horst. 1985. "Primate Communication, Comparative Neurology, and the Origin of Language Re-Examined." *Journal of Human Evolution* 14:157–73.

Swartz, Sharon. 1989. "Pendular Mechanics and Kinematics and Energetics of Brachiating Locomotion." *International Journal of Primatology* 10:387–418.

Tattersall, Ian, Eric Delson, and John van Couvering. 1988. *Encyclopedia of Human Evolution and Prehistory*. New York: Garland.

Turner, Jonathan H. 1986. "The Mechanics of Social Interaction." *Sociological Theory* 4:95–105.

———. 1987a. "Toward a Sociological Theory of Motivation." *American Sociological Review* 51(1):15–27.

———. 1987b. "Analytical Theorizing." In *Social Theory Today*, ed. by Anthony Giddens and Jonathan H. Turner. Cambridge: Polity.

———. 1988a. *A Theory of Social Interaction*. Stanford, Calif.: Stanford University Press.

———. 1988b. "A Behavioral Theory of Social Structure." *Journal for the Theory of Social Behavior* 18(4):354–72.

———. 1989. "A Theory of Microdynamics." *Advances in Group Processes* 6:1–26.

———. 1992. "The Production and Reproduction of Solidarity: A Synthesis of Two Rational Choice Theories." *Journal for the Theory of Social Behavior* 22(3): 311–28.

———. 1995. "Roles and Interaction Processes: Toward a More Robust Theory." In *Self, Collective Action and Society*, ed. by G. Platt and C. Gordon. Greenwich, Conn.: JAI Press.

Turner, Ralph H. 1962. "Role Taking: Process versus Conformity." Pp. 20–40 in *Human Behavior and Social Processes*, ed. Arnold Rose. Boston: Houghton Mifflin.

———. 1974. "Rule Learning and Role Learning: What an Interactive Theory of Roles Adds to the Theory of Social Norms." *International Journal of Critical Sociology*, 1:52–73.

White, Tim, and Gen Suwa. 1987. "Hominid Footprints at Laetoli: Facts and Interpretations." *American Journal of Physical Anthropology* 72:485–514.

Wrangham, Richard W. 1980. "An Ecological Model of Female-Bonded Primate Groups." *Behaviour* 74:262–99.

## Chapter 6

# The Body and the Social

*Lloyd E. Sandelands*

This volume dwells on human society. It asks whether society is a fact, whether it reduces to other facts, and whether the perceiving subject must be included in its definition. In contemplating these questions we retrace steps taken long ago by Durkheim, Weber, and others. Perhaps there is something wrong with the questions that we never quite answer them.

I believe society eludes us because we think about it inaptly. Although it is an instance of life (see Sandelands 1995), we treat it as a structure, as if a life could be reduced to elements. And although it is something we feel (see Sandelands 1994), we treat it as an object we can see. Perhaps society is not the structured object we take it to be.

The challenge for social science is to bring feelings of society within the compass of conceptual analysis, to know society in light of its feeling. Durkheim (1915) identified this problem in his study of the elementary forms of religious life, noting that mythological systems for interpreting social life, such as totemism, exist because people cannot see the social facts they feel. "Social action follows ways that are too circuitous and obscure, and employs psychical mechanisms that are too complex to allow the ordinary observer to see when it comes" (p. 239). This insight not withstanding, Durkheim's objective sociology regarded feeling as a bare hint of society, not the stuff of rigorous conceptual analysis. Elsewhere Durkheim (1895/1982) wrote:

> Feelings relating to social things enjoy no pride of place over other sentiments, for they have no different origin. They are a product of human experience, albeit confused and unorganized. They are not due to

some transcendental precognition of reality, but are the result of all kinds of disordered impressions and emotions accumulated through chance circumstance, lacking systematic interpretation. Far from bringing enlightenment of a higher order than the rational, they are composed exclusively of states of mind which, it is true, are strong but also confused. To grant them such a predominant role is to ascribe to the lower faculties of the intelligence supremacy over superior ones and to condemn oneself more or less to a rhetorical logomachy. A science constituted in this way can only satisfy those minds who prefer to think with their sensibility rather than their understanding, who prefer the immediate and confused syntheses of sensation to the patient, illuminating analyses of the reason. Feeling is an object for scientific study, not the criterion of scientific truth. (p. 74)

Against Durkheim, I take the view that feeling is more than a confused acknowledgment of social life. Feeling is an invaluable clue to the forms of social life and indispensable for conceptual analysis. Durkheim errs in regarding feeling a subordinate mental faculty to be supplanted by the higher mental faculty of reason. There is no refusing those who "prefer to think with their sensibility rather than their understanding" because there is no alternative. Everyone thinks with feeling *in order to* understand. Feeling is the basis of all conception, including that exalted as scientific. The forms of social life appear in feeling and there we must look to find them.

In this chapter I ask where do ideas of society come from. I trace an argument in four parts—a creature of four legs. First, I find as a general principle of psychology that ideas of things begin in feeling. Ideas are construed feelings, some no more articulate than vague intuitions. Second, I find that such ideas have a real existence in the body. They are forms of bodily activity that take on meaning and include perceptions, gestures, art, and language. Third, I find that ideas of society in particular take shape in bodily symbols of social life. These symbols consist of certain visual or auditory percepts and physical gestures. And finally, on the basis of the foregoing, I argue that social science must turn to the body and its symbols to develop empirically based ideas of society. A science of society must be built upon objective experiences, not disembodied verbal formulations.

## From Feeling to Idea

The first leg of the argument is a general proposition of psychology that ideas of things begin in feeling. Feeling is lived experience. All feeling is of life, proximally of the body that is its playground, and distally of objects and dynamics that impress upon the body from outside. An idea, on the other hand, is a symbol, an element of a system of meanings. The process that finds ideas in feelings is mind. Ideas are integrations and distillations of feelings.

Following Langer (1967), mind may be conceived broadly as a canalization of feeling into a matrix of symbols. Feelings induced in the sympathetic nervous system enter mental phase when two or more of them are integrated to comprise a symbol. This is more than a labeling of arousal, as proposed by Schachter and Singer (1962), but a genuine synthesis whereby feelings interact to form a compound with a new property: meaning. Thus channeled into symbols, feelings become part of a person's mental life and biography.[1] Symbols are a residue and record of feelings that otherwise are spent in nervous activity. Symbols can be retrieved, feelings only reconstructed and relived. Language (with its names and object-predicate logic) is one way to symbolize (canalize) feeling. Art (with its sensuous forms and presentational logic) is another. Both modes of thought are evolved means of dealing with our species' enlarged capacity for feeling.[2]

Mind works on feelings by using them to synthesize concepts that can be reasoned about and acted on. Mind is how feelings of a situation, which well up immediately and involuntarily as an intensification of sensations and internal dynamisms, are put into the service of thought and action. Thus, feeling and idea are entwined in human mentality. To think is not simply to manipulate symbols, but to have and handle feelings in acts of conception.[3]

Since Durkheim social scientists have failed to see society as a feeling, seeing it instead as a construct, typically of individuals and relations. Thus, Campbell (1958) defined group as an inference drawn from the proximity, similarity, common fate and *pregnanz* of persons. By the same token, social network theorists define group by 'distances' between persons, as indicated by how often they interact or how much they like one another. The more tightly packed the persons, the more 'groupy' the network. In both instances the group is not a feeling of something but an imagination, an intellectual construct.

These theories of society suffer two faults. First, they are incomplete. There is no telling how parts of a group or society are known without prior knowledge of the whole. It is significant that Campbell's model of group perception includes *pregnanz* as a basis for inferring entativity. Unlike the other criteria of the model, *pregnanz* is a principle of good form that applies not to elements of the group but to the group as a whole. It is a feeling of the whole. And its inclusion means perception could not be the logical affair it is supposed to be. Second, and crucial for this chapter, these theories ignore the central role played by feelings. The vicissitudes of life—its risings, fallings, starts, stops, swellings, contractions, and cadences—are song to the heart but strange to an intellect that measures, catalogues, and infers. Life is known only to feeling—that office of mind prior to thought.

In moving from feeling to idea, mind objectifies feeling by transforming its diffuse vitality into discrete and stable symbols. From the whole cloth of feeling are fashioned objects that can be pointed to, thought about, compared, and evaluated.[4] Mind brings feeling into the realm of reflection where a science can make something of it.

## The Principle of Embodiment

The second leg of the argument moves in stride with the first, in the proposition that ideas of things arise in the body. Ideas are meaningful organizations of bodily activity.

### The Body in Psychology

The body is all but ignored by a modern psychology that indulges a morbid fascination with digital computation and information processing (e.g., Simon 1992). Mind today is as Descartes left it, a realm apart from body.

Still there are voices in exception. Gestalt psychology, for all its concern for appearances and illusion, was formulated as a study of brain processes (Kohler 1947). And Bartlett's (1932/1964) once influential theory of mind conceived of thought as a living organization of experience never far from the body. "All incoming impulses of a kind or mode," wrote Bartlett, "go together to build up an active, organized setting"(p. 201). And this setting cannot be decomposed. He continues, "There is not the slightest reason, however, to suppose that each set of incoming impulses, each new group of experiences persists as an isolated member of some passive patchwork. They have to be regarded as constituents of living, momentary settings belonging to the organism." (p. 201). For Bartlett, thinking is suffused with feeling. Ideas and memories evince and justify the vital energies that produced them.

Lakoff (1987) has called for a return to the body. Against the idea that thought is a logical manipulation of abstract, disembodied symbols, he begins with the body and the premise that thought is a biological event. Conceptual systems, according to Lakoff, grow out of bodily experience and make sense in terms of it.

> Thought is embodied, that is, the structures used to put together our conceptual systems grow out of bodily experience and make sense in terms of it; moreover, the core of our conceptual systems is directly grounded in perception, body movement, and experience of a physical and social character. (p. xiv)

For Lakoff, ideas reside in biological capacities. The most basic ideas, which he calls kinesthetic image schema, are rooted in the body and take their form from body processes. Higher-level ideas of category and model are related to the body indirectly as concretions of kinesthetic images. Cognitive science, argues Lakoff, must be based on bodily experiences (a doctrine he calls *experiential realism*), not on abstract symbols that take their meaning from a domain of information.

Lakoff's ideas about body and mind resonate in those precincts of evolutionary psychology where mind is argued to have evolved from the body among our remote prehominid and hominid ancestors. For Sheets-Johnstone (1990), ideation began in tactile-kinesthetic awareness. The living body is the mold from which all fundamental human practices and beliefs are cast—all knowledge is based on analogy to the body. She details how mind develops from body, and specifically from tactile-kinesthetic feeling. Feeling and movement are not stimulus and response, as behaviorists suggest; they are modes of symbolization. The human animal comes to terms with the world through bodily processes. Primitive concepts of substance, enclosure, efficacy, number, and subjectivity develop by analogy to bodily feelings of weight, ingestion of food in mouth, mastication, binary periodicity of gait and breathing, and sound making.

Evolutionary psychology thus makes bold the principle that mind begins in the vastly complicated field of organic activity and, further, that feeling is its first psychical moment. Mind arises on the occasion of feeling. Its key principle is embodiment. Knowledge of objects or events outside the body is possible to the degree they are represented in bodily activity. This idea is well expressed by Whitehead (1934) in his philosophy of organism:

> The world for me is nothing else than how the functionings of my body present it for my experience. The world is thus wholly to be discerned

within those functionings. Knowledge of the world is nothing else than an analysis of the functionings of the body. And yet, on the other hand, the body is merely a society of functionings within the universal society of the world. We have to construe the world in terms of the bodily society, and the bodily society in terms of the general functioning of the world. (pp. 86–7)

This idea also resonates with James's (1890) suggestion that the human organism be considered a 'sounding-board' on which we hear (or feel) the innumerable and subtle changes of somatic and cerebral activity. For James, too, experience and ideation are tied to body consciousness. And for James, knowledge of the world is nothing else than an analysis of the functionings of the body.

**Body and Symbol**

Having identified mind as an operation on feelings, it remains to say *how* it operates. *How* does the body figure in the process? *How* are body feelings made into ideas? And, more specifically, *how* could feelings of social life culminate in an idea of society.

Ideas are symbols that result from the brain's ability to structure feelings. Feeling in one sensory mode is projected on feeling in another sensory mode (e.g., sight on sound, or kinesthesis on sight) and thereby experienced as a quality of the second. By referring to another feeling it functions as its symbol. It is about that feeling, an idea of it. This dynamic is especially potent when bodily feeling is projected on a distance receptor such as the eye or ear, in which case that feeling returns as an impingement, as if brought about by an outside stimulus.

As a folksy example, consider the idea of a cow. One way this idea might come about is by interaction of body sense and visual sense, where these two senses work together to define an experience of a cow as an object having certain properties. In this marriage of senses, the objectness of the cow originates not as a received property of the actual cow but as a feeling of the perceiver's own body projected on his or her visual image of the cow. The perceiver knows his or her own body to be a real object by its constant interplay of outside impacts and inside impulses. The perceiver imparts this personal bodily feeling of objectness, together with closely allied bodily feelings of weight, balance, symmetry, and vitality, to the cow by assimilating them to his or her visual experience.[5] As Sheets-Johnstone (1990: 59) puts it, "vision is *impregnated* with tactile values."[6] The result: the cow is known as a thing in the world because this is how the perceiver knows him- or herself. At the same time, and by the same token, visual sense imparts properties of shape, color, depth, and 'out-there-ness' to kinesthetic feeling, thus conferring on the cow properties it did not have before. This interleaving of sense experiences results in an idea of cow that is more than a visual percept and more than a kinesthetic percept. It is a compound that supervenes over the two (as table salt supervenes over the poisons sodium and chlorine). It is also an idea that begs for a name, such as 'cow' (which is why language has the object-predicate structure it has). Behind idea and name are two symbols: the body symbolizes vision by associating bodily aware-nesses with what the eye sees, and the eye symbolizes bodily feeling by associating a visual image with what the body feels. Working together the senses comprise the dynamic alchemy of symbols we call mind.[7]

In contrast to the example of the cow we can now see why it is difficult to form an empirically based idea of society. Because we have neither a strong visual nor auditory impression of society, we have no distance sense of its shape, color, depth, or 'out-thereness' to coordi-nate with our bodily sense. Lacking these, the fact of society remains maddeningly elusive. We cannot quite point it out.

### Two Types of Body Symbols

Mind involves two kinds of body processes: coordinations of differ-ent sensory inputs, and coordinations of body feelings with physical gestures. Although these two processes are not everywhere distinct, they are usefully separated for purposes of analysis.

The first type of body process to result in symbols consists of the coordinations of sensory modes described earlier. These are the most primitive ideas. Such symbol processes, which are innumerable, are ordinarily of such a low and unconscious level that only labored introspection brings them to the surface, if at all. However, as noted earlier, these subterranean processes, built upon collateral processes across sensory domains, are largely lacking in our experiences of society, much to our chagrin.

A second type of body process resulting in symbols is gesture. Gestures are overt physical movements that have become symbols by their associations with body feelings. Two properties of overt physical movements destine them to become symbols and not simply symptom-atic expressions. First, they are formalized through habituation. Habit supplies repeated patterns of movement that unfold on their own and thus can be sundered from eliciting circumstances and used for symbolizing purposes.[8] And second, by being visible, they are experienced by others who understand them intuitively.

Most gestures develop as transformed signs. Body movements once part of particular actions are dissociated from their original setting and used as symbols for those actions in other settings. They become a means of thinking about those actions. Thus, an embrace or kiss, at one time an integral element of an instinctive behavior complex, comes to symbolize a social encounter or bond. It becomes an idea of that encounter or bond. This distancing of body movements from their original circumstances is crucial for their functioning as symbols. Movements can be symbols—that is, media of thought—only when released from the tyranny of stimulus control. Thinking about something means standing back from it without being compelled to respond.

Gesture's development can be traced in ontogeny and (more speculatively) in phylogeny. The human infant begins life in crisis. What was originally a seamless tie with mother in the womb becomes, with birth, a problem of identity. Society with mother is lost, never quite to be reclaimed, although, as Freud pointed out, a lifetime may be spent in unconscious attempt to do just that. Instead, the infant is reminded of its separateness by its dependence on an inconsistently available mother. After parturition the infant's first vocalizations appear as a preadapted signal for attention from mother. First comes the cry, and later the sweet affiliative sounds of cooing and laughter. That these vocalizations mostly occur when mother is out of touching distance but in sight attests to their role in maintaining the mother-infant bond. Later, by about twelve months, a change occurs and the baby begins to vocalize and gesticulate self-consciously, with purpose and for effect. The child's actions become dissociated from their eliciting conditions and increasingly function symbolically. Cries and other calls begin to be employed strategically and are sometimes exaggerated in awareness of their likely effects. At this point the infant has become aware of self in relation to other. From this point forward, his or her social behavior is tinged with gesture. As every parent knows, questions arise about the meaning of the infant's overtures. A cry is not just a cry. It may be a real cry, and as such a sign of need or trouble. Or it may be a pretense or subterfuge, a self-conscious ruse to attract or divert attention. As pretense the cry is a symbol or mark of society; a kind of thought about it. The infant-child has entered a world of symbols, and its actions increasingly become full-fledged gestures, ideas. Finally, around the age of four years, when the child becomes aware of social roles and conventions, gesture becomes a potential source of embarrassment. The child experiences being out of face or countenance. As Goffman (1967) well described, embarrassment arises when a person's idea of a situation is contradicted by others.

In phylogeny gesture takes its root in mime, to which it relates as an abbreviation. Mime is a rudimentary symbolism whereby whole sequences of action are used as figures for actual sequences of the self-same action. It is distinguished from simple 'aping', which probably is not a symbolism at all.[9] The movements of mime are metaphorical; they are ideas of actions, as a dance may be an idea of a prior or planned hunt, or an idea for a night's sexual passion. Typically, these movements are distinguished by a style that results from repetition outside the exigencies of circumstance—exaggerated in certain emphases, diminished in others, and stereotyped. Its only discipline is that of conveying a feeling and idea of action. Seen in this light, gesture is cryptic mime, a foreshortening through repetition and economizing.

## Ideas of Society

Langer (1976) has speculated that the original reason and motivation for gesture and higher symbolisms of language and art was not, as commonly supposed, to communicate ideas but to uphold an animal feeling of communion. Ideas of society thus may have arisen to hold onto life with others.

> What may have led to the formation of linguistic utterance and understanding was a prior sort of symbolic action, the vociferous accompaniment of the earliest communal expression of formalized feeling, ritual dance. Its motivation was not communication, but communion, though not the sheer desire for bodily contact or at least intimate nearness of ape and monkey bands; what found expression in the dance was the sense of a power residing in the horde as a single agent pervading the holy place, and perhaps made visible in a fetish. The reason for fomalizing the expression of group feeling was that in this way it was enhanced, sustained and upheld when subjectively it might have breaks and lapses. (pp. 301–2)

The third leg of the argument applies the principle of embodiment described previously to propose that we know society—our life together with others—by symbols. These symbols of society are of two types, corresponding to the two types of bodily symbols described earlier. First, there are projections of bodily feelings onto naturally occuring distance percepts of sight and sound. These are perceptive ideas of society. Second, there are projections of bodily feelings onto perceptible movements in gesture. These are enactive ideas of society.

## Perceptive Ideas of Society

Society is symbolized when one of its felt embodiments is integrated with another of its felt embodiments. When this occurs, each serves as symbol for the other and each announces the fact of society. The idea of society begins with embodiment of social life in multiple sensory modes.

The earliest and surest embodiment of society appears in kinesthetic sense. We are indelibly impressed by the feeling of union with mother—a bond that begins as physical communion in the womb and upon partuition develops into an increasingly psychological and anxiety-bound connection punctuated by interludes of physical intimacy. Infant attachment is supported by myriad bodily activities, including touch, embrace, cuddling, stroking, nursing, kissing, gaze, cooing, and, later, verbalization—all of which recapitulate, to a greater or lesser degree, the original identity of the womb.

What begins as a bodily drama of mother and infant is repeated endlessly throughout life. Adult sociality, and especially adult sexuality, reenacts this drama in many details, repeating basic bodily motifs—of touch, embrace, cuddling, stroking, kissing—and adding dazzling imaginative reconstructions and elaborations. In contact of flesh and exchange of body fluids, lovers reproduce the interpenetration and unity that constitutes their basic tactile-kinesthetic experience of communion. As Freud described, this drama is the model on which all society is conceived as analogue. We feel society in a thousand quotidian acts—of handshake, hug, kiss, embrace, dance, wave, a returned smile or gaze, and sheer copresence—that we do not think of as sexual. We feel it also in the pain of isolation (as every jailer knows). These bodily acts and states comprise the felt substance of society.

Ideas of society are established when kinesthetic sense is coordinated with other senses, particularly vision or audition. Frequently, such ideas are worked up collaboratively in communal activities, such as dance or choric shout. By coordinating kinesthetic feelings of group with strong public visual and auditory percepts, communal activities are occasions for ideas of society. Such collaborative assimilations of group feelings and visual and auditory percepts abound today in stadium chants, folk dances, marches, religious liturgies, sing-alongs, candlelight vigils, and even moments of silence. Indeed, such symbols can be the group's main reason and reward, as is suggested in Sata's (1988) study of a Japanese motor cycle gang. According to one gang member:

> Seventy to one hundred vehicles start their engines all at once. We can hear nothing but the exhaust noises. Nobody can, even the police, cannot, stop us. The moment the engines are started the disorderly crowd becomes a dinosaur. It's really overwhelming. (p. 101)

Here an inchoate bodily feeling of the crowd is integrated with a definite auditory sensation (the sound of exhaust noises in unison) that gives an objective referent to the feeling. The ensuing din is symbol of the dinosaur the group has become. The group is a real something 'out there'.

Another gang member confirms the developing group, this time alluding to its visual aspect as the coordinate sensation to bodily feeling. The group forms as it begins to move in concert; as it "wags the tail of the band."

> When running, we are not in complete harmony at the start. But if the run begins going well, all of us feel for others. How can I say this? When, when we wag the tail of the band. When our mind becomes one. At such a time, it's a real pleasure. When all of us become one, I understand something. All of a sudden, I realize "oh! we're one" and think, "If we speed as fast as we can, it will become a real RUN." When we realize that we become one flesh, it's supreme. (p. 113)

A similar visual aspect of the felt group often is noted in athletic contests when a well-drilled team operates in concert. For example, when discussing the play of the University of Nevada at Las Vegas men's basketball team during the 1990 NCAA championship game, the television announcers referred often to its "amoeba defense"—a defense so named for its fluidity and tenacious envelopment of opposing players (see Sandelands and St.Clair 1993). At such times the group crystallizes to form an entity over and above the players that comprise it. The feeling of the team is corroborated visually and in this way the team is substantiated as an object.

**Enactive Ideas of Society**

There are also ideas of society based on conjunctions of body feelings with physical movements that have been dissociated from their usual eliciting conditions (i.e., gestures). Gaze, wave, smile, and embrace are among the oldest and most universal of these gestural symbols. They mark society so that we can see it. Research on eye contact, for example, finds it a means of approach (to the point of threat sometimes), a factor in impression formation and persuasion, and a mechanism that maintains social relations.[10] For the sighted, gaze figures centrally in ongoing social behavior to maintain contact and coherence (Argyle and Cook, 1976). Interactants look to each other for information and for assurance that the group is intact. Other 'immediacy behaviors', such as head and body orientation, touching, and smiling, function the same way (Argyle,1975). Moreover, these behaviors are meaningful to non-participants who recognize in them an idea of affiliation (Kleinke et al. 1974).

Argyle (1975) proposed that nonverbal immediacy behaviors (including gaze, proximity seeking, body orientation) comprise an equilibrium-seeking system whereby interruptions in one behavior (such as gaze) are compensated by other behaviors (such as proximity seeking). These movements are necessary, he argued, to maintain social order and life. Langer (1976) speaks more generally and incisively of the same dynamic:

> With the overgrowth of mental functions in hominid phylogeny the need of contact between individuals, found in all degrees in various animals, undergoes a change from bodily contact to mental contact. Communion becomes an elaborate emotional need, in which the simple impulses to grooming, clinging or going to sleep in each other's arms are gradually replaced by symbolic collective acts. The mental contact among the proto-human beings which displaces the constantly needed physical contact of gregarious simians is most readily made by celebration, dance, choric shouts and gestures, centering around some symbol of potency. By such acts all the participants are joined in one performance and feel themselves as one. (pp. 302–3).

The significance attached to gaze as a symbol of society is plain in a wide variety of cultures, particularly in primitive cultures where it defines the sacred and profane. In many cultures it is said to be impossible to stare into the face of God and live to tell the tale. In cultures where the divine takes human form, it may be forbidden to gaze upon that person. According to Frazer (1922/1951), in Loango a penalty of death awaits any who dare or happen to see the tribal chief eat. Elaborate precautions therefore are taken to ensure this does not happen. It is likewise a capital offense to see the King of Dahomey at his meals. When he drinks in public he hides himself behind a curtain, or hankerchiefs are held up around his head, while the people throw their faces to the ground. In cultures where the divine is not confined to a tribal chief or figurehead but is spread out among all the people, strictures on gazing at others apply more generally, though they are weaker and not so dramatically sanctioned. The Navajo, for example, are taught not to gaze directly at another person during a conversation (Hall 1963). Among the Wituto and Bororo of South America, a speaker and listener look at outside objects during a conversation; and a storyteller turns his back to his listeners and addresses himself instead to a hut (Whiffen 1905). Similar traditions appear in modern Eastern and Indian cultures where eyes are averted in a bow when greeting another person. This is likewise in homage to the divine in each person (Zen or Bhudda nature). What is true of the sacred is true also of the profane. Tabooed persons are likewise shunned from gaze, either by confinement to a hut or ward or by banishment from the group altogether. Frazer (1922/1951) cites numerous examples of such treatment of strangers, warriors, and menstruating or childbearing women.

Gaze is restricted because it symbolizes intimacy with the sacred or tabooed figure. This symbol is deeply rooted as vision accompanies the earliest and most profound contacts of child at mother's breast. The power of gaze in symbolizing society is dramatically illustrated by the belief of some primitive peoples (and some moderns too) in the 'evil eye'. This belief announces the idea that vision connects the subject with its object. The evil eye is the way malevolent spirits project their baleful influences (Argyle and Cook, 1976).

Other gestures function symbolically in social regulation, for example, to guide the taking of turns in conversation, hold the attention of a listener during a monologue, and seek support. Bavelas et al. (1992) call these 'interactive gestures' because they symbolize the fact of a relationship between interactants, irrespective of its content (which is the domain of 'topic gestures'). Indeed, it is Bavelas et al.'s basic thesis that such interactive gestures "constitute a class with the common function of *including the listener* and thereby counteracting the beginning of a drift toward monologue that is necessarily created every time one person has the floor" (p. 476, emphasis in original).

Gestures such as gaze, embrace, or hand motions objectify society, making it visible. They are not only symbols of society but figures of its felt form. There are formal parallels yet to be explicated between gestures and society, as, for example, between gaze and group psychology. Hints of concord are suggested by our near primate relatives. Among chimpanzees, all eyes are on the alpha male who is thereby fixed both geographically and psychologically at the epicenter of the troop. Sometimes, as in our own case, gaze upon the leader seems to involve a profound, even hypnotic, fascination, a dramatic symbol of a strong tie and a clue perhaps to an underlying group psychology (see, e.g., Freud, 1922/1959). It is likely that the vital tensions and conflicts of human gaze tell a similar tale of the vital tensions and conflicts of human society.

From gesture it is but a short step to the more complex and abstracted symbolisms of society that appear in mime, ritual, music, visual art, and language. To the great benefit of social science, these lattter symbolisms project bodily feelings of society outward into isolable and analyzable performances and objects, such as ceremony, story, dance, song, sculpture, painting, or speech act. Unencumbered from the slow and often discursive mechanics of gesture, these symbolisms indicate more of the feeling and form of human society, and they thus afford a more comprehensive and nuanced object for study. It is possible to discern felt forms of human society in such diverse symbols as a Japanese tea ceremony, square dance, stadium chant, and organizational chart (Sandelands 1996). These symbols represent the vital dynamics of social life—dynamics known to us as feelings of society.

Although we have much to learn about gesture and more advanced symbols of society, there is no doubt of their role in making and maintaining society. Everywhere they affirm the idea of society—a passing glance of solidarity, a handshake of trust, a bowed head in respect, an embrace of sympathy, a dance of sexual intent, or a sacrament of communion.[11] For being visible, these quotidian acts comprise a realm of social fact from which an emprically verifiable idea of society can be built.

## A Challenge for Social Science

In closing, I append a final leg to the argument to give it the wherewithal to run. If the chief problem for social science is to bring our sure feelings of society to conceptual analysis, then its main challenge is to take the body as a focus of study. Human society is of the body. There is a great deal to learn about human society from those whose business it is to understand the social significance of the body, such as dance instructors, figure painters, mannequin makers, acting coaches, and even morticians. These people must be able to read the social meanings of the body. If social science is to deal in fact, it must likewise be conversant with the embodied symbols that comprise our intuitive ideas of society.

This chapter has touched on a few such symbols; there are many others. As Langer (1962) points out, social life is shot through with symbols of society. "All fantastic beliefs in a great ancestor are symbolic of the original and permanent life of the stock from which every individual life stems. The totem, the hero, the sacred cow, these are the most elementary social symbols" (p. 120). These symbols sustain our involvement with others, particularly against our counter-vailing interest to distinguish ourselves as individuals:

> We can give up our actual, instinctual involvements with our kind just to the extent that we can replace them by symbolic ones. This is the prime function of social symbols, from a handshake, to the assembly of robed judges in a Supreme Court. In protocol and ritual, in the investment of authority, in sanctions and honors, lies our security against loss of involvement with mankind. (pp. 121–2)

This chapter has emphasized gestures as embodiments of feelings of society that can be studied objectively. They are our most elementary marks of the social. Yet, for being elementary, they offer limited insight into the nature of society. We need symbols that can objectify society even more comprehensively—higher-level symbols tied less to the body and more to conception. Language is unsuited to the task because its discursive form is incomensurate with the all-at-once dynamisms of society (see Sandelands 1995). Too often its symbols multiply unchecked by concerns for their tie to experience, leaving discourse to outrun its subject (Sandelands and Srivatsan 1993).[12] Art is more promising because its symbols are compatible with the vital forms of society. Society is more revealingly symbolized by artistic images such as totems, logos, mascots, artworks, chants, song, and architecture, because these symbols better convey its vital substance.[13] They keep more faithfully to the restless dynamisms of society and to the restless dynamisms of our bodily awareness of it. Art objectifies what the body knows by expressing its forms of feeling. In art we can discern the forms of society. Artworks are social facts fitted for objective scientific study.

In sum, society is known to us through the body, as feeling. Feeling, however, is elusive; it collapses into condensed and forshortened memory as soon as our contact with it ends. Thus, we need symbols to fix our feelings of society in awareness so we can think about them. By making feelings of society manifest, such symbols make them objects for public evaluation and thereby objects for a science of society. As shown, a study of gesture offers a start. As argued, a study of art (so-called 'frozen gesture') promises even more because its objects are better symbols of social life. I believe we must turn to the body and to art to grapple more effectively with social life and society. It remains to show how social facts are encountered in the body and in art and to show how these symbolisms can be used to further conceptual understanding of society. When we have done so, we can lay aside the foundational questions of existence and meaning that perplex us and step out of Durkheim's large footsteps.

## Notes

Thanks to Jane Dutton, Martha Feldman, Dan Friedland, John Greenwood, Karl Weick, and Mayer Zald for their contributions to this work. Correspondence should be addressed to Lloyd Sandelands, Department of Psychology, University of Michigan, 525 E. University Drive, Ann Arbor, MI 48109-1109.

1. Uncanalized feelings are what psychologists call moods. For want of a symbol, moods are shapeless, unthinkable. People come to grips with them by symbolizing them. To discover that one is feeling 'blue' is the first step toward mastering that feeling.

2. The emotional and intellective life of non human primates make an interesting comparison. The chimpanzee, for example, is racked by feeling. Whereas we dissipate feeling through cerebration, the chimpanzee has no choice but to act them out. We are freed from the tyranny of feeling by our ability to symbolize. Instead of responding immediately to every circumstance on the basis of feelings, we can decide whether and how to respond.

3. This psychological principle is noted by the physicist Albert Einstein who saw his own thinking as a play of feeling below the level of language.

The words of the language, as they are written or spoken, do not seem to play any role in my mechanism of thought. The psychical entities which seem to serve as elements in thought are certain signs and more or less clear images which can be 'voluntarily' reproduced and combined. The above mentioned elements are, in my case, of visual and muscular type. Conventional words or other signs have to be sought for laboriously only in a secondary stage, when the mentioned associative play is sufficiently established and can be reproduced at will. (cited in Damasio 1994:107)

4. According to Langer (1976), this objectification of feeling distinguishes human mind from animal mind.

In a symbol-making brain like ours, every internal feeling tends to issue in a symbol which gives it an objective status, even if only transiently. This is the hominid speciality that makes the gulf between man and beast, without any unbiological addition, and probably goes back as far as any possible division between our kind and other primates. (p. 342)

5. Writes Langer (1982):

Bodily feelings may be the first thing man projected and thus, all unwittingly, imputed to everything he objectified as material bodies in his world. The very existence of 'things' is modeled on his own inward expectation of strains, directions, and limitations of his felt actions; the wholeness and simplicity of molar objects is that of his own soma. (p. 48)

6.Sheets-Johnstone (1990) writes:

The relationship of the one modality to the other cannot be treated simply under the rubric of coordination—of eye and hand typically—but must be more deeply understood as a *transposition of meanings* from an original datum to a second: as a transfer of *sense* in the double meaning of that word. (italics in original, p. 59)

Although the interaction of sense modes is the central dynamic of perception, the process cannot unfold as a transposition of meanings. This implies that meanings preexist transfer of sense across modes. Rather, it is this transfer that creates meaning. Sense experience has no meaning *until* it is brought into contact with other sense experiences.

7. Langer (1982) illustrates the human capacity for cross-modal transfers of sensation and feeling by comparing it to that of our nearest primate relative, the chimpanzee. Citing Kohler's study of the mentality of apes, she shows how Kohler's descriptions of the chimps' use of material objects seems not be informed by the same degree of cross-modal interchange. For example, to reach a desired object out of arm's reach, a chimpanzee will show humanlike resourcefulness in using available materials to make a ladder to reach the object. However, unlike his human cousin, the chimpanzee exercises none of the same care in amassing materials to climb upon. Whereas a person can and

will visually assess the weight, balance, and sturdiness of a prospective ladder, the chimpanzee seems unable to do so and relies instead on a separate and fortunately more acute bodily sense of balance when climbing. Langer surmises that the chimpanzee capacity to symbolize is small in relation to humans.

8. Writes Langer (1982):

> On this habitual round of behavior, the dreaming, inventing, apprehensive mind imposes itself, giving all the familiar recurrent acts—shooting, fishing, planting, and above all the daily occasions of eating—a heavy cargo of symbolic functions. Being repetitious, their various detailed subacts have attained a natural economy and order; it is this fixed design of concatenated subacts, rather than the purposive act as a whole, that offers models for expressive gestures and manipulations. (p. 60)

9. Apes are often observed to repeat the actions of others, including their human trainers (see, e.g., de Waal 1989). However, it is not established that these repetitions are employed symbolically as mime, or even that they comprise genuine imitation in the sense of a deliberate literal recapitulation of a sequence of actions.

10. A charming illustration of this last point is Bruner's (1976) study of the game of peek-a-boo in mother-infant interactions. This game, which is quite common, consists essentially of moves that establish, break, and reestablish mutual gaze between mother and child. It seems likely that such games, which are among the child's first forms of social interaction, function to develop and maintain the mother-child bond. It seems likely too that such games are the origins of the infant's idea of this bond, as gaze comes to be appreciated as its symbol.

11. The extent to which these acts and innumerable others symbolize society is suggested further by the cultural variations in their meaning. Eye contact may be an intimacy everywhere, but its meaning differs from place to place. Whereas in the West it is good breeding to look a business associate squarely in the eye, in the East this degree of eye contact may be seen as a sign of disrespect or even vague threat.

12. Development of a verbal symbolism, in particular, brought substantial changes. It made possible an internal cerebration almost completely divorced from motor centers of the body. The person could have private ideas and think for him- or herself. Increasingly, the person came to inhabit a world of his or her own making, an individual world apart from the social world.

13. This point was brought home to me in a class exercise in which students were asked to create an image of an organization using office supplies, such as paper, ink, glue, scissors, paper clips, and the like. This assignment was difficult for most students. Most admitted to having no image of organization whatsoever. The result was a wide variety of visual objects and an even wider variety of interpretations to make sense of them. Most interestingly, when it was suggested to them, in view of their lack of a clear idea of organization and

the disparateness of the images they produced, that there is no such thing as organizations, they met this suggestion with incredulousness and denial.

# References

Argyle, Michael. (1975). *Bodily Communication.* London: Methuen.

Argyle, Michael, & Mark Cook. 1976. *Gaze and Mutual Gaze.* New York: Cambridge University Press.

Bartlett, Frederic. 1932/1964. *Remembering: A Study in Experimental and Social Psychology.* Cambridge: Cambridge University Press.

Bavelas, Janet B., Nicole Chovil, Douglas A. Lawrie, and Allan Wade. 1992. "Interactive Gestures." *Discourse Processes* 15:469–9.

Bruner, Jerome. 1976. "Early Rule Structure: The Case of Peek-a-Boo." In *Life Sentences*, ed. Rom Harré. New York: Wiley.

Campbell, Donald T. 1958. "Common Fate, Similarity, and Other Indices of the Status of Aggregates of Persons as Social Entities." *Behavioral Science* 3:14–25.

Cheney, Dorothy L. and Richard M. Seyfarth. 1990. *How Monkeys See the World.* Chicago: University of Chicago Press.

Damasio, Antonio R. 1994. *Descartes' Error.* New York: Putnam.

de Waal, Frans. (1982). *Chimpanzee Politics.* Baltimore, Md.: Johns Hopkins University Press.

Donald, Merlin. 1991. *Origins of the Modern Mind.* Cambridge, Mass.: Harvard University Press.

Durkheim, Émile. 1895/1982. The Rules of Sociological Method, ed. Steven Lukes, trans. W.D. Halls. New York: Free Press.

———. 1893/1933. *The Division of Labor in Society*, trans. G. Simpson. New York: Macmillan.

———. 1915. *The Elementary Forms of the Religious Life.* London: Allen & Unwin.

Frazer, James G. 1922/1951. *The Golden Bough: A Study in Magic and Religion.* New York: Macmillan.

Freud, Sigmund. 1922/1959. *Group Psychology and the Analysis of the Ego*, trans. J. Strachey. New York: Norton.

Goffman, Erving. 1967. *Interaction Ritual.* Chicago: Aldine.

Hall, Edward T. 1963. "A System for the Notation of Proxemic Behavior." *American Anthropologist* 65:1003–26.

James, William. 1890. *Psychology*, Vol. 2. New York: Holt.

Kleinke, Chris L., Frederick B. Meeker, & Carl La Fong. 1974. "Effects of Gaze, Touch, and Use of Name on Evaluation of Engaged Couples. *Journal of Research in Personality* 7(4):368–373.

Kohler, Wolfgang. 1947. *Gestalt Psychology.* New York: Liveright.

Lakoff, George. 1987. *Women, Fire, and Dangerous Things*. Chicago: University of Chicago Press.

Langer, Susanne K. (1962). *Philosophical Sketches*. Baltimore, Md.: Johns Hopkins University Press.

———. (1967). *Mind: An Essay on Human Feeling*, Vol. 1. Baltimore, Md.: Johns Hopkins University Press.

———. (1976). *Mind: An Essay on Human Feeling*, Vol. 2. Baltimore, Md.: Johns Hopkins University Press.

———. 1982. *Mind: An Essay on Human Feeling*, Vol. 3. Baltimore, Md.: Johns Hopkins University Press.

Sandelands, Lloyd E. 1994. "The Sense of Society." *Journal for the Theory of Social Behavior* 24(4):305–38.

———. 1995. "The Idea of Social Life." *Philosophy of the Social Sciences* 25(2):147–79.

———. 1996. "Feeling and Form in Social Life." Unpublished manuscript, University of Michigan, Ann Arbor.

Sandelands, Lloyd E. & Vatsan Srivatsan. 1993. "The Problem of Experience in the Study of Organizations." *Organization Studies* 14(1):1–25.

Sandelands, Lloyd E. & Lynda St. Clair 1993. "Toward an Empirical Concept of Group." *Journal for the Theory of Social Behaviour* 23(4):423–458.

Sata, Ikuya. 1988. "Bosozoku: Flow in Japanese Motor Cycle Gangs." In *Optimal Experience*, ed. Mihalyi Csikszentmihalyi and I. Csikszentmihalyi. Cambridge: Cambridge University Press.

Schachter, Stanley and Jerome E. Singer. 1962. "Cognitive, Social and Physiological Determinants of Emotional State." *Psychological Review* 69:379–99.

Sheets-Johnstone, Maxine. 1990. *The Roots of Thinking*. Philadelphia: Temple University Press.

Simon, Herbert. 1992. "What is an 'Explanation' of Behavior?" *Psychological Science* 3:150–61.

Whiffen, Thomas. 1905. *The North West Amazons: Notes on Some Months Spent among Cannibal Tribes*. London: Constable.

Whitehead, Alfred N. 1934. *Nature and Life*. Chicago: University of Chicago Press.

# Chapter 7

# Social Explanation

*Peter T. Manicas*

I approach the central question of this volume indirectly, by considering what seems to me to be a central fallacy, or series of fallacies, regarding the task of a human science. To illustrate the issues I begin with a sketch of a very impressive study now under way, a $32 million project entitled "The Project on Human Development in Chicago Neighborhoods." Its size and expense suggests that what it represents is not marginal in the human sciences. Quite the contrary, very much of social science shares in its most fundamental assumptions.

Writing in defense of this project, James Q. Wilson, perhaps the nation's best-known criminologist, notes that "two children of the same family often turn out very differently. This casts doubt on the notion that the shared environment of the children is the principle—or even a very important factor in their development." He asks "what is going on?" "Correlational studies," he says, cannot help much since they "can tell us next to nothing about what causes what." Thus:

> We may find that crime and unemployment are correlated, but we can't tell from this association whether unemployment causes crime, whether crime causes unemployment (as it would if people found drug dealing more profitable than work), or whether some common factor (such as impulsiveness or poor work habits) causes both crime and unemployment.

Some of what we know, he says, comes from longitudinal studies, but "most longitudinal studies cannot tell us very much about causality because they did not begin when their subjects were young enough and did not involve a sufficient number of measures, such as looking at early patterns of mother-child bonding."[1]

The Chicago study, directed by Harvard psychiatrist Felton J. Earls and Yale sociologist Albert J. Reiss, Jr., is interdisciplinary and begins with the assumption that previous research "doesn't go far enough." It includes a selected sample of eleven thousand research subjects, grouped into overlapping cohorts. Along with community studies, each will be "followed" for eight years. "By the year 2001 data will be available on the entire development process of a large number of criminals and non-criminals."[2]

It is clear that Wilson thinks that to explain crime, one needs to find the causes in individual biography (or perhaps in individual biology—a crime gene, perhaps). He thinks that if we look at enough individual cases and do enough multiple regressions, we will find the key "factor" or perhaps the right combination of factors. We will have the causes of crime.

## Human Development

It is surely true that "two children of the same family often turn out very differently." But Wilson draws the wrong conclusion from this. Indeed, it is easy enough to explain why this happens and why it also is a mystery. Before looking critically at the guiding assumptions of the study, let us consider what are, I think, some fairly elementary general facts.

As seems clear, the psychological traits of persons—personality, cognitive ability, and so on—are causal outcomes of a complex epigenetic process that begins with conception and ends with the death of the organism. A particular and *unique* genome, itself the product of the conjunction of haploid sex cells, is in embryogenesis, the locus of continuous transactions both in itself and in relation to its 'environment.' It subsequently emerges from the womb and is then in a continuous transaction with a natural and human environment, acquiring a language and basic conventions of human interaction, eventually forming a self and traits of personality. Through both of these conditions, in the womb and then after, as the biologist Paul Weiss remarks,"the latitude for epigenetic vagaries of the component elements on all levels is immense."[3]

To say that the process is epigenetic is to say that in this immensely complicated process—misleadingly called a chain—the causes are transactional and not additive.[4] With the exception of mechanical causation where forces are interactive and can be added (as vectors), this is true of all causality. For example, a plant's growth depends on water, fertilizer and a host of other "factors." But as Lewontin remarks, it would be "absurd to say what proportion of the plant's height is owed to the fertilizer it received and what proportion to the water."[5]

As regards human development, many causes are working at various levels. Biochemical processes (and interventions at the biochemical level, e.g., nicotine) have effects on molecular processes that then have effects on higher-order complexes, organelles, organs, organ systems, finally to the intact functioning organism. And these causal transactions are both "bottom-up" and "top-down." As Pattee writes: "Coordination in biological organisms takes the form of hierarchical controls which at each level provide greater and greater freedom or adaptability for the whole organism by selectively adding more and more contraints to its component parts."[6] Not only is there considerable contingency between levels in this dynamic process, but our knowledge of interlevel processes is still very much incomplete. Indeed, as Hull remarks, "in some cases, the analyses are not even compatible."[7]

Since each moment of development establishes new conditions for what comes after, time is also critical. Some changes are unimportant relatively; others, including those that are irreversible, are not. Although preceded by a host of more marginal changes, the emergence of the self, for example, is monumental.

The epigenetic "vagaries," of course, are not unlimited; they are, if you will, restricted by our 'biologically determined' human nature. It may be useful here to give a restricted meaning to a term used widely but vaguely (and usually wrongly). We can say that some trait, capacity, or difference is a feature of our (biologically determined) 'human nature' only if the person realizing that trait would have realized it had she been in any other time or place. That is, time and place are irrelevant as regards features of 'human nature'.

There are some obvious biologically determined traits: our human anatomy and physiology is one. Others, related to this, include manifest physical traits that mark family resemblances, such as facial features, body type, and skin color. (Race is *not* biologically determined since on all the evidence there are no biological grounds for grouping people according to race. Race, like ethnicity, is a social construction, a fact of some importance.)[8]

We can also distinguish realized capacities (e.g., the ability to speak

Dutch) from capacities as potentialities, the ability to acquire language, and hold that the latter are biological determined although the former are not. There are a host of distinctly human (species-specific) capacities that presuppose our distinct evolutionary history. These are a critical part of 'human nature'. *Homo sapiens* everywhere and at any time can acquire language. But, of course, depending on the time and place, children acquire some very different languages. There are as well biologically grounded propensities or tendencies of other sorts— for example toward cancer and schizophrenia. Like the human powers just mentioned, these need not be realized, and, like these other capacities, they are still very poorly understood. We do know, however, that *all the distinctly human capacities require for their realization a human environment*. It follows, accordingly, that all these realized capacities are social in a very obvious sense.[9]

## The Mark Of The Social

What then is the special or defining character of a human environment? Although there are alternative ways to approach this question, George H. Mead's account is powerful and convincing.

> The 'peculiar' character possessed by our human social environment . . . is to be found in the process of communication, and more particularly in the triadic relation on which the existence of meaning is based: the relation of the gesture of one organism to the adjustive response made to it by another organism, in its indicative capacity as pointing to the completion or resultant of the act it initiates. Such a response is its meaning, or give it its meaning . . . . When this conversation of gestures can be taken over into the individual's conduct so that the attitude of the other forms can affect the organism, and the organism can reply with its corresponding gesture and thus arouse the attitude of the other in its own process, then a self arises.[10]

Mead's formulation (not to be developed here) generates some important implications. First, the self (personality) is a concrete, and thus idiosyncratic, incarnation of a local community: a particular instantiation of the social mind. As Dewey says, there is a radical difference between 'individuals with minds' and 'individual minds'. It follows that, for example, a Harlem youth will incarnate a social world common to many Americans but that he will also incarnate a local world shared by 'significant others.' Second, humans act on the basis of the meanings that are not merely "in the head" but in public space. These are reproduced and transformed through an interpretative process. One illustration must suffice. Brent Staples comments:

> I'd been a fool. I'd been walking the streets grinning good evening at people who were frightened to death of me. I did violence to them by just being. How had I missed this? I kept walking at night, but from then on I paid attention. I became expert in the language of fear.[11]

His decision to use his blackness on his walks near the University of Chicago depended on some distinct meanings derived from interactions on those walks. The 'interpretative process' is, as Mead analyzed it, a conversation of the actor with himself employing the materials at hand. Blumer puts the matter clearly: "the actor selects, checks, suspends, regroups, and transforms the meanings in the light of the situation in which he is placed and the direction of his action."[12] Following on this, finally, the self is not fixed but is being transformed through action in a continuous process. Differences will emerge in the possibilities for change and the degree of change, critical junctures in the maturation process and in the life history of selves. These last, of course, will vary widely in individual life histories.[13]

## The Chicago Study

If the foregoing is even approximately correct, then there is *no* possibility that the Chicago study will produce what it aims to produce. My criticism begins with some broadly philosophical concerns regarding causality and agency and concludes with some methodological remarks about some standard statistical techniques.

First, the study assumes a fundamentally flawed notion of causality and explanation, an essentially Humean picture in which causes are construed as invariants of the form "whenever this, then that." This has been usefully termed "regularity determinism."[14] It depends on a false model of science constructed on the paradigm of classical celestial mechanics. Unfortunately, it is an idea still very much alive in the human sciences.

There is an alternative, realist view. For the realist, the world is not a determined concatenation of events, but a contingent concatenation of real structures. The world is stratified and contains "powerful particulars" that conjointly but contingently produce what is actual.

Laws of nature are not, as regularity determinists hold, "invariant relations of succession and resemblence" (to quote Comte's classic formula). They must be analysed, as Bhaskar argues, as tendencies "which may be possessed unexercized and exercised unrealized, just as they may be realized unperceived (or undetected)."[15] Because the world is not a Laplacean closed system, there is genuine novelty and in principle unpredictability as regards everything that happens, even while, at the same time, everything that happens is caused and thus, in principle, can be explained.[16] Versus the conventional deductive-nomological model of explanation, there is, accordingly, a radical asymmetry between explanation and prediction.[17] There is a stability in the world, and this gives rise to patterns. We can, therefore, establish true generalizations. But there are also surprises. Sugar *usually* dissolves in water and does not explode. Regularity determinism is *not* consistent with the developmental process sketched in the foregoing. The realist alternative is.

Second, because the Harvard study assumes regularity determinism, it must deny human agency. It assumes that the "factors" identified by the study as potential causes of crime *determine* the behavioral outcomes: The criminal acts of Sam, Edith, Joe, and so on, are the result of factors X, Y, Z, and so on. As stated earlier, these "factors" are causes in the sense that if they are present (usually in this or that combination), they explain given instances of behavior.

But once we have genuine contingency and novelty in the world, it is possible to make a place for genuine human agency—and, I would hasten to add, responsibility. Persons are 'powerful particulars' in that they are causes. Once self is decentered from consciousness (as in Mead's formulation), we can see that, as Giddens says, "agency refers not to the intentions people have in doing things, but to their capability of doing those things in the first place."[18] Indeed, it is analytic to the concept of action that the agent could have done otherwise.

The idea should not be either minimized or misunderstood. It is not an anti-naturalistic concession to 'free will' as an uncaused cause. Rather, it means that by virtue of our emergent minded capacities, persons act for reasons (which are causes), and that action is characterized by radical contingency. I may reach to close the window but stop because a bee suddenly flies into my field of vision. I may decide to marry but get cold feet at the last moment. As argued, what we are, including our personalities, skills, habits, attitudes, beliefs, and so forth, is the product of a complex epigenesis and of course, this gives us some measure of confidence in what others *might* do. But 'might do'—even with a strong probability—is not 'will do.' The in principle unpredicability of action is a consequence, not only of the open-system character of the world—the flight of the bee in the window—but of reflexivity, a process, as George H. Mead insisted, of communication of the actor with himself.

Third, the Chicago study cannot hope to establish causality (or causal chains) because it must rely on multiple regression as the preferred method of inquiry.

## The Limits of Multiple Regression

We can think of the longitudinal study as an extended effort at applying a version of Mill's joint method: Look at a large number of positive and negative cases, and identify the potential "causes" by seeing whether there is some "factor" (or factors) present in the positive cases and absent in the negative cases.

We should note, first, that there are severe limits on the use of this method *where experimentation is possible*. We must assume, for example, that the positive cases represent a unitary phenomenon and that our analysis has not obscured some common factor, perhaps at a different level of analysis. Moreover, where experiment is possible, the *most* that can be said is that some identified factors are eliminated as not necessary conditions, and some identified factors are eliminated as not sufficient conditions. This mode of proceeding is essential to causal analysis even if inferences to causality are always tentative and revisable. But, of course, experiment is not possible in our case. Characteristically, in the social sciences, one appeals to multiple regression as a second best alternative.

Roughly the idea is this: We have a "dependent variable" (crime) and number of independent variables, for example, IQ, family environment, race, income, and educational level—each operationally defined. By the use of well-known mathematical techniques, we hold each of the "variables" constant and then consider the relation of the others to the dependent variable. We hope to find differences in the beta coefficients of the variables, thus establishing the relative importance of the factors as regards the outcomes.

The National Longitudinal Survey of Youth (NLSY), a two-year study of a "nationally representative sample" of some 12,686 American youths, compares neatly with the Harvard study. It was employed heavily by Murray and Herrnstein in *The Bell Curve*. To focus our discussion, we can provide one result reported by them. With reference to IQ and SES (socioeonomic status), they produce the results of a multiple regression which shows that the probability of being in poverty is considerably higher as IQ goes from high to low than if parental income goes from high to low. Murray and Herrnstein ask, "How does each of these causes of poverty look when the other is held constant? Or to put it another way: If you have to choose, is it better to be born smart or rich? The answer is unequivocally 'smart'."[19]

There are some obvious criticisms to make. First, it is no longer possible to assume that IQ measures a real property of the person.[20] Second, we need to assume the accuracy of self-reports of participants.[21] Gould summarizes a third criticism: "almost all their relationships are weak; very little of the variation in social factors is explained by either independent variable." He points out that they admit as much when they say that "one cannot predict what a given person will do from his I.Q. score."[22]

These remarks lead to the deeper criticism. Gould comments: "But a few per cent of statistical determination is not causal explanation." We need here to distinguish analysis of variation and causal explanation.

Assume first a set of dependable, meaningful independent variables with a linear relation to the dependent variable.

$$Y = a + b_1 + b_2 + b_1b_2 + e \text{ (Equation 1)}$$

The problem is then one of variable selection. The goal of the analysis is a "good fit." If we do our work well, what we end up with is "a useful statistical description defensible against plausible alternative interpretations."[23] It is critical to emphasize that *the very best result is a statistical description*, a point nearly always missed. At best, the result is a highly simplified picture, a statistical snapshot, of a fantastically complicated concrete social situation. For example, as an abstract ratio, the crime rate represents a picture of crime in the real world. It leaves much out—obviously. On the other hand, as Achen remarks, "A picture of a friend is useless if it covers a football field and exhibits every pore. What one looks for instead is an interpretable amount of information, with the detailed workings omitted."[24] As regards the crime rate, the "detailed workings" include, of course, the specific structured actions of *everyone* in society: both criminals and noncriminals. While it would be agreed that a crime rate is such snapshot taken from a very long distance, the same is true of all other statistical results, including the results of regressions.

A useful description—a good fit—is not so easy to come by. One test of this is the coefficient of determination, $R^2$. It is usually said that

$R^2$ gives "the percentage of variance explained" in the dependent variable by the regression. But as Achen commends, this is an expression that, "for most social scientists, is of doubtful meaning but great rhetorical value."[25] The rhetorical values lies in the supposition that first, a large $R^2$ guarantees "a good fit" and second, in the more radical confusion, that the number represents the causal importance of the factor in the regression.

Neither supposition can be sustained. As Achen says, $R^2$ "is best regarded as characterizing the geometric shape of the regression points and nothing more"[26] It is easy to see why this is so. Achen says, "The central difficulty with the $R^2$ for social scientists is that the independent variables are not subject to experimental manipulation."[27]

There are several lines of argument. One regards the problem that "variances are a function of the *sample*, not the underlying relationship." That is, the linear model (Equation 1) is a *local analysis* whose result depends upon the actual distributions of the variables in the population sampled. Thus, "in some samples, they vary widely, producing large variance; in other cases, the observations are more tightly grouped and there is little dispersion."[28] For this reason, then, "they cannot have any real connection to the 'strength' of the relationship as social scientists ordinarily use the term, i.e., as a measure of how much effect a given change in the independent variable has on the dependent variable."[29]

Second, there is the problem of assuming that the measured variables "add up" to 1.0. Achen offers an example:

> If the regression describes, say, domestic violence in countries as a function of violence in prior years plus economic conditions, can one say which variable is more important in causing violence? For most purposes the answer is no. The units of one variable are violence per amount of prior violence; the units of the other are violence per amount of economic dislocation. One can say only that apples differ from oranges. *As theoretical forces abstracted from any historical circumstances, they have no common measure* .[30]

Equation 1 makes us believe that the variables are both additive and independent (with $b_1 b_2$ taking into account the interaction effects of the variables.) But this is (almost?) never the case. The best sort of example to illustrate the general principle is to see the confusion in the mostly meaningless discussions of the relative effects of heredity and the environment. Consider a parallel (idealized) biological study.

Take a genotype replicated by inbreeding or cloning. This minimizes genotypic individuality. Place them in various carefully controlled environments. It is then possible to establish rough tables of correspondence between phenotype on the one hand and genotype-environment combinations on the other. The results, called the norm of reaction, are *never* predictable in advance. They are not predictable since genetic and environmental factors are not additive (and hence cannot be represented by linear equations.) They are causes in transaction in exactly the sense that genes cause different outcomes in different transactional environments.

If such norms could be experimentally established for persons in their development, then across the range of controlled environments and (cloned?) genotypes, one could relate the variances in outcomes with the changes in the independent variables. This would still not provide the proportion of causation since causation does not suddenly become additive. But one could talk sensibly about their relative "importance." One could "explain the variance" sensibly. More dramatically, as Achen says, put some children in middle-class homes and the others in closets. There surely will be differences in cognitive ability, personality, and so forth. Almost certainly, most of the differences in personality will be "explained" by environment. Conversely, put them all (*per impossible*) in *the same* environment; most of the variation surely will be "explained" by heredity.

I hope, however, it is obvious that, except for identical twins, not only are no two genotypes the same but that in the concrete real world, there is not any way *in principle* to specify all the relevant environmental "variables"—exactly because *these are not independent*. The social world is real enough, but the mere fact that *necessarily* it is mediated by the consciousness of agents makes it impossible to say how a condition will be experienced and understood by the agent, and thus what effect it will have on him and his behavior. Accordingly, there is no hope that the Chicago study will produce anything like what it hopes to produce.

## Social Explanation and the Explanatory Goals of Social Science

If the foregoing is correct, does it follow that we cannot hope to explain crime? Not in the least. But we need first to offer some preliminary considerations.

What are we asking for when we are asked to explain crime? I have argued that it is not sensible to hope for a scientific explanation of the particular criminal acts of concrete persons (e.g., why Sam mugged a woman in Central Park on the eighth of July, 1994). Our ordinary, unscientific explanations will have to suffice. Yet, it is true and important that there is a crime rate because of the criminal actions of Sam and the many others who end up in crime statistics. We need a way to acknowledge this and at the same time have explanatory goals that can be realized.

Although it is too often overlooked, the explanatory goals of the successful sciences are modest. Physics does not try to explain the trajectory of a leaf falling in Central Park, even though the processes are very well understood. Chemistry does not try to explain the failure of my sugar to dissolve in my iced tea, although, again, the processes are very well understood. In general, science seeks an understanding of the causal mechanisms at work in the world. Molecular chemistry gives us an understanding of processes in its domain, similarly regarding particle physics or the physics of space and time. Of course, these very powerful—and abstract—theories can be put to work in explaining events and kinds of events and in designing technologies. But application brings in all the problems of the concrete: complexity, the open-system character of outcomes, contingency, and predictive failure. We can expect no more—or no less—from social science.

We can think of social explanation, then, as explaining social phenomena in terms of *social mechanisms*. Since I do not think that there is a useful way to define or classify "social phenomena," I shall mean by "social phenomena" *everything but* the concrete acts of individuals.[31] Thus, I include poverty, crime, revolution, electoral victories, war, marriage, inflation—including the descriptions of these as provided by statistical analysis. But I also include group behavior, the genesis (and reproduction) of institutions (e.g., the current system of criminal law), institutional changes, and changes in norms, values, and much else besides.

As regards 'social mechanisms,' the root metaphor is the famous text from Marx's *Eighteenth Brumaire*: "[Persons] do make their own history, but do not make it just as they please; they do not make it under circumstances chosen by themselves, but under circumstances directly encountered, given and transmitted from the past."[32] Giddens has suggested that his entire body of work is an extended gloss of that text[33], but one can find variant formulations from among a wide range of recent writers, including recent Marxist writers who insist on the need for a microfoundation for so-called "macro-explanations" and in the recent work of James Coleman, who identifies himself as pursuing a "special variant" of methodological individualism.[34] The thesis I will defend is well put by Daniel Little:

> An assertion of an explanatory relationship at the social level (causal, functional, structural) must be supplemented by two things: knowledge of what it is about the local circumstances of the typical individual that leads him or her to act in such a way as to bring about this relationship and knowledge of the aggregative processes that lead from individual actions of that sort to an explanatory relationship of this sort.[35]

In what follows, I try to illustrate this, but we should note here, perhaps, that this is not methodological individualism as that is usually understood. There is no claim here that the *meaning* of social concepts is translatable without residue into terms that refer only to individuals. Indeed, not only can we not translate, e.g., the concept of a bureaucracy in terms of predicates that refer only to persons and their actions, but we cannot talk about human action without appeal to predicates which are irreducibly social. That is, as I argued, *persons* are irreducibly social beings.

Nor is it assumed that social phenomena can be *explained*, without residue, in terms of the psychological attributes and actions of persons. As Little argues, we must allow that social facts supervene upon individual action. He gives an excellent example. There are true generalizations about bureaucracies, for instance, that they tend to be conservative. But this statement is not about ensembles of persons but about bureaucracies. What is critical is the fact that the activities of persons in bureaucracies are structured by the form of a bureaucracy. It is this that gives bureaucracies properties that are not reducible to the properties of individuals and their actions. There is a sense that the particular characteristics of the persons are wholly irrelevant. Who the individuals are—whether, for example, they are individually conservative or altruistic, and so forth—is irrelevant insofar as the concern is properties of bureaucracies.

On the other hand, it is surely true (versus many readings of Durkheim) that there are no independently existing social forms, and no such thing as 'society.' There are only persons engaged in interaction. Thus all the 'institutions' and/or 'social structures' that comprise 'society' are constituted soley and entirely by persons and their interactions. Social forms exist only as incarnate in persons and their interactions, or, as Giddens has put it, they have but 'virtual existence'.[36] This means, critically, that there are no 'social forces.' Persons are the sole causal agents of social phenomena: every social phenomenon is what it is because of the actions of persons, past and present–and nothing more.

This is, of course, a powerful reason for insisting that a social mechanism be unpacked in terms of the actions and the consequences of actions of individuals using materials at hand, but there is another relevant reason: Once we abandon the regularity determinist theory of science, we see that it is silly to suppose that there could be *causal* regularities at the level of social phenomena.[37] The assumption that there could be, of course, is symmetric to the assumptions made by the Chicago development study. Instead of trying to be "interdisciplinary" and include biological, psychology and social "factors" in explaining behavior, the typical "sociological" explanation makes both dependent and independent variables "macro" (social phenomena). The interest is not in individuals. Indeed, as in most forms of structuralism (Parsonian and Marxist), persons simply drop out. Instead of trying to explain the social in terms of the acts of individual, there is an inversion: what persons do is "explained" by the causal regularities at the macro level. For quantitative applications of this, the regression, then, looks for 'strong relations' between "social facts," (e.g., anomie and suicide rates).

Antinaturalistic writers rightly reject both versions of regularity determinism. In despair, they give up hope for *scientific* explanation and retreat to description, 'thin' or 'thick', to 'interpretation' or 'geneaology', or merely to storytelling!

The other alternative is the one promoted here, to turn to an analysis of the underlying social mechanisms that produce the weak generalizations, probability statements, and exception-laden patterns and regularities—the very stuff of statistical description.

## Explaining Crime

What follows is not meant to be either complete or definitive. It is meant to be an illustration—and, if you will, to offer that we know a great more about crime and its causes than our social scientists often tell us that we do. It may also suggest that studies of the Chicago type serve only to obscure matters, not to help us to understand them.

As is obvious, 'crime' is a social construction in the very straightforward sense that acts are criminal only insofar as they are proscribed by the criminal law. (The idea that there could be genetic or biological cause of crime is, accordingly, patent nonsense.) Morality (moral codes, norms, values, etc.) is also a social construction. But the relation between crime and morality is contingent—a consequence of the fact that the social mechanisms that produce them are different, though related. There need not be universal agreement among members of a society on what counts as moral (and immoral). Not everyone thinks that sodomy or smoking marijuana, for example, is immoral. There are a number of important consequences of this contingent relation. For example, if morality is a constraint on behavior, morality may not constrain people from doing things that are illegal, and, conversely, laws will not make people moral.

Moreover, not all acts that are harmful to others are criminal. For example, willfully ignoring work safety regulations that lead to the unnecessary death of workers is not a crime.[38] And not all criminal acts are harmful to others (e.g., prostitution and possession or use of marijuana).[39] This leaves us with a set of illegal acts that are not harmful to others and contestably immoral and another set of acts that are manifestly harmful (and thus presumably immoral) and yet are not illegal. One may wonder why we allow tens of thousands of workers to die because we lack adequate laws and we fail to enforce those that we have, and at the same time, we put millions of dollars into enforcing laws to prohibit behavior that does not harm others.

Answering this will require a social explanation. It will no doubt be complicated, and I do no more than suggest here what would be involved in such an explanation. It will involve giving a historical account of the genesis of the relevant institutions and beliefs, and it should include an account of how these are reproduced by individuals: lawmakers, police, the media, schools, and ordinary citizens. We will need to discriminate between the explicit goals of typical agents and the consequences, intended and unintended, of their (typical) actions. We will need also to consider whether the typical beliefs and attitudes of legislators, enforcement agencies, teachers, journalists, and ordinary citizens are heavily ideological in the clear but restricted sense that these beliefs are (1) distorted, (2) essential to the reproduction of existing institutions, and (3) in the interests of those with power in society. And if so, we will need to consider how this has been produced and gets reproduced.[40]

There is a second set of preliminary considerations. We need to be clear that there are at least three very different sorts or kinds of crime: crimes without victims (acts that are not harmful to others), white-collar crime, crimes whose victims are usually indirectly affected (e.g., embezzlement, bribery, fraud, fee splitting), and what is perhaps best termed one-on-one crime—murder, rape, assault, robbery, and so on. That is, sociologically, crime is not a unitary phenomenon.

Talk about crime, including "wars" on crime, is *never* about white-collar crime, even if the costs of such crime are quite astronomical.[41] The fixation on drugs, one-on-one crime, and prostitution by the general public and lawmakers—and one should not exclude criminologists—also cries out for explanation. And no doubt, the explanation will take much the same form as the previous explanation. I do not attempt it here.

Keeping these considerations in mind, consider again the explanation of crime. Of course, we cannot "predict" *who* will become criminal. There are criminals of every class, gender, race and ethnicity, age, religion, and so forth. But suppose, instead, that we tried to explain these social facts.[42]

1. Between 1987 and 1992, Federal bank regulators investigating the Savings and Loan scandal, filed 95,045 criminal referrals with the FBI. Of these, 75 percent were dropped without prosecution. Those convicted served an average of 2.4 years in minimum-security prisons, compared with 7.8 years for those convicted of bank robbery. From October 1988 through June 1992, courts ordered defendents to pay more than $846.7 million in fines and restitution. As of 1992, 4.5 percent of this amount had been collected.[43]

2. In 1993 the United States lost its lead in incarceration rates. Russia led with 558 incarcerations per 100,000, the United States was second with 519, and South Africa was next at 368. France had a rate of 84; The Netherlands, 49; Japan 36.[44]

3. In 1992, 58 percent of persons in federal prisons and over 30 percent in state prisons were sentenced for drug offenses. Over two-thirds of drug arrests were for possession and less than a third for the sale or manufacture of drugs. According to the U.S. Justice Department (February 1994), over 21 percent of all federal prisoners were "low-level offenders with no current or prior violent offenses on their records, no involvement in sophisticated criminal activity and no previous prison time." They served an average of 81.5 months.

4. White high school students are twice as likely to report using illegal drugs as African-American students. Twenty four percent

of whites report marijuana and 3.3 percent report cocaine; 11.5 percent of black students use marijuana; 1.3 percent use cocaine. But young black males account for 40 percent of drug arrests and 60 percent of prison commitments for drug offenses.

5. Between 1987 and 1991, juvenile arrests for murder climbed 85 percent. Arrests on charges of robbery, assault, rape, and other violent crime rose by 50 percent among juveniles, double the adult rate.[45]

6. Perhaps 85 percent of those processed through the criminal justice system come from the lowest 15 percent in income.[46]

7. In Chicago, 80 percent of the men jailed are high school dropouts; since 1973, the income of dropouts has declined 37 percent.[47]

Unsurprisingly, class, race, gender, age, and drugs leap at us as critical variables in explaining these social facts. We can think of these as structuring the activities of typical persons: they are "materials" that enable and constrain activity and, insofar, structure opportunities, expectations, values, attitudes, and so forth.

We can start with a fairly simple model. Individuals are reared in households characterized by class, race, and family condition (e.g., male or female headed, two parents, one working, both working, etc.). Households are in neighborhoods structured by race and class. Schools are in neighborhoods structured by race and class. So much, perhaps, is obvious.

Begin the explanation of white-collar crime. Because committing white-collar crime requires institutional access to a position of trust and authority, white-collar criminals are *never* either poor or uneducated, and, with some exceptions, they were not reared in slums in broken homes. They were seldom "problem children" and did not appear in juvenile courts. Why do they commit these crimes?

Social theory has tended to be divided into two schools concerning 'social control': Durkheimians, who hold that internalized social norms constrain behavior, and utilitarians, who hold that individuals act on the basis of a cost/benefit analysis. Actual motivated behavior, of course, does not so easily get divided up, and, I think, it is always overdetermined. But no sophisticated psychological theory is necessary here, neither a strong theory of rationality nor a Freudian theory of superego domination. Still, accepting that the distinction is useful as far as it goes, we can say here that as regards white-collar criminals, neither constraint would seem to be operative. Indeed, as is well understood—but evidently ignored—white-collar crime does pay! One anecdote, not in the least an exception, makes the point.

John McNamara defrauded GM of $436 million. In exchange for his freedom, he agreed to testify in a bribery trial. The officials he testified against got off and Mr. McNamara kept nearly $2 million. *The New York Times* commented, "But with all the tough 'three strikes' talk, he'd better watch out: If he steals $436 million from G.M. two more times, he's going to be in *real* trouble."[48] Sutherland summarizes the issue well:

> The crimes of the lower class are handled by policemen, prosecutors, and judges, with penal sanctions in the form of fines, imprisonment and death. The crimes of the upper class either result in no official sanction at all, or result in suits for damages in civil courts, or are handled by inspectors, and by administrative boards or commissions, with penal sanctions in the form of warnings, orders to cease and desist, occasionally by the loss of a licence, and only in the extreme cases by fines or prison sentences.[49]

White-collar criminals know that they will not be arrested; if they are, they will not face criminal charges; if they do, they will pay a fine or serve a light sentence in a comfortable prison. There is, accordingly, next to nothing to lose and very much to gain. Explaining this stunning difference in the structure of law enforcement will, of course, require a social explanation. It will parallel or be part of the explanation of what social mechanisms produces the criminal law and the criminal justice system.

What then about the criminals who fill our prisons? As noted earlier, two social mechanisms are at work. One structures choices for crime; the other structures who ends up in prison. Concerning much one-on-one crime, prostitution, and drug possession and sale, poverty is a cause of crime in the sense that it makes these sorts of criminal activities rational alternatives. We can draw on a vast ethnographic literature.

Felicia Lee comments on the circumstances of Lakeshea Hill, a sixth grade graduate at PS 158 in East New York:

> For Lakeshea and the other students who graduated in the past week, the choices are complex and painful, like staying in school or dropping out, selling drugs or fast food, carrying a gun for protecting themselves or staying in the house. They ask themselves: "Can I make it?"[50]

A classmate, Pedro, knows kids who sell drugs because it is the only way to make money. He comments, "If you don't wear name-brand sneakers, they dis you." The principal of PS 158, Anita D. Harrison, wept at the graduation:

> Some of these kids, this is the only graduation they will have. Some of these kids, by some quirk of fate, might be killed. Some girls might have babies. They're good kids and the opportunities aren't there for them. The experiences aren't there for them.

Terry Williams shows that the young drug dealers he spent several years with are deeply committed to mainstream values, including the work ethic and the American dream.[51] Says Masterrap, "Selling dope is just like any other business. You gotta work hard, stay on your toes, protect what's yours." Williams makes it clear that the drug business is a direct response to the absence of legitimate opportunities. Charlie reports:

> I don't plan to be in this business forever; I've got potential to do better, and I will. But right now, the thing is to make some money. After I do that, I can think about college and all that.

Charlie knows, of course, that what he is doing is illegal. But is it wrong? How can one criticize a hardworking young man like Charlie? He is not harming anyone. After all, he is merely providing others what they want. Yet, as Gina Kolata remarks:

> Despite the popular notion that crack sellers wear gold jewelry and get rich quick, most of the people in the business work round the clock, six to seven days a week, for low real wages in an atmosphere of physical threat and control.[52]

Most are, of course, on the bottom rung of the distribution chain. But because it is easy to believe that there is opportunity for those who are sufficiently clever and hardworking, it is easy to find new recruits.

Richard Price, researching for his novel *Clockers*, reports the observation of a drug dealer:

> The scariest thing to a kid out here in the streets is not drugs, AIDS, guns, jail, or death. It's words on a page. Because if a 15-year old kid could handle words on a page, he'd be home doing his homework instead of selling dope with me.[53]

There is a vicious trap. Not only are his opportunities structured by his circumstances but because he is intelligent, he knows what he can expect from life. He has no good reason to struggle with the books if he is not likely to find more than part-time work in a dead-end job.[54]

It is often said that, like crime, poverty is ill understood, that it is, for example, the complicated result of family breakdown, lack of education, poor motivation, welfare dependency—one could go on. But this is so much nonsense. It confuses three different questions: the explanation of poverty, the explanation of what groups will likely be poor, and the explanation of who in these groups will likely be poor.

The explanation of poverty is easy. As is very well understood, in a capitalist economy there is no mechanism that guarantees enough jobs for all those who want to work, far less enough jobs which pay wages which would put a family above the poverty line.[55] Who then will be poor?

We know too why African Americans are disportionately poor: about three in ten versus one in ten whites. Explaining this requires looking at the history of African Americans in America, beginning with slavery and its effects up to the present. For example, as late as 1930, 54 percent of men were in agriculture, and 5 percent were white-collar. Since World War II some four million African Americans were driven from Southern fields and immigrated to northern cities. But, as Harrington writes, by the 1960s, "there was no growing industrial sector to absorb them."[56] It requires noting that *only* African Americans suffered net employment losses in the recession of 1990–91 and that, as Ellis Cose notes, even the most successful African Americans "find themselves haunted by racial demons."[57]

The microfoundations of reproduced black poverty are also well understood. As Elliot Liebow argued as early as 1967, each man on Tally's Corner

> comes to the job with a long job history characterized by not being able to support himself and his family. Each man carries this knowledge, born of his experience, with him. He comes to the job flat and stale, wearied by the sameness of it all, convinced of his own incompetence, terrified of responsibility—of being tested still again and found wanting. Marriage is an occasion of failure. To stay married is to live with your failure. It is to live in a world whose standards of manliness are forever beyond one's reach.[58]

Can one hardly be surprised if, among a minority, there are patterns of abuse, abandonment, womanizing, drinking, or drugs? Indeed, the real question is how so many manage to avoid these patterns given the conditions of racism and poverty.[59]

This is, however, but one side of the 'crime problem.' The other is the criminal justice system itself. As the discussion of white-collar crime has already suggested, it, too, is structured by class and race. Arrest records are just that. We do not know how many crimes are committed.[60] But that means that the allocation of law enforcement resources will be critical.

We must begin by looking at resources devoted to enforcing safety regulations whose violation often causes loss of life. As Labor Secretary Robert Reich noted,[61] the 2,300 employees of the Occupational Safety Safety and Health Administration (OSHA) cannot hope to police the nation's six million employers. While it is difficult to determine from police departments how many officers are assigned to vice squads, almost certainly the number in a dozen or so of our major cities will exceed the number of OSHA inspectors. With the Reagan cuts, these number now approximately seven hundred.

We then can look at other government agencies responsible for enforcing, for example, laws regulating the $20 billion coal industry. According to inspectors who head regional offices of the Office of Surface Mining, the director, Harry M. Snyder, ordered them "to end investigations of violations, reduce fines, eliminate penalties, divert prosecutions and prevent inspections." As it turned out, ranking officials, including Secretary Manuel Lujan, Jr., knew of Mr. Snyder's actions and "by not interfering, in effect sanctioned them."[62] No one served prison time.

Next, we can look at the practices of other critical regulatory commissions, for example, the Securities and Exchange Commission or the Commodities Futures Trading Commission (CFTC). For example, Thomas Collins defrauded investors of some $40 billion. He had been under investigation for five years. Edward T. Joyce, a lawyer representing some of Collins's former clients, asserted that the "CFTC was utterly and totally incompetent." The *Wall Street Journal* commented that if this were an exception, it would not be worrisome, but it is not. Indeed, critics contend that "the CFTC remains undermanned and beholden to the interests it is supposed to police."[63] Collins has disappeared.

Finally, we must look at police resources and practices. The United States doubled the number of police officers between 1980 and 1990. The 1994 Crime Bill will add another 100,000—even though according to official victim surveys, the crime rate has not changed significantly.[64]

What of police practices? Between 1985 and 1989, the number of white juveniles in locked detention declined, while during the same period, the number of imprisoned nonwhite juveniles increased by 259 percent. But it has been well established that young males who live in poor neighborhoods and are apprehended for delinquency are many times more likely to appear in an official record than males from wealthier neighborhoods who commit the same offenses. Since a criminal record is the scarlet letter of our era, this is highly significant. Indeed, not only does it nearly guarantee a low-paying job, but it ensures that any subsequent apprehensions will guarantee prison time.

Chambliss's recent work with the Rapid Deployment Unit (RDU) of the District of Columbia Metropolitan police shows that there are two distinct sets of practices for black and white neighborhoods. It is not merely that the RDU does not patrol predominately white neighborhoods, but the governing assumption in black neighborhoods is that a black male is presumptively guilty of some crime. We can get a sense of this by quoting one field note from Chambliss:

> After midnight. The driver of the patrol car points out a car driven by two black men. He tells his partner to check for violations. The partner says, "pull him over. Broken taillight."
>
> The officers call for backup. Two other RDU patrol cars arrive and the suspect's car is surrounded by the three cars. Two officers approach the car on each side. The driver rolls down his window, and the officer asks to see his license, which is given without comment. The officer on the other side of the car asks to see some identification of the passenger and is given his driver's licence. The licenses are given to a third officer who removes himself to his car to check for warrants and to check the license of the car.
>
> The officer on the driver's side asks: "Can we search your car?" The driver says "No." The officer then says "You know what will happen if you refuse a police officer's request?" The driver then says "OK, you can look." Both occupants are told to get out of the car and the car is searched. The officers find nothing.
>
> Apparently satisfied that there are no drugs or guns in the car, the officer says: "OK. You can go; but don't let us catch you with any shit, you understand." The driver nods yes, everyone returns to their cars.[65]

But, of course, the class and race bias in the system does not end here. While the U.S. Constitution requires that all defendants have attorneys, it does not guarantee that they should put equal time into a defense, or have psychiatric services, investigatory assistance, expert witnesses, or bail. Not only are the indigent found guilty more often, but they are less likely to be recommended for probation or granted suspended sentences. And mandatory sentencing and the "three strikes" policy has exacerbated the differences. Since stiff mandatory sentences for crack have been instituted by the the U.S. Congress, very few whites have been federally prosecuted in the region from San Luis Obispo to the Mexican border while hundreds of blacks and Hispanics have been imprisoned. Nearly all white crack offenders are prosecuted in state courts where the sentences are far less—up to eight years different! Remarkably, the average sentence for murder is six and half years. Possession of seven hundred marijuana plants has a federal mandatory sentence of eight years, with no possibility of parole.[66]

I have argued that too much social science misconceives the proper task of a social science. It asks the wrong questions, too often misunderstands the legitimate role of its methods, and draws conclusions that cannot stand up to critical scrutiny. Worse, too much of this is ideological in that it serves the interests of the powerful. Crime has been my example. I think that we can explain crime. But, of course, much depends, as I have argued, on what one thinks one is explaining and how this is to be explained.

## Notes

1. James Q. Wilson, "Scholars Must Expand Our Understanding of Criminal Behavior," *Chronicle of Higher Education*, June 22, 1992, p. A40.

2. Felton Earls, quoted from *Chronicle of Higher Education*, April 27, 1994. Earls went on to say, "When we try to predict from those profiles to actual outcomes of children who go on to show delinquency and criminal behavior, it turns out the predictions are pretty weak" (p. 9).

3. Paul A. Weiss, "The Living System: Determinism Stratified," in *Beyond Reductionism: New Perspectives in the Life Sciences*, ed. Arthur Koestler and J. R. Smythies, (New York: Macmillan, 1970), p. 38.

4. Reporting on very recent research in evolutionary theory that shows that a common genetic key triggers the development of eyes of vastly different constructions, Peter Monaghan refers to the process as a "cascade of biochemical events that take place in eye development" (*Chronicle of Higher Education*, May 26, 1995).

5. Richard Lewontin, "Analysis of Variance and the Analysis of Causes," reprinted in *The Dialectical Biologist*, ed. Richard Lewins and Richard

Lewontin, (Cambridge, Mass.: Harvard University Press, 1985), Chapter 4, p. 111.

6. Howard H. Pattee, "Physical Theories of Biological Coordination," in *Topics in the Philosophy of Biology* , ed. Marjorie Grene and Eliot Mendelssohn, (Dordrecht: Reidel, 1976), p. 154.

7. David Hull, *Philosophy of Biology* (Englewood Cliffs, N.J.: Prentice Hall, 1974), p. 134.

8. For an excellent review and summary of the evidence, see Emanuel Drechsel, "The Invalidity of the Concept 'Race'," in *Restructuring for Ethnic Peace* , ed. M. Tehranian, (Honolulu: Matsunaga Institute for Peace, 1991).

9. This is true, I believe, of language, the emotions, perception, and cognition. For language, see Derek Bickerton, *Language and Species* (Chicago: University of Chicago Press, 1990). For the emotions, see Rom Harré, "Social Sources of Mental Content and Order," in *Psychology: Designing the Discipline*, ed. Joseph Margolis, Peter Manicas, Rom Harré and Paul F. Secord, (Oxford: Blackwell, 1986). For perception, see J. Van Brakel, "The Plasticity of Categories: The Case of Colour," *British Journal for the Philosophy of Science* (1993) 44:103–35. For cognition, see most recently, Marshall Sahlins, *How "Natives" Think about Captain Cook, for Example* (Chicago: University of Chicago Press, 1995).

10. George Herbert Mead, *Mind, Self and Society* (Chicago: University of Chicago Press, 1967), p. 145.

11. Brent Staples, *Parallel Time: Growing Up Black and White* (New York: Avon, 1994), p. 202.

12. Herbert Blumer, *Symbolic Interactionism: Perspectives and Method* (Englewood Cliffs, N.J.: Prentice Hall), p. 5.

13. In addition to Staples's fine book, a small sample of recommended accounts by African-American males would include the following: Claude Brown, *Manchild in the Promised Land* (New York: Penquin, 1965); Sanyika Shakur, *The Autobiography of a Gang Member* (New York: Penquin, 1993); Henry Louis Gates, Jr., *Colored People* (New York: Vintage, 1995); Ellis Cose, *The Rage of a Privileged Class* (New York: Harper, 1993). Each of these accounts illustrates clearly how selves get constructed and changed and how remarkably contingent most of this all is. They also show the depth of racism as a social mechanism (see later discussion).

14. The philosophical argument against 'regularity determinism' was set out by Roy Bhaskar, *A Realist Theory of Science*, 2d ed. (Atlantic Highlands, N.J.: Humanities Press, 1978). Jonathan Turner has most recently attempted a compromise that moves in the right direction but falls very short. "We should," he writes, "still view as our goal the isolation and understanding of invariant and basic features of the social universe, but we should be intellectual fascists about it. Moreover, analytical theory must not be concerned with regularities *per se* but with the 'why' and 'how' of invariant regularities" ("Analytical Theorizing," in *Social Theory Today* , ed. Jonathan Turner and

Anthony Giddens (Oxford: Polity Press, 1987), p. 159. Not only is the search for "invariant regularities" misplaced, but for Turner, the "hows" and "whys" should be "abstract and not tied to the particulars of an historical/empirical case." This seems to me to be exactly the opposite of what we should be doing.

15. Roy Bhaskar, *A Realist Theory of Science*, 2d ed. (Atlantic Highlands, N.J.: Humanities Press, 1978), p. 96.

16. Just as genuine emergence and novelty are perfectly consistent with causality, order and structure are perfectly consistent with chaos and complexity—as argued by current complexity theory. One way to say this is to note that "a lot of nature is not linear—including most of what is really interesting in the world. Indeed, except for the simplist physical systems, virtually everything and everybody in the world is caught up in a vast, non-linear web of incentives and connections. The slightest change in one place causes tremors everywhere else" (M. Mitchell Waldrop, *Complexity* [New York: Touchstone, 1992], p. 65). Waldrop remarks:

> Physicists had begun to realize that by the early 1980s that a lot of messy, complicated systems could be described by a powerful theory known as "non-linear dynamics." And in the process, they had been forced to face up to a disconcerting fact: the whole of reality can be greater than the sum of its parts.
>
> For most people that fact sounds pretty obvious. It was disconcerting for the physicists only because they had spent the past 300 years having a love affair with linear systems—in which the whole is precisely equal to the sum of its parts. (p. 64)

17. Most social scientists, of course, would admit that we should be content with statistical regularities (but see note 14.). If so, however, we lose hold of the individual case, a point of some importance. We can grant that some substantial percentage of those who smoke get lung cancer, but Sam wants to know why he did and his wife did not.

18. Anthony Giddens, *The Constitution of Society* (Berkeley: University of California Press, 1980, p. 9. For a superb account of agency, see Roy Bhaskar, *The Possibility of Naturalism* (Atlantic Highlands, N.J.: Humanities Press, 1979), Chapter 3.

19. Charles Murray and Richard J. Herrnstein, *The Bell Curve*, (New York: The Free Press, 1994), p. 127. See their diagram, p. 134.

20. This was beautifully argued by Stephen Jay Gould in his *Mismeasure of Man* (London: Norton, 1981), but it seems that the lesson has been hard to learn.

21. See Richard Lewontin's critique of the sample survey as a technique in his review, "Sex, Lies, and Social Science," *New York Review of Books*, April 20, 1995. His general conclusion is worth quoting:

The social scientist is in a difficult, if not impossible position. On the one hand there is the temptation to see all of society as one's autobiography writ large, surely not the path to general truth. On the other, there is the attempt to be general and objective by pretending that one knows nothing about the experience of being human, forcing the investigator to pretend that people usually know and tell the truth about important issues. How, then, can there be a "social science"? The answer, surely, is to be less ambitious and stop trying to make sociology into a natural science although it is, indeed, the study of natural objects. There are some things in the world that we will never know and many that we will never know exactly. Biology is not physics, because organisms are such complex physical objects, and sociology is not biology because human societies are not made by self-conscious organisms. By pretending to a kind of knowledge that it cannot achieve, social science can only engender the scorn of natural scientists and the cynicism of humanists. (p. 29)

22. Quoted by Stephen Jay Gould, "Curve Ball," *New Yorker*, April 28 1994.

23. Christopher H. Achen, *Interpreting and Using Regression* (Beverly Hills, Ca.: Sage, 1982). I am indebted to Achen's clear account.

24. Ibid., p. 13.

25. Ibid., pp. 58–59.

26. Ibid., p. 59.

27. Ibid., p. 59.

28. Ibid., p. 59.

29. Ibid., p. 59.

30. Ibid., p. 70.

31. As I noted, we are not likely to improve on our ordinary unscientific explanations of concrete acts. These are usually 'psychological' or better, biographical, and employ, inevitably, 'social factors'. See Peter Manicas, "The Human Sciences: A Radical Separation of Psychology and the Social Sciences," Chapter 8 in *Explaining Behavior: Consciousness, Behavior and Social Structure*, ed. Paul F. Secord (Beverly Hills: Sage, 1982), pp. 155–73.

32. Karl Marx, The *Eighteenth Brumaire of Louis Bonaparte*, (Moscow: Progress, 1852/1934), p. 18.

33. Anthony Giddens, *The Constitution of Society* (Berkeley: University of California Press, 1984).

34. James S. Coleman, *Foundations of Social Theory* (Cambridge: Belnap Press of Harvard University, 1990).

35. Daniel Little, *Varieties of Social Explanation* (Boulder, Colo: Westview, 1991), p. 196. In my view, Little remains captured by regularity determinism, which leads him to some barely concealed inconsistencies. For example, he takes seriously what he calls "predictive theory naturalism," an unabashed neopositivism (p. 224), and then offers that this is not a useful model for social science. But it is not useful for natural science, either.

36. For some discussion, see my *A History and Philosophy of the Social Sciences* (Oxford: Blackwell, 1987), pp. 154–8.

37. Little wants to perserve this assumption, a bedrock assumption of regularity determinists.

38. We lack accurate statistics here, but in 1992, Senator Edward Kennedy reported a Labor Committee report that held that forty workers were killed every day from occupational injuries. Another four hundred per day will die of occupationally inflicted disease. Of course, not all of these are victims of violations of safety regulations. The absence of sufficient numbers of OSHA inspectors guarantees countless needless deaths (see text).

39. Strictly speaking, we should include here *all* drugs *and* their sale, but I do not to avoid needless controversy. The analogy to alcohol is quite exact. Buying drugs can only be harmful to the user, assuming that drug use is harmful to the user. One might argue that the harm to others is indirect. There are no laws proscribing either drinking or drunkenness, although, of course, there are laws against "driving under the influence." This is a paradigm of indirect harm. But if so, any disanalogy would seem to favor drugs! Indeed:

> In reality, the heavily advertised legal drug alcohol is the drug most likely to lead to violence and death. Alcohol is associated with more homocides nationally than illicit drugs, and almost the same number of people are killed annually by drunk drivers as are murdered. (Peter Medoff and Holly Sklar, *Streets of Hope: The Fall and Rise of an Urban Neighborhood*, Boston: South End Press, 1994, pp. 210–11.)

We know not only that prohibition did not reduce consumption but that educational programs have worked best to reduce alcohol consumption (see text).

40. The only systematic effort to address this is Jeffrey Reiman's excellent, *The Rich Get Rich and the Poor Get Prison: Ideology, Class and Criminal Justice*, 2d ed. (New York: Wiley, 1984).

41. Edwin H. Sutherland, who introduced the term "white collar crime" only in 1939, was arguing then that we lack any sort of accurate statistical comparison of the numbers of white-collar criminals and the costs, financial and social, of white-collar crime. This is still the case. Using a 1974 Chamber of Commerce source, Reiman estimated a total of $75.2 billion for 1980. This is many times the cost of all crimes generally thought of as "the crime problem."

42. And some crime (e.g., so-called "crimes of passion" and crimes committed by geniune psychopaths) will not call for a social explanation.

43. Stephen P. Pizzo and Paul Muolo, "Take the Money and Run," *New York Times Magazine*, May 9 1993.

44. I draw much of what follows from the work of William J. Chambliss, "Policing the Ghetto Underclass: The Politics of Law and Law Enforcement," *Social Problems* 41(2) (May 1994) 41(2):177–94; and "Another Lost War: The

Failure and Consequences of Drug Prohibition,'' unpublished manuscript, N.D.

45. *New York Times*, December 1, 1994.

46. Indeed, while the FBI tabulates arrest rates by race, sex, age, and geographical area, neither the FBI nor any other government agency collects statistics on arrest rates by income.

47. Bob Herbert, *New York Times*, June 12 1994. Herbert's data comes from a report of the Alternative Schools Network, compiled by Jack Wuest, its executive director.

48. *New York Times*, October 3, 1995.

49. Edwin H. Sutherland, "White Collar Criminality" (1940), reprinted in *Readings in Criminology and Penology*, ed. David Dressler, 2d ed. (New York: Columbia University Press, 1972), p. 125. The list of persons who escaped punishment and gained huge profits would be a truly impressive list. As role models, we should add also the Casper Weinbergers and Oliver Norths.

50. Felicia R. Lee, "Sixth-Grade Graduation: Moment for Pride on Treacherous Path," *New York Times*, June 28 1992, p. 17.

51. Terry Williams, *The Cocaine Kids* (Reading, Mass.: Addison-Wesley, 1989), p. 47.

52. "Despite Its Promise of Riches, the Crack Trade Seldom Pays," *New York Times*, November 26 1989, p. 1.

53. "Kilos of Crack and $200 Sneakers: Young Dealers Confide in a Novelist," Bruce Weber, *New York Times*, September 6, 1992, p. 11.

54. See John Ogbu, *Minority Education and Class: The American System in Cross Cultural Perspective* (New York: Academic Press, 1978). Ogbu's point was simply that persons who are members of a poor minority group know the limits of their adult roles. They behave toward school accordingly. Compare here also Paul Willis's brilliant study, *Learning to Labor: How Working Class Kids Get Working Class Jobs* (New York: Columbia University Press, 1981).
A recent study by my colleague Herbert Barringer on marginal income for additional education completed for minorities makes the point in a stunning way. For Filipino males, the marginal increase of income with a high school education is $1,251; for Hawaians, $1,922; for whites, $4,968! With a college education, the marginal increase for Filipino males is $5,450; for Hawaiians $2,451, for whites, $10,142. See H. Barringer and Nolan Liu, "The Demographic, Social and Economic Status of Native Hawaiians, 1990," a study for *Alu Like*, Inc., Honolulu. 1994.

55. It is also easy to provide the microfoundations for this consequence: capitalists facing competition will seek to reduce costs. Since Say's so-called law does not hold, even in a perfectly competitive economy, there will be at least periodic unemployment, and, since workers are in competition for available jobs, there will be low wages for many of those who find work.

56. M. Harrington, *The New American Poverty* (New York: Penguin Books, 1985), p. 134.

57. Ellis Cose, *The Rage of a Privileged Class* (New York: Harper, 1993).

58. Elliot Liebow, *Tally's Corner* (Boston: Little, Brown, 1967), p. 223.

59. In the words of Orlando Patterson and Chris Winship, we need to remember "the forgotten majority of working class black men who pay their bills, fear their god, respect their women, and cherish their friendships," *New York Times*, May 3, 1992, p. 60. For a recent study, see Mitchel Duneier, *Slim's Table: Race, Respectibilty and Masculinity* (Chicago: University of Chicago Press, 1992).

60. Keeping in mind all the problems of such research, Reiman reports that a Presidential Crime Commission survey of 10,000 in which 91 per cent reported that they had violated laws that could have subjected them to imprisonment. Domestic violence, income tax evasion, and drunken driving would surely figure hugely here.

61. Robert Reich, *New York Times*, January 23, 1994, p. 25.

62. Keith Schneider, "US Mine Inspectors Charge Interference by Agency Direction," *New York Times*, November 22 1992, p. 1. Or consider the Food and Drug Administration. In 1987, Beech-Nut paid $2 million in fines for illegally selling "apple juice" that was nothing more than sweetened water and chemicals. But the practice, widespread in the industry, continued, nonetheless. The *New York Times* reported:

And while Federal officials say they are committed to pursuing adulteration cases, court exhibits and interviews with investigators and juice industry executives show that enforcement efforts are still haphazard, plagued by inadequate resources and an institutional tradition that has put a low priority on cases that, at least until recently, were not considered a threat to public safety. (October 31, 1993, p. 1.)

63. Jeffrey Taylor and Jeff Bailey, "CFTC Failed to Halt Trader Accused of Scam," *Wall Street Journal*, October 4 1994, p. C1.

64. Chambliss, "Policing the Ghetto Underclass," p. 184. It is easy to confuse arrest rates, incarceration rates and rates of victimization (e.g., the number of persons who report being robbed or raped).

65. Chambliss, "Policing the Ghetto Underclass," p. 18. Police concentrate on minority neighborhoods in all U.S. cities on grounds that this is where the crimes are committed. California counties have now moved to a new form of "prevention" in which named males, "incidentally" black, who are suspected of being gang members are prohibited in engaging in what would otherwise be quite legal activity. Putting aside the manifest attack on civil liberties, the costs of this sort of police activity are, of course, extraordinary.

66. *New Yorker*, April 13, 1992. In Los Angeles County alone, while hundreds of whites have been prosecuted for crack between 1988 and 1994, not one white was prosecuted federally. Demands on the criminal justice system in California have reached crisis proportions. There are not enough prosecutors, public defenders, or courts—not to mention prisons. The fantastic expense, of course, is at the expense of education and social services. To

make room for persons convicted of possessing small amounts of crack who will, as three-time offenders, serve mandatory life sentences, charges are being dropped for other kinds of offenses, especially misdemeanors, that seriously affect the quality of life. One consequence, already feared by prosecutors, is the further erosion of any possible deterrent effect for committing violent crimes. If a person is guaranteed a life sentence for possession of drugs, he or she has nothing to lose.

# Chapter 8

# The Meaning of "Social"

*Joseph Margolis*

Asked to say what we should take to be the mark of the "social," I concede that it would be a thankless scruple to begin by announcing that Max Weber and Émile Durkheim were fundamentally muddled in their understanding of the idea, in the midst of their otherwise important discoveries. You may, patronizingly, ask how so, and I should answer, by a deliberate evasion, that they misunderstood the conceptual distinction between existence and reality and reference (or denotation) and predication. Both Weber and Durkheim, attempting to demarcate the proper "subject" and range of the science of sociology, take social life for granted and worry only about what, disjunctively, we should assign individual human agents and social groups or collectivities. That is not a perspicuous beginning.

Let me press my evasion one sentence further: effective causality, I should say, can only be assigned to what exists; the effectiveness of causal explanation, on the other hand, is a matter of selecting which predicative descriptions to favor. If, therefore, one supposes that corporations or collective entities (nations, peoples, societies) are fictions (do not exist), then either they have no causal efficacy, or attributing causality to them is as much a fiction as their existence. Durkheim, of course, believes that there are (exist) collective entities distinct (but not separable) from individual persons. He cannot be said, therefore, to be making fictional causal attributions when, in *The Rules of Sociological Method*, he says:

A social fact is any way of acting, whether fixed or not, capable of exerting over the individual an external constraint; or, which is general over the whole of a given society, whilst having an existence of its own, independent of its individual manifestations.[1]

The phrasing is hardly fortunate, since "any way of acting" is plainly a predicative expression, although it is obviously intended metonymically to signify the existent collectivity to which a way of acting is ascribed. The only reason for supposing that there are (exist) collectivities or collective agents is that there are collective attributions that cannot be ascribed to individual persons as such, except derivatively—the occurrence of a war, for instance. The matter is partly empirical and partly conceptual. For, as I should argue, all the fundamental attributions of distinctly human forms of life—those in particular (if the claim is thought vague) that bear on culturally formed competences, language paradigmatically—are collectively defined attributes ascribable to and only to individual human agents, whether singly or aggregatively. "Engaging in war," I should say, is a collective attribute ascribable to aggregates of individuals.

If I am right in this, then, empirically, Durkheim is wrong in claiming that collective attributes require the admission of existent collective entities; conceptually, the claim I offer is sparer than Durkheim's—without sacrificing any pertinent facts. It is true that we must "adequate" our attributions to the "natures" of our denotata: for instance, in denying that it makes sense to affirm or deny that a stone has (literally) smiled. But we do meet our adequational intuitions if we regard human persons or selves as *sui generis* "culturally emergent" entities first formed by the infant members of Homo sapiens internalizing the collective competences of the human society to which they belong.[2] For selves are formed as selves by acquiring (internalizing) the collective "nature" of their existing society. That will have to be explained. But on the argument, Ockham's razor may be fairly invoked against Durkheim. In any case, I advance my claim as a challenge to any Durkheimian who supposes that there is something "left over" from whatever we ascribe to individual persons that requires the admission of collective entities. I cannot see that there is any such remainder.

I admit that one may construe a "collective agent" in a way other than Durkheim's. One notable such view is offered by Margaret Gilbert, on the strength of claiming Georg Simmel "as an inspiration and an ally." Gilbert admits to "having some affinity with Simmel's claim" to the effect that "a society is an 'objective unit' of a special kind"—namely, where "the consciousness of constituting with the others [with other members of a supposed society] a unity is actually all there is to this unity."[3] Gilbert then goes on to sketch her own "Simmelian" variant: "Human beings X, Y, and Z constitute a collectivity (social group) if and only if each correctly thinks of himself and the others, taken together as 'us*' or 'we*'."[4] The asterisked expressions are explicated a bit later as terms of art in such a way that it is clear that "collectivity" marks a distinctive "way of acting" of aggregated individuals, not collectivities in Durkheim's sense. Gilbert sees an affinity between her own view and Paul Grice's but also serious inadequacies in Grice's account.[5] Fair enough. But her own view (and, I think, Simmel's) requires that the members of a putative "social group" must "have similar equipment," possess "common knowledge" regarding one another and certain other facts, and be "open*" to one another in ways pertinent to same.[6] I say that such concessions actually favor collective attributes, but they are not acknowledged to be such. The same is true of Grice's account. ("Open*," by the way, is another reasonably intuitive term of art.)

Two observations are in order. First, Simmel's thesis (which Gilbert appears to accept but adjusts) rests on a predicative distinction regarding an aggregate of individuals. Second, the shared "consciousness"— like Gilbert's "similar conceptual equipment," "common knowledge," and "openness*"—are presupposed as defining conditions of "social groups"; they are not artifacts of that group's existence (even if further such artifacts obtain). I therefore conclude (i) that the Simmel/Gilbert option does indeed offer an "ontological" economy over Durkheim's thesis (which, to that extent, I favor) but (ii) there is a deeper "collectivity" Gilbert ignores—which I think Weber and Durkheim also fail to do justice to—that threatens the adequacy of the option Simmel and Gilbert offer. For what is it, if not a collective competence, that aggregated individuals share in sharing "the consciousness of constituting" or "similar conceptual equipment," or "common knowledge"? I see an aporia there, one that is identical (if I am not mistaken) with the one Rousseau famously exploits in his social contract theory, namely, that the status assigned the parties to the effected contract must, in some measure, already be presupposed in their being parties to it. I say that to form a social group in Simmel's and Gilbert's sense is already to share the collective competence to do so. That is also why Durkheim's conception of a "social fact" (already cited) goes so wildly astray.

Let me return to Durkheim to make this clear. It will affect the

assessment of Gilbert's alternative. Speaking of a "sociological phenomenon" or a "social fact," Durkheim says rather pointedly:

> If it is general, it is because it is collective (that is, more or less
> obligatory); but it is very far from being collective because it is general.
> It is a condition of the group repeated in individuals because it imposes
> itself upon them. It is in each part because it is in the whole, but far from
> being in the whole because it is in the parts.[7]

I think this is extraordinarily perceptive—also dead wrong. It is perceptive because it recognizes that the "general" is (pertinently) such
because it is "collective", but it is dead wrong because it fails to see
that it is collective because it is already such "in the parts," that is,
"in" the individual members of a human society. Failing to grasp that,
Durkheim was forced to invent existent collectivities, but collectivity
is never more (and need not be more) than a predicative distinction.
Gilbert and Simmel rightly avoid Durkheimian collectivities, but, on
the evidence, they fail to account for the predicative role of the
"collective." The finding is also lacking (even more strenuously) in
Weber. It belongs originally to the tradition that links Hegel and Marx
and Gadamer and Foucault—and, more eccentrically, Nietzsche and
Heidegger and Wittgenstein. If I am not mistaken, you will not find, in
Marx, that the notion of a socioeconomic class is treated in the
Durkheimian way, that is, in the existent sense, denotatively; contrary
to Jon Elster's reading, Marx seems always to have nominalized
a merely predicative distinction.[8] Remember: what, denotatively or
referentially, is real, exists; but what is real, predicatively, is only
what answers to what is truly or validly predicable of what exists.
Anything else would oblige us to admit Platonic Forms or medieval
Universals as existent tertia mediating between what we believe (predicatively) and what is real in the natural world. I shall come to the
import of these distinctions in a moment. They hold the key to my
charge against Durkheim and Weber—and now, more interestingly,
against Simmel and Gilbert.

I need to dwell a little longer on the strategy of the argument before
moving forward. I am, of course, claiming that the "social" includes
or presupposes attributes that are inherently collective. I am not
insisting that all attributes or all "social" attributes are explicitly
collective—greeting a friend in the street, for instance. I am entirely
willing to admit (with Gilbert) that (say) the description of the state of
"readiness" of an aggregate that assents to something like an invitation

to play bridge need never use explicit collective predicates, but that, I claim, says altogether too little. Gilbert offers the following example:

> Enemy troops can be heard advancing through the woods. The partisans pick up their weapons. They exchange glances. One says to the others: "Well, we're ready." From this scene we can abstract a concept of joint readiness. I propose that we can best sum up the conditions of appropriateness for "Shall we do A?" in terms of this concept.[9]

I cannot afford to pursue Gilbert's elaboration of "joint readiness," since it would require a good deal of special labor to do justice to her numerous terms of art. But I assure you that the term *joint* captures the sense in which, although "social groups" are taken to exist (by Gilbert), they are not collective in Durkheim's sense, and the explication of "joint readiness" does not require the use of any explicit collective predicates. So a part of my strategy requires agreeing with Durkheim that we need collective predicates, but it also requires insisting (against Durkheim) that we do not need (and cannot justify introducing) existent collective entities. A second part of my strategy requires agreeing with Simmel and Gilbert that we need only admit "social groups" as existent aggregates (though Gilbert is willing to call such groups "collectivities"). I insist, however, that we do need to admit collective predicables, and Gilbert does not acknowledge that. Third, I wish to concede that the quarrel about collective entities and collective predicables is entirely formal (in the logical sense) and does not yet capture what, qua collective, the "social" actually signifies! I need to say something further about that. So our work stands before us.

# I

There is a very large mystery about reference and denotation, on the one hand, and predication, on the other. I shall not pursue their narrowly linguistic and logical features, but you must bear in mind that the linguistic—*a fortiori*, the referential and predicative—is the very paradigm of the "social." Modern analytic philosophy has indoctrinated us so thoroughly into accepting the good sense of its logical economies that it has all but dismissed the social import of doing that.

Consider, for the moment, a few specimen theories. Quine, for one, claims to be able to retire denotative devices (proper names, say) in favor of the resources made available by a first-order predicate logic. For example, Quine believes, notoriously, that the name "Socrates" (used to name the historical Socrates) may be replaced by a uniquely instantiated predicate, "socratizing," so that, *salve veritate*, one may render (in canonical terms) the sentence "Socrates was the teacher of Plato" as (roughly) "There is an x such that x socratizes and x was the teacher of Plato."[10] Quine completely ignores Leibniz's indisputable observation that one cannot mount any purely logical objection against conceding that, in principle, any general predicable ("blue," "round," "just," "socratizing") is, if instantiable at all, always multiply instantiable.[11] Again, to continue by way of example, Nelson Goodman holds that there are no real general predicables, so that the successful use of general predicates can be accounted for in the nominalist's manner.[12] But Goodman does not see that even the nominalist's success requires the admission of "real generals";[13] his own account betrays that failing.

You may well wonder how these considerations bear on the analysis of the "social." The answer is remarkably important. Reference and predication are essential to linguistic communication, but there is no algorithmic—no purely formal or extensionally definable—conditions under which they succeed. Both reference and predication are insuperably informal in the logical sense. But they obviously do succeed. My own analysis leads me to the conclusion that they succeed consensually, that is, in and only in the ongoing collective practices of a given society. Here, "consensus" is meant holistically, never criterially; that is, it signifies the open-ended tolerance of a society regarding what is to count as (1) the identification and reidentification of existent particulars and (2) the admissible extension of general predicates to new instances (beyond paradigms). The members of a society remember (in idiosyncratic ways) how their practices play out; they have no algorithm to fall back to, and whatever referential or predicative criteria may be admitted depend on the same consensual informality that has just been acknowledged. If there were strict epistemic constraints, then, for one thing, Quine would be right and Leibniz wrong; and, for another, there would be Forms or Universals functioning as existing tertia by which to assess predicative validity. The fact remains that no one has been able, without pretending to some form of privilege, to solve these two puzzles except in the consensual way. The slimmest anticipation that I know of of the "consensual" solution is the one Wittgenstein puts forward in his account of "following a rule."[14] Socially or culturally formed behavior said to accord with a practice (as with a "language game") is rightly characterized in rulelike terms, except that there is no antecedent rule that we follow, in "following a rule." Only the apt members of a society can reflect on their ongoing practice and propose a "rule" that fits their remembered practice (there may be many such rules), but their ongoing practice is not bound by any such formulation; on the contrary, subsequent extensions of that practice are likely to result in revised "rules" for the then newly reviewed continuum. That is what I mean by consensual tolerance.

If you understand that, you have the sense in which discourse and all its distinctions are collective: as infants, we internalize the referential, predicative, and other practices of our society. We share a practice aggregatively, but what we share is collective—ranges (predicatively) over an entire aggregate, but not individually, except in the derivative sense in which what we say and do as individual agents is "consensually" tolerated, as instantiating those practices, by the aggregated membership of the society in question. I take this to explicate the meaning of Rousseau's *volonté générale*.

Hence, when Gilbert explains "joint readiness" in terms of how we should understand the responsiveness of individuals to something like the question, "Shall we do A?" she fails to take account of the collective import of the question.[15] The "collective" cannot be confined to the explicit use of collective terms. The collective is rather the enabling preformative medium of human discourse and culturally significant activity. That is what Durkheim dimly grasped (if I may say so) and what Simmel and Gilbert—and Weber—risk losing. The same is true of Grice's analysis of linguistic intentions and David Lewis's analysis of social conventions.[16]

If you compare Weber's best-known account of "social action," offered in *Economy and Society*, you will find two themes emphasized: one, that he rejects altogether anything like Durkheim's collectivities; and, two, that a "social action" lies in an agent's taking account "subjectively" (I should say, in a "methodologically solipsistic" way) of another's behaviors or interests.[17] Gilbert shows very effectively the limitations of Weber's formula,[18] without, however, going beyond the methodological solipsism I detect. I do not say that either Weber or Simmel or Gilbert—or Grice or Lewis, for that matter—really believes that there is no socially shared cultural space in virtue of (sharing) which individual and aggregated agents function "socially." But they fail to identify the very mark of the "social"—in particular, the fact that the social is insuperably collective. I am speaking, of course, of the social at the human level. Bear in mind: wherever prelinguistic infants, sublinguistic animals, the human unconscious, or intelligent machines are concerned, the attribution of any form of cognition or intelligence is anthropomorphized—in terms of the paradigmatically human. Think, for instance, of the propositional modeling of perception among infants and animals.[19]

Now, if Gilbert is right about Weber's conception of "social action"—and I think she is—then Weber's account is nearly completely irrelevant, despite the great power of any of Weber's actual sociological analyses. That is startling, I admit, but perhaps no less startling than the oddity of Durkheim's theory at the opposite extreme and (if I may now add) the threat of irrelevance in Simmel's and Gilbert's account. In any case, here is what Gilbert says about Weber:

> Weber's technical concept of social action has two general features. First, it involves a strongly intentional conception of what makes a piece of behavior social: whether one performs a social action or not depends not on factors such as the influence of others or consequences for others, but rather on the ideas and conceptions of the agent. In particular, the agent must have the conception of an animate being other than himself, and the social meaning of his act must involve that conception. Second, at least on the face of it, the definition of social action involves no collectivity concepts. One who performs a social action in Weber's sense need not, from a conceptual point of view, either be or see himself as a member of a social group or see that other to whom his act is oriented as the member or co-member with himself of any group.[20]

This strikes me as a decisive blow against Weber if, as seems true, the summary is accurate.

The trouble is, it is, ultimately, as effective against Simmel and Gilbert. Not that Gilbert does not introduce with considerable care the idea of perceiving one's membership in a "social group"; it is just that Gilbert's idea presupposes an unacknowledged condition of collectivity: the sine qua non, in fact, on which her own examples (the enemy troops case, for instance) count as examples of social action. For Gilbert, "social action" requires the presence of a "plural subject." The presence of a plural subject defines the strict sense of "we*" broached in her Simmelian variant (previously mentioned) of what it is to be a "social group." This is meant to identify the middle ground between Weber and Durkheim. But if you look at it with care, you will see that it too is Weberian—though a distinct improvement on Weber himself. The term *plural subject* applies to cases of "joint action" in which what obtains is (roughly) that "each [member] must make clear his willingness to accept a certain goal jointly with certain others."[21] This may be endlessly improved—for example, along lines similar to disqualifying Weber's views or Grice's or Lewis's—but the would-be improvements are meant to do no more than preclude or avoid trivial or irrelevant or paradoxical or inadvertent possibilities within the general compass of (Weber's) "methodological solipsism." That may not be believed. We shall have to see. Nevertheless, Gilbert is certainly right to note that a game-theoretic model, which Lewis, for one, espouses and then sets aside in his account of social convention (language), fails to invoke "the concept of a plural subject."[22] In any case, Lewis opts for what I am calling a "solipsistic" theory; whether he finds the game-theoretic model adequate or not, he also fails to hit on the "mark of the social." Curiously, Lewis actually touches on Rousseau's paradox, though he does so only in the sense of acknowledging a marginal feature of "tacit convention," that is, conventions not created by explicit agreement.[23] What is needed is a deeper analysis of "tacit convention" itself: a mere convention cannot neutralize the force of Rousseau's original paradox. But then neither can the notion of a "plural subject."

Lewis apparently means to construe social institutions and traditions as themselves resting on tacit conventions. There is a related suggestion in the game-theoretic work of Thomas Schelling.[24] But Gilbert's suggestion centers on the fact that game theory and its analogues are not forms of social action at all. Hence, when she formulates her account of a "group language," although it is true that she employs the notion of a "plural subject" or ("social group"), that, too, is solipsistic in the way I have suggested. The following is a crude approximation to what she intends, but she herself offers it. My objection is not with its crudity but rather that it too falls afoul of Rousseau's paradox. Here is what she says:

A group's having a language is not, intuitively, a function of social convention in the intuitive sense, though it is a function of something in the plural subject family. The existence of a group language may now be characterized in terms of the joint acceptance of particular sound-sense links. That is, for a variety of terms, the people concerned must jointly accept that the term in question means such-and-such. If a group accepts that, say, "red" mean red, "socks" mean socks, and so on through the English dictionary, and given that they also accept that certain syntactical forms are correct, then we can appropriately say that English is the group's language.[25]

Yes, of course. But how can that agreement be achieved or shown or discerned? There you have the knockdown relevance of what I offered earlier about reference and predication. Gilbert cannot show what she needs to show. Because the condition that makes social agreement social agreement is our grasping that what the aggregated members of a group say or do is, may be, or will be tolerated (or not tolerated) within the consensual collective practices they share. There are no rules, algorithms, or criteria to invoke, because invoking such considerations can only obtain against the background of already sharing a run of collective practices. Gilbert's "invention" of a group language is hardly different from Lewis's "invention" of a linguistic convention: although she invokes a "plural subject" where Lewis does not, her "group subject" is as solipsistic as Lewis's game-theoretic rational agent. Collective practices cannot be invented; they are a theoretically abstracted dimension of everything we do or say in the distinctively human way, and they are effective in what we say and do. You will find this elaborated in rather similar ways (within entirely different traditions) in Gadamer and Bourdieu.[26]

## II

It is time to rein the argument in. My principal claim is this: (i) that whatever is "social" in the distinctive way in which culturally competent persons are first formed by internalizing the natural language and associated practices of the society in which they mature from infancy is already collective; (ii) that whatever we do, as apt persons or selves, has been enabled by, and implicates in every deed, such collective competences; and (iii) that there is no way to explicate or generate collective practices by exercising the native abilities of the individual members of Homo sapiens (whether singly or aggregatively) if construed as not yet formed persons or as individual persons said (whether singly or aggregatively) to be apt in ways that do not yet assume the collective competences (language, for example) that we seek to explain. I take the denial of point (ii) to be tantamount to adopting "methodological solipsism"—with Noam Chomsky and Jerry Fodor, for example.[27] Chomsky and Fodor succumb to the charms of an extensionalist account of grammar and concepts[28]; doing that, they risk scanting the puzzles of reference and predication, which (I remind you) are paradigmatic of our "social" abilities and which (I claim) cannot be resolved without presupposing the sharing of collective practices. If I am right, reference and predication cannot function in primarily extensional ways. (That was also the reason for opposing Quine's and Goodman's strategies.)

But if extensionalism fails, and if cognitive privilege is precluded, then the spontaneous success of natural-language reference and predication cannot be explained in methodologically determinate ways at all. The only available option admits consensual (not criterially operable) processes by which we extend and test the tolerance of our extended application of the collective practices we share. Those cannot but be open-ended, in the sense that, in acquiring them, we learn to improvise by small increments ranging beyond their remembered (consensually tolerated) regularities. No one (and no aggregate) knows their correct pattern: according to Wittgenstein's acute remarks about "following a rule," there is no such pattern to learn.

Selves are essentially the contingently empowered individual sites of collective competences—in short, effective agents. Persons are cultural artifacts, therefore, that cannot emerge (exist) except in a suitably enabling social or cultural space. Such a space requires an aggregate of mature selves that already share the collective practices that a new cohort of *Homo sapiens* will (somehow) internalize by maturing among their number. If something of this sort captures the sui generis "nature" of human selves—entities that are "socially constituted" as artifacts of cultural history ("embodied" in *Homo sapiens*[29])—then (1) the admission of existent selves entails the admission of collective practices (real, in the predicative sense), and (2) the admission of real practices entails the existence of a society of selves. Furthermore, (3) the paradigmatic powers of such creatures (selves) are their referential and predicative competences, and (4) the successful exercise of those powers is inseparable and inexplicable apart from the enabling collective practices of the society of which they are members. There you have the hidden dimension of human agency scanted by Weber and Simmel and Gilbert and Grice and Lewis—and, I should add, by the entire tradition of philosophy from Descartes to Kant and, in the twentieth century, by the return to seventeenth- and eighteenth-century thinking, as in Husserlian phenomenology and Anglo-American analytic philosophy. You see, therefore, the immense importance of the issue that lurks beneath the request to specify the mark of the social.

I must say a little more about collectivities or collective attributes. First, on the argument, cultural attributes are collective at their source, whether or not they are explicitly collective in sense. "Engaged in war"—Gilbert's example—is, in my view, an explicitly collective predicate: wars can only be fought by aggregates committed (by way of ideologies) to the purported interests of collective entities (nations, for instance). That nations are legal or ideological fictions does not affect the fact that human aggregates commit to them. They postulate collective entities as the referents of certain relevant predications. Similarly, "baroque," "in the baroque style," is an implicitly collective predicate by which we mark an individual painting (an El Greco, say) as a variant of a period style. Secondly, specifically cultural or social or historically pertinent predicates are, I should say, Intentional. "Intentional" is a term of art.[30] I signify by it any of a range of predicables that are intrinsically interpretable, that is, inherently structured as significative, significant, symbolic, semiotic, linguistic, "lingual,"[31] rhetorical, stylistic, traditional, institutional, rulelike, purposive, rational, historical, intentional (in Brentano's or Husserl's sense), or the like. You cannot fail to see that Intentional phenomena are inherently "intensional" as well. If you understand this in terms of the open-ended, historically evolving practices of a society, the admission of the Intentional will be seen to undermine completely the (extensionalist) optimism of nearly the whole of analytic philosophy.

Finally, the entities and the characteristic phenomena of human societies (selves, linguistic communication, art, and manufacture) are inherently historicized, meaning by that that the conceptual and active powers of human agents (their "thinking") are both formed and continually transformed by the ongoing exercise of their collective practices. This again is paradigmatically illustrated by the exercise of our referential and predicative powers. For, for example, what a general predicate "means," rightly applied, will be a function of its evolving application within the tolerance of its accommodating society. That is why the total absence of algorithmic criteria for referential and predicative success is so important philosophically.

The argument applies with equal force to predicates like *saline* and *baroque*. Predicates are artifacts of collective origin: *saline* is not collective in its signification; *baroque* is implicitly or explicitly collective. But the very process of speech is both collectively empowered and collectively structured in such a way (Intentionally) that its successful issue can be marked only in terms of an imputed consensus (among already competent agents). To be Intentionally structured is to be significant in a consensual way; thus, that this solution is saline implicates the collective practice of predication—in accord with which the attribution is "possible" (in something like the Kantian sense of "possible," the same sense Simmel invokes)—but that hardly requires that *saline* be a collective predicate. If this be granted, then Gilbert's analysis will be seen to be question begging at its very inception; for all the usual activities of competent selves are (as enabled) collectively structured even if particular predicates (thus enabled) are not actually collective in the narrow sense of what they "mean."

This also signifies that the solution to the famous mind/body problem cannot be entirely separated from the solution to the larger problem regarding the relationship between (human) culture and (physical) nature. The reason is simply that the paradigm of the "mental" is what it is in the human case; and, there, it is always already linguistically informed or else anthropomorphized (as with prelinguistic infants). Obviously, also, whatever is a specimen of anything is such only on the sufferance of a human posit, but the very competence entailed in such a posit is a socially acquired competence.

By collective, then, I mean an attribute (or a run of subaltern attributes) that applies only or in the first instance to an aggregate of existing individuals, formed as apt selves, such that (i) their individual aptitudes are or include variants of one another's aptitudes ("common" to them all) when (ii) viewed as instantiations of practices idealized from just such instantiations ("common" to the entire society). Selves have collective "natures," and collective attributes are applicable to selves (and the phenomena and artifacts of their world) as and only as instantiating the "nature" of their society—the "nature" imputed to the idealized nominalization of their inclusive practices. A society (*Gemeinschaft*) is a unified nominalization ranging over an aggregate of selves, where to be a self is to instantiate the practices ("nature") of some enabling society, and to be a society is to be an aggregate of such selves. Hence, self and society implicate one another: the apparent circularity is real enough but benign; for societies are prior to selves (generation by generation) in enabling new selves to be formed, and selves are prior to societies in being (at any time) the only effective "agents" there are. In this sense, the mark of the social is the collective or the Intentional. The social is causally effective through the agency of selves, but effective agency is itself collectively structured.

## Notes

1. Émile Durkheim, *The Rules of Sociological Method*, trans. W. D. Halls (New York: Free Press, 1982), p. 59. I should say at once that I have benefited

a great deal from a careful reading of Margaret Gilbert, *On Social Facts* (Princeton, N.J.: Princeton University Press, 1989), though I do not share her account of the "social." You would not be wrong to view this essay as a running debate with Gilbert.

2. I have developed this notion in many places. See, for instance, Joseph Margolis, *Culture and Cultural Entities* (Dordrecht: Reidel, 1984), Chapter 1; and *Texts without Referents: Reconciling Science and Narrative* (Oxford: Blackwell, 1989), Chapter 6.

3. Gilbert, *On Social Facts*, pp. 146–147. The line from Simmel is from Georg Simmel, "How Is Society Possible?" in *Georg Simmel: On Individuality and Social Forms*, ed. D. N. Levine, (Chicago: University of Chicago Press, 1971), p. 75, cited by Gilbert.

4. Gilbert, *On Social Facts*, p. 147.

5. Ibid., pp. 490, n. 109.

6. Ibid., pp. 185–99.

7. Durkheim, *The Rules of Sociological Method*, p. 54. Gilbert cites the passage as she does the other I have mentioned.

8. See Jon Elster, "Marxism and Individualism." In *Knowledge and Politics: Case Studies in the Relationship between Epistemology and Political Philosophy*, ed. M. Dascal and D. Gruengard. (Boulder, Colo.: Westview Press, 1989). I have seen the essay in manuscript only.

9. Gilbert, *On Social Facts*, p. 185; cf. the rest of Section 3.7.

10. See W. V. Quine, *Word and Object* (Cambridge, Mass.: MIT Press, 1960) Sections 37–38.

11. See *The Leibniz-Clarke Correspondence*, ed. H. G. Alexander (Manchester: Manchester University Press, 1956), Leibniz's fifth letter.

12. See Nelson Goodman, "Seven Strictures on Similarity." In *Experience and Theory*, ed. Lawrence Foster and J. W. Swanson (Amherst: University of Massachusetts Press, 1970).

13. For a somewhat fuller account of the issue, with regard to both reference and predication and to Quine and Goodman, see Joseph Margolis, *Historied Thought, Constructed World: A Conceptual Primer at the Turn of the Millennium* (Berkeley: University of California Press, 1995).

14. See Ludwig Wittgenstein, *Philosophical Investigations*, trans. G.E.M. Anscombe (New York, Macmillan, 1953). Sections 201–202.

15. Gilbert, *On Social Facts*, p. 185.

16. See H.P. Grice, "Meaning," in *Philosophical Review* (1957) 66:377–88; and "Utterer's Meaning and Intentions," *Philosophical Review*, (1969) 78:147–77; also, David K. Lewis, *Convention: A Philosophical Study* (Cambridge, Mass.; Harvard University Press, 1969). Grice, I may say, risks subverting his "solipsistic" account by introducing, much later, his interesting notion of "conversational implicatures," which seem to me to be plainly collective, though he dampens the account along the lines of his earlier papers. See Paul Grice, *Studies in the Way of Words* (Cambridge, Mass.: Harvard University Press, 1989).

17. See Max Weber, *Economy and Society: An Outline of Interpretive Sociology*, ed. Guenther Roth and Claus Wittich (Berkeley: University of California Press, 1978), Vol. 1, pp. 102, 88.

18. See Gilbert, *On Social Facts*, Chapter 2. John Greenwood offers a mild criticism of Gilbert's account of Weber, attenuating the picture of Weber's treatment of "others." But Greenwood confirms Weber's opposition to the "reification" of collectivities. See *Weber, Economy and Society*, p. 27, cited by Greenwood in John D. Greenwood, *Realism, Identity, and Emotion: Reclaiming Social Psychology* (London: Sage, 1994), Chapter 5. Greenwood himself is a "social constructionist" in the sense that he takes "collectivities" to be "real" and "ontologically distinct from aggregate groups" (p. 90) but also formed or "enacted in accord with a set of recognized arrangements, conventions, or agreements between individuals" (p. 86). By the latter, he specifically means to treat "enacting" such forms of "arrangements" and the rest as "forms of association" (p. 101, n. 7). But, of course, that is precisely the issue at stake. My own suggestion is that we treat collectivities predicatively rather than denotatively.

19. See, for instance, Joseph Margolis, *Culture and Cultural Entities*, Chapters 2, 6.

20. Gilbert, *On Social Facts*, p. 33.

21. Ibid., p. 199.

22. Ibid, p. 321. See the rest of Chapter 6.

23. Lewis, *Convention*, p. 3.

24. See Gilbert, *On Social Facts*, p. 322; also, Thomas Schelling, *The Strategy of Conflict* (Oxford: Oxford University Press, 1960).

25. Gilbert, *On Social Facts*, pp. 389–90. Gilbert explicitly says, "To my knowledge, I have not used any notion approximating to Rousseau's concept of the general will, which I make no attempt to characterize here" (p. 438). That, I think, is precisely what is needed. See Jean Jacques Rousseau, *On the Social Contract*, trans. D. A. Cress (Indianapolis: Hackett, 1983). See, also, the candid and devastating reflections regarding "Gricean conditions for speaker meaning" offered in Stephen Schiffer, *Remnants of Meaning* (Cambridge, Mass.: MIT Press, 1987), Section 9.2. It seems to me that analogous constraints apply very easily to Gilbert's (and Lewis's and similar "Weberian") solutions.

26. See Hans-Georg Gadamer, *Truth and Method*, trans. Garrett Barden and John Cumming (New York: Seabury Press, 1975), Second Part, II; and Pierre Bourdieu, "Structures, Habitus, Practices," in *The Logic of Practice*, trans. Richard Nice (Stanford, Calif.: Stanford University Press, 1990).

27. See, for example, Jerry A. Fodor, *Representations: Philosophical Essays on the Foundations of Cognitive Science* (Cambridge, Mass.: MIT Press, 1981), Chapter 10.

28. See, for instance, Jerry A. Fodor, *The Language of Thought* (New York: Thomas Y. Crowell, 1975).

29. This is no more than a compressed hint of a much larger argument that I cannot possibly provide here.—The argument I am offering must, therefore, be considered conditional. Fair enough. But it is a thesis I have been exploring for many years—most compendiously perhaps in *Historied Thought, Constructed World*.

30. See, further, Joseph Margolis, *The Flux of History and the Flux of Science* (Berkeley: University of California Press, 1993), and *Interpretation Radical but not Unruly: The New Puzzle of the Arts and History* (Berkeley: University of California Press, 1995).

31. By "lingual" I mean any competence (the ballet, cooking and preparing food, making love) that presupposes linguistic competence but not its explicit exercise.

## Chapter 9

# Crews, Clubs, Crowds, and Classes: 'The Social' as a Discursive Category

## Rom Harré

I am disinclined to try to define the 'mark' or characteristic features of something until I am clear about what sort of thing is the focus of concern. We need a rough ontological specification before we try to lay down necessary and sufficient conditions for a type-identity or try to delineate the relevant field of family resemblances among the members of a diverse extension in detail. For instance, compare the tasks of seeking the mark of the tiger, the diplodicus, or the unicorn. Without a prior investigation of the presumed ontological category of these beings, the actual, the extinct, and the mythological, the project of seeking a characteristic mark is hopelessly underdetermined. Again, compare any of these tasks with setting about finding (specifying) the mark of the quark, beings that may never appear in *propria persona*. Perhaps 'the social' is more like 'the quark' than it is like 'the tiger'. Some prior work on the metaphysics of the relevant entities seems to be in order.

All sorts of expressions invoke 'the social'. There are social acts, social clubs, social problems, social events, social work programs, social climbers, social misfits, and social disasters. Somehow or other these expressions all point to collectivities.

The idea of 'the social' clearly has something to do with the idea of 'a collective'. But what makes a real or notional multiplicity of animate beings, a special case of which would be a multiplicity of persons, a collective? I shall assume that the minimal mark of a collective is given by the rule that a multiplicity is a collective only if it admits of the application of the intension/extension distinction. There is some common property or set of properties, a putative intension, that could serve as a criterion for admitting beings as members of the collective, that is, to its extension. But the idea of a collective so identified is radically multivocal. There are at least the following distinct kinds of human collectives:

1. There are those groups we could roughly designate as 'classes'. I shall call these 'taxonomic groups'. They include the extensions of such collectives as nations, ethnicities, and socioeconomic categories.
2. Then there are those multiplicities of persons we could identify roughly as institutions. Among these are crews, teams, and families. I shall call these 'structured groups'.
3. Then there are those puzzling collectives we could roughly call 'crowds'. Though many headed and in some way coherent, crowds are neither institutions nor classes, neither structured nor merely taxonomic groups.

'Between' each of the three kinds here distinguished there are all sorts of possible intermediaries. Between types (1) and (2) are certain common kinds of associations, such as the American Association of Retired Persons (the AARP). It is more coherent than a taxonomic collective, but less organized and differentiated than a political party. Between types (2) and (3) are such carefully crafted multiplicities of persons as those 'street armies' that figure in planned demonstrations. I shall take it that 'sociality' admits of degrees (as Gilbert has argued). It reaches a maximum in structured groups and falls away through crowds to reach its lowest 'value' in taxonomic groups.

## Some Preliminary Observations

Problems of definition abound once we try to give more detailed accounts of the kinds of groups I have distinguished here in which we might seek the mark of 'the social'. Each kind of group has some claim to fall under the supertype 'social collective'.

### Taxonomic Groups

If citizenship is a taxonomic group, does this not tacitly invoke the distinction between natural and artifactual kinds, between 'people *qua* human beings' and 'people *qua* citizens'? A group is logically a set, the members of the extension of which are collected conceptually by their each instantiating a characteristic property or cluster of properties that have been declared to be the intension of the set. The relations between the members of a merely taxonomic group are logical, not substantial. The members are related neither by common descent nor by currrent interactions. Of course, there may be substantial relations between the members of a group thus designated, but those relations are irrelevant to their forming that particular collectivity. Members of the upper middle class may also be supporters of the local opera society, but that is not part of the intension of the class of which all the upper-middle-class folks of the area are the extension.

## Structured Groups

The members of structured groups are usually related by some physical bond, and characteristically each member differs in some membership relevant way from every other. Cox and Stroke are members of the College Eight by virtue of those roles; thus, they differ by reason of the way they instantiate the very attribute that binds them into the collective, namely 'boatsman'. Taxonomic groups and crews differ on another dimension. While the members of taxonomic groups are externally related—that is, one can add or subtract a member from the collective without altering any of the other members—members of crews are internally related. If we took away Stroke from the College Eight, every other member is affected. When a member of a rugby team is sent off for foul play, the remaining players must adjust their game accordingly. One Welshman more or less makes no difference to any other *qua* ethnicity.

## Crowds

Crowds are distinguished from the non-social multiplicities of folk about the city or on the beach by their exhibiting a common purpose, say, to burn the Atlantian Embassy. (Contrast here the *'unanime'* collected round a street accident, suggested by Margolis as a group that is neither just there by happenchance nor united by a common purpose.) However, we can read nothing of the thoughts of the individual members of the crowd from the common purpose they exhibit. There are postural balances and interactions of bodies that result in a coherent motion quite independently of any formulated plans. There are the *chronotopoi,* of Bakhtin (1981), the temporally enduring orientations to a common goal that do rather well for describing the coherence of the crowd that flees from the Cossacks across the snowy streets of St. Petersburg.

## Belief

To be a member of a taxonomic group, it is not necessary to have any beliefs about other members of the group, even that there are any. However, sometimes the discovery that there are others fulfilling the same membership criterion may be of profound psychological importance. Someone may be astonished and relieved, when diagnosed as having some rare disease, to learn that there are other sufferers. But to be a member of a team, crew, or family, it is necessary both to believe in the existence of other members and to have beliefs about them, including, from time to time, quite strong expectations about their behavioral propensities and skills. If I am playing fly-half and the full back calls to field a 'Gary Owen' (ed.—a play in rugby), then, believing him to have 'safe hands', I step back. The psychological state of members of a crowd has provoked speculations from Le Bon to Moscovici and may detain us at a later stage of the argument. For the moment it is necessary only to point out that it seems to be neither the indifference of ethnicity nor to have the explicit character of the beliefs of team members about one another.

## Internal and External Relations

Why would we refuse the title of 'social unit' to the persons congregated at a bus stop or in the carriage of a subway train? They are doing something together, namely, waiting or riding. It seems to me that the description ''member of the group waiting for the 35 bus at the junction of Wisconsin Avenue and P Street'' characterizes these beings as people only in the most minimal way, in that it implies that they are waiting intentionally. By joining the waiting group, one is not in any way changed as to the social category to which one belongs. The relations these people bear to one another and to the bus stop are characteristically 'external'. But standing before the minister and exchanging vows, ''taking the Queen's shilling'' (ed.—joining the army), and so on are quite different kinds of joinings, since the relations into which one enters through these ceremonies are 'internal'. One is changed hereafter in social category, in particular, with respect to ascribed rights and duties. One becomes a husband or wife, a soldier or sailor, and so on.

Here is the interesting point: there are taxonomic groups in the joining of which one is transformed in social category. For example, when one takes up the citizenship of a country to which one has emigrated, one is transformed in social category, from 'alien' to 'citizen', in that one's rights and obligations are thereby changed. This is a different kind of transformation from that which occurs when one is adopted by a family. In both cases the cluster of membership relations is internal—that is, the being is transformed as to type, but in the case of citizenship the group one has joined is unstructured and purely conceptual. (Or not quite—there are some presumed material relations, though of a weak kind, such as living on the same piece of land, which are sometimes nearly sufficient but rarely absolutely necessary.)

**Provisional Summary**

This brief ontological survey has yielded three major categories of person multiplicities, to each of which in certain contexts one would wish to attribute the accolade 'social'. They seem to have little in common except many-headedness. Faced with this situation, we may note two obvious possibilities for its resolution. In everyday use the category 'social' is highly abstract and thin in content in some contexts. In others it is multivocal. We could take a surview of the senses in actual use of the expression 'social'. These already reveal a field of family resemblances. Or we might attempt a preemptive semantic strike, setting out criteria for the use of the concept 'social', which would do some of the work of distinguishing person multiplicities that is done by the actual usage but which, as inventors, we would control. In the first case, we are in Wittgenstein's medieval part of the city. In the second case, we are laying out the plan for a new suburb. Both tasks are worth doing. Greenwood (1994), for instance, has done some of the antiquarian map making. I am going to try to do some town planning on the outskirts of the city of language.

## Commonality: Teams and Crews

### Merging Skills and Shared Aims

Having a certain skill, one that is needed for successfully occupying a place in a team, is a necessary but not a sufficient condition for membership of the team. What was it that made Joe DiMaggio a member of the New York Yankees? At least he needed a special ability to hit the ball. Furthermore, different skills are required of different members. Alley Reynolds, who pitched for the Yankees in those years, was on the team for his 'arm'. Though each member of a team may differ from every other with respect to the attributes that make him or her suitable for team membership, one psychological factor is common to those who are actually members of a team: namely, the aim of the project, the point of the joint activities they believe themselves to be undertaking. Someone who 'throws' a game for a bribe is morally and metaphysically a member of the rival team. His or her contribution is directed (covertly) at a different goal from that of the other team members. The family of common aims is enormously diverse. The yacht must sail a course faster than its rivals; the excavation should culminate in the uncovering of the tomb and the preservation of its contents and so on. But having a common aim is still inadequate as the general mark of membership of a structured group. Families, for instance, do not always or perhaps even often present themselves as teams or crews. Members may have divergent aims and purposes and still count as family members in good standing. Is this just a matter of common biological origins? I think not, but that remains to be demonstrated. Neither interlocking skills nor shared aims makes this group of people the 'Clinton White House' or the 'crew of the *Santa Maria*' or the Chicago 'Bears'. Something else is required.

## Metaphysics of Structured Groups

In what does the reality of the U.S. government, 'New York's Finest,' the House of Windsor, the crew of the Oxford boating team consist? It is salutary to wander around downtown Washington and imagine the sound turned off, the marks on the trillions of pieces of paper fading into illegibility and so on. What would there then be? Some primates in a warren! Legislative acts, tax demands, investigations of savings and loan scams, the scams themselves, press conferences, debates, changes in the base rate, and so on, are through and through and exhaustively characterizable as discursive. They are one and all forms of conversation. A state is brought into being as a way of talking and writing. But a social kind of way, in that if and when it goes right, and in Washington the John Locke–inspired Constitution is almost purposely built to prevent it, people act in coordinated ways.

The House of Windsor is metaphysically more complicated. It is not only a talk show, enmeshed in a worldwide discourse, but also a biological entity, whose members are materially connected by a variety of reproductive links. Superimposed on these material links are evolving conversational patterns, some of which have appeared reprinted in the public domain, which is, of course, part of the conversational flow that is constitutive, on the platform of the biological structure, of the House of Windsor.

For the being of a state, the order of influence is from conversation to material coordination, while for a family the order of influence is from a material relationship to a conversation. But what is constitutive of a biologically grouping as a family is not who has sexual intercourse with whom, who bore whom, and so on, but the conversational (ceremonial) forms we call betrothals, marriages, divorces, or their informal equivalents (e.g., the source of palimony suit). In both cases the material aspect is a contingent matter, though if there were no material outcome or element at all, the state would wither away and the marriage would be annulled.

It looks as if conversation or discourse is coming to the fore as somehow the bearer of the 'mark of the social'. But wait! Would not that consequence force us to deny the accolade 'social' to all those fellow Tellurians to which the word has been traditionally applied—ants, termites, chimpanzees, elephants, and so on? Well, alright, but that is just a bit of lexicography I want to leave to others. It is just the kind of usage that can exert a mesmerizing effect on our ways of thinking about ourselves by importing a grammatical model that seems so natural. Wittgenstein warned against taking a pattern of family resemblances in grammar for a metaphysical premise of deep import.

The term 'discursive' is now in the height of fashion, displacing the tendentious expression 'social construction'. It is used to maintain the link with the idea of the centrality of linguistic modes of interaction, while the relativist implications of some of the social-constructionist literature are less central. However, the scope of the term 'discursive' needs to be made clear. Margolis has used the term 'lingual' to identify those symbolic interactions that are language-like in certain important respects. I would take these respects to include intentionality of the display, the conventionality of its symbolic force, the requirement that these actions are subject to normative constraints, the extent to which the distinction between illocutionary and perlocutionary acts can be applied to it, and, finally, the extent to which the use of these devices subserves expressive rather than practical matters. This extension of the scope of 'the discursive' allows us to comprehend such matters as gestures, postures, dress, styles of talk and action, and even the choice of cars as part of discourse.

## A Conversational Ontology

To get a view of this complex mode of being, I offer two snapshots taken from different directions in different lights. In one the conversation as a flow of social acts will be highlighted, while in the other the multiple and overlapping networks of speaking rights and obligations will be in focus. An ontology must specify three main features of a 'world'. It must list the types of beings of that world, and in detailed exposition it must offer criteria for their identity and individuation. In the physical world, the Newtonian scheme, for instance, listed material things and certain of their dispositional properties, the realizations of which defined the kinds of events recognized in that scheme. An ontology must also define whatever arrays of locations there are at which beings of the sorts specified could be found, and what the status of locations in those arrays could be when no being is actually present. In the physical world, these arrays are condensed into 'space-time'. Finally, an ontology must specify the network of relations that tie the array of beings into a world. In the ontology of physical science, these relations are condensed into various kinds of causality.

In the ontology I shall sketch for a social world, the 'things' of that world are acts, the locative manifold is the array of people capable of performing acts (whether licensed to or not), and the cement of the social world is composed of the complex hierarchies of rules and conventions, including narrative schemes by which acts are taken to form up into social episodes.

But in the ontology as so far presented, people appear as dimensionless points. It is an ontology in which as yet there is no place for psychology or for a moral order. Yet not everyone has the right or the obligation to speak or otherwise perform, or listen to or otherwise register, every possible kind of act recognized in the culture whose sociality we are trying to specify. It might be thought that from the point of view of an ontology for sociology, the private world of each human being, the flux of subjectivity and so on, has no part. Yet I believe that the psychology of each human being is no more than, but at least as much as, a partially privatized part or aspect of the larger conversation that is constitutive of the social world.

Furthermore, there are moral orders of acting, and above all of speaking and listening, that are best expressed, I believe, in terms of the concept of 'position', a psychosocial concept most fully developed by feminist authors such as Hollway (1984). A position in an interaction that is literally a conversation is a set of moral rights and duties of speaking and listening, and it may or may not be occupied by a particular person at a particular moment. It is usually true that any one person may have a number of positions to which he or she can aspire, and some of which that person has the right to occupy. Positions, like everything else in the social world, can be more or less determinate, and since they are linked into a kind of 'triangle' with acts and story lines, the realization of local narrative schema and conventions, each of which in being made more determinate (that 'making' being itself a social act or acts) makes the other members of the triangle more or less determinate.

So far I have presented this ontology in such a way that it might seem that individual persons were capable of performing the acts that, linked into narratives, constitute this or that social world. But every act is actually a joint action. To make this clear, we need the distinction between actions and acts. An 'action' is that which someone does intentionally (be the intention conscious to the actor as a plan or aim or, more commonly, immanent in the action unreflectingly performed as the situation seems to demand it). An 'act' is the social meaning of an action or commonly of a cluster of actions. But an action can have no social meaning without the interaction of others (and in the zero-th case, that other may be oneself). The words I utter, meaning to invite you to tea, do not constitute the social act of inviting unless they are taken as such and completed by acceptance or refusal in the words you utter or the gestures you make. Sometimes an act may need the joint actions of hundreds or millions of people—for example, the act of electing a leader.

More needs to be said about acts. Only as acts do actions have social consequences. Austin's distinction between the illocutionary force of what is said or done and its perlocutionary force can be generalized to acts of all kinds, though his exemplars were acts accomplished by actions of speaking. The perlocutionary force of an act is its power to bring about consequences. For instance, the perlocutionary force of an action of signing a treaty may be what brings about the withdrawal of your nuclear warheads. But, according to Austin, an action has perlocutionary force only in so far as it has illocutionary force, that is, is taken up as a social act in a joint creation. Compare the explanation of how my utterance can deafen you with how it can commit you. It follows in one short step that the social world is knitted up of threads that are not causal, though they have efficacy. Or if you insist, despite my warnings, that only confusion can come of it, that all cases of efficacious bringing about of consequences are instances of causality, then two quite different modes or categories of causality must be recognized, and care must be taken to see that natural assumptions involved in the use of the one concept do not leak over into the other. The word 'efficacy' and other causal expressions, I would like to say, is a field of family resemblances, not a family hierarchy of genus and species.

Keeping this in mind should help with the problem of properly categorizing the life forms of ants and bees, the 'social insects'. It should also help with finding a proper account of the life forms of chimps and dogs, which are also 'social animals' but of a different dye. To the latter, a fairly straightforward application of the action/act distinction can be made. George H. Mead begins his great work with a description of the life form of a pack of wolves. Their social order is maintained by all sorts of 'ritual' performances, in which the causality of the action, say, as sexual, is suspended or, better we should say, is metanymically transformed and is taken up as an act of submission. The life forms of 'higher' social animals are shot through with this duality, between an action or action sequence and the taking of that action up, not as it is, so to say, in the basic behavioral repertoire of the species but as a 'social signal', as the ethologists say—that is, as an act, jointly constituted by both performer and recipient. In that role it is, of course, just as active as that of the initiator of the action sequence through which the two or more creatures jointly constitute the act. Only as so constituted does the action sequence play a part in the social life of the animals. We have no reason to believe that the action/act distinction has any useful analytical role in describing or explaining the life forms of termites and the like. A whiff of phero- mone, the prevailing scent of the hive, is the causal substrate of the illusion of sociality that we have in ant watching.

### Individualism: The Last Temptation

With the sound off, we see hominids in a hive, moving about in mysterious but orderly ways. With the sound on, we see Georgetown University, its faculty and students engaged in the social production of knowledge, aided by the campus cops, the cleaners, the librarians, and more or less facilitated by the 'administration'. The 'sound off' picture would lead us to look for the mark of the social in patterns and agents of causality. But only in the 'sound on' picture does this group display itself as what it is, a human institution. The occurrence of actions, meant and taken as acts, that serve to create the internal relations by which the group is constituted as a university is the mark of the social.

But now we ask, How is it that a group of hominids can perform in these complex ways, constituting not only the institutions in which human sociality is found but at the same time the very persons that occupy them? Perhaps the true mark of the social has not yet been identified. Perhaps it lies somehow in the creatures that bring these things about. My argument so far was intended to establish that macrosocial 'entities' are logical constructions, spun out of conceptual distinctions and having their being only in discourse. Microsocial 'entities' too are discursive constructions, but through the action-act patterns which are thereby constituted some robust realities are accomplished, such as parenthood, victory on the river, graduation *summa cum laude*, and so on. Should we not look for the mark of the social in individuals, in their skills and capacities, in particular, to follow the argument so far, in their discursive skills and capacities?

To follow this line of argument down to a basic individualism would be to join with Piaget and (seemingly paradoxically) the sociobiologists in their view that each individual is a native source of those actions through which the social is constituted. Egocentric speech defines the alleged basic solipsism of the infant for Piaget (1926), while genetically programmed fixed action patterns merge to be integrated into a tribal whole for Wilson (1980). In opposition one can rank Vygotsky (1986) and Wittgenstein (1953), and the contemporary social theorists such as Giddens (1976) and Bhaskar (1979), as well as ancients such as Aristotle, who have emphasized reciprocal structuration. The organization of individual mentation to make it capable of performing socially constitutive action patterns with others is appropriated from discursively realized social interactions, while the structured orderliness of those very social interactions is produced by beings who have themselves been made orderly and structured in Vygotsky's zone of proximal development, in which their incomplete and fumbling attempts at action are supplemented by the contributions of others. Individuality as a personal being is as much a product of interpersonal processes as one's role in a collectivity, a team of social beings.

## Failures of Sociality

Another way of marking off the 'societies' of ants from the societies peopled by human beings can be discerned in the ways we would explain the collapse of social structures in typical cases. We do know that the 'evaporation' of the pheromone that binds the population of the ant heap into a coherent order brings that order to an end. Soap and deodorants have not brought Western civilization crashing down into chaos. When sociality 'evaporates' in human groups, we diagnose a failure to share meanings. Actions are performed, the act force of which is not taken up by the others in a joint construction. If you do not know what acts are incipient in the gestures, grimaces, nods, and utterances of the others, social relations are impossible. There could be no Bhaktinian chronotopoi if the orienting gestures of the crowd could not be taken up as directors of attention, and so ultimately of the organization of joint action.

## Conclusion

In the introduction I remarked that a variety of expressions incorporated the notion of 'the social'. We are now in a position to locate their referents somewhere in the spectrum between the taxonomic group, the crowd, and the structured group. It seems to me that most of these expressions refer to collectivities that fall within the central category of structured groups and, as I have shown, thereby are to be conceived as discursively constituted and maintained. A social club is created and maintained by shared aims, interlocking skills, and a common discourse. A social disaster—say, the distinguished guest is so drunk he presses unwelcome attentions on the hostess—is the product of slippage between one discursive mode and another, between one set of projects appropriate to one milieu and those proper elsewhere. A social climber is one who is native to one discursive frame in the process of acquiring those skills necessary to enter into another. And so on.

## References

Bahktin, Michael. 1981. *The Dialogical Imagination*, trans. C. Emerson and M. Holquist. Austin: University of Texas Press.
Bhaskar, Roy. 1979. *The Possibility of Naturalism*. Hassocks: Harvester.
Giddens, Anthony. 1976. *New Rules of Sociological Method*. New York: Basic Books.
Greenwood, John D. 1994. *Realism, Identity and Emotion: Reclaiming Social Psychology*. London: Sage.

Hollway, Wendy. 1984. "Gender Difference and the Production of Subjectivity." Pp. 227–263 in *Changing the Subject*, ed. Julian Henriques, Wendy Hollway, Cathy Urwin, Couze Venn, and Valerie Walkerdine. London: Methuen.

Piaget, Jean. 1926. *The Language and Thought of the Child*, trans. M. Worden. New York: Harcourt, Brace & World.

Vygotsky, Lev S. 1986. *Thought and Language*, trans. A. Kozulin. Cambridge, Mass.: MIT Press.

Wilson, Edward O. 1980. *Sociobiology*. Cambridge, Mass.: Harvard University Press.

Wittgenstein, Ludwig. 1953. *Philosophical Investigations*. Oxford: Blackwell.

## Chapter 10

# Social Theory in Context: Relational Humanism

*Kenneth J. Gergen*

What is the "the mark of the social" in contemporary theory? Or, more generally, how are we to regard the demarcation of a phenomenon or a domain of scholarly inquiry? If we remain within the long-honored and companionate discourses of the Enlightenment and "the scientific worldview," the answers are readily forthcoming. In comprehending the world in which we live, in submitting it to rational analysis and empirical scrutiny, we see that ontological clarity is imperative. We must carefully delineate among entities, or else thinking becomes clouded and research may become irrelevant. Clarity in such matters is also important for purposes of professional efficacy. With domains of study carefully delineated, the goals of the various professions are legitimated, we avoid redundancy of effort, and we encourage scholarship in depth. In the present context, to distinguish the social from the psychological, the interpersonal from the societal, the relational from the autonomous, then, is to lay the foundations for productive and complementary disciplines of inquiry.

Yet, as scholarship has accelerated exponentially within the present century, we have also become fitfully aware of the limitations of this "rage to order." As various enclaves lay claim to territories of the real, so do they insulate themselves from the dialogues of neighboring (and typically "less important") domains. When experts from otherwise alienated encampments do attempt collaboration, their models are often ill fitting: hypothesis testing in one domain conflicts with multivariate modeling in another; the organismic metaphors favored

213

by one clash with the mechanistic metaphors of the other; nativist explanations collide with environmentalist; and so on. Further, each circumscribed basis of explanation appears capable of infinite expansion, ultimately absorbing all human action in its propositional corpus (for example, tracing all action to cognitive schemata, biogenetics, microsocial process, etc.). All contending forms of explanation are reduced to the single frame and alterior argots dismissed as irrelevant or obfuscating. Finally, we have witnessed in the past decade a mushrooming of hybrid areas of scholarship—black studies, women's studies, environmental studies, cultural studies, queer studies, and more. Here and elsewhere we find a generalized restlessness with the traditional disciplinary boundaries. Urban sociology begins to converge with anthropology, social psychology with social linguistics, psychology with evolutionary biology, cultural anthropology with literary analysis, and so on. In all these adventures, demarcation on either phenomenal or explanatory grounds is obstructive. We gain most, it is argued, when "language goes on holiday."

More important, various intellectual movements of the past thirty years raise serious questions with attempts to delineate domains of study. Quine's *Word and Object* (1960) raised early doubt in the possibility of tying a descriptive language unequivocally to an array of observables, and Saussurian semiotics demonstrated the fundamentally arbitrary relationship between language and referent. Developments in both the history of science and the sociology of knowledge place in jeopardy all demarcations based on characteristics of "phenomena in themselves." As widely demonstrated, ontological commitments and their instantiations are byproducts of communal interchange; the world as it is makes no obvious demands on our forms of theorizing. With referentially based meaning thus replaced by a communal (cultural, historical) account, the particularly political and ideological components of demarcation are drawn into focus. To demand a particular arrangement of discourse, and a related domain of practices, can be seen as authoritarian, self-serving, and oppressive to all who fail to acquiesce. Developments in literary deconstruction theory lend further credibility to this view. For Derrida (1976) and others, the meaning of any utterance is not self-standing but dependent on a vast history of language use in which this utterance is embedded. To treat the meaning of a word as transparent and transcontextual is to deny its history, suppress its broad web of interdependencies, and prevent its potentials for creative and variegated usage.

It is against this backdrop that I wish in the present exercise to move more dialogically. I do not wish to argue against drawing any distinctions but, rather, against distinctions removed from historical and cultural context. Drawing from the previous analysis, to remove distinctions threatens the destruction of community. The challenge, then, is to place distinctions into the context of ongoing interchange. Rather than determining in the abstract and in advance what constitutes the "mark of the social," my attempt here will be to enter a long-standing dialogue of broad significance and to introduce a particular conception of the social that may press that conversation forward in interesting and potentially significant ways. The impetus then is not toward Apollonian purity, an ultimately satisfying point of respite, but a Dionysian brawl in which a catalytic clash of discourses may yield unanticipated moves in meaning. The experiment is one in which I wish to enter a specific dialogue of long-standing, introduce adversarially a preliminary and necessarily ambiguous conception of the social, and in pressing the dialogue forward move toward a richer and more pragmatically useful conception. The more elaborated view will attain its meaning within, and because of, its placement within this specific context.

## Social Construction in the Humanist Tradition

In the halcyon years of French existentialist thought, a broad stirring developed among many French humanist thinkers. Existentialist theory did seem to embody much that was essential to the humanist. The pivotal commitment of existentialist theory was to individual agency; the theory was preeminently a celebration of human subjectivity and freedom. Yet, existentialist thought also seemed to lack a very special ingredient, any sense of moral or ethical direction. Too often, it seemed, existentialists sacrificed ethical sensibility for the "gratuitous act"—the spontaneous burst of unencumbered action. In doing so the existential hero denied the significance of history, culture, and community—any commitment to the good of others. Sartre's (1977) little volume, *Existentialism and Humanism*, served as a reply to his critics, and in this volume he attempted to show that existentialist theory did indeed lay the groundwork for moral concern.

Sartre's particular arguments were scarcely convincing. As he proposed, we are essentially responsible for our actions. But in our choices for ourselves, we "choose for all men [*sic*]" (p. 29). We do this because we always chose what we feel is valuable, estimable, or better, "and nothing can be better for us unless it is better for all" (p. 29). Why one person's good should speak for all, what we are to do with competing goods, and how such a position can speak to any of the abiding evils of society are left unanswered. These problems notwithstanding, the present offering echoes Sartre's concern with reconciling a thesis that ostensibly flies in the face of the humanist concerns with certain aims of the humanist tradition. Specifically, I shall argue, as we move toward a theoretical imaginary in which the social precedes the personal, so do we undermine major tenets of the humanist intelligibility. Because many humanist ideals are deeply woven into the fabric of Western tradition, and because the erosion of these ideals would constitute a major loss, the "shift to the social" must be viewed with circumspection.

I shall carry out this analysis from the standpoint of what may be viewed as a radical social constructionism. I am here taking constructionist texts to include all recent sources treating the manner in which language is used by persons to generate intelligibility, and the repercussions of such intelligibilities for the human condition—thus including within the dialogue a substantial range of writing in the sociology of knowledge, the history of science, discourse analysis, critical theory, feminist theory, semiotics, literary theory, rhetorical analysis, communication theory, hermeneutic theory, and postmodern political theory and philosophy.[1]

These dialogues scarcely yield a univocal account of social construction; there are numerous tensions among grounding assumptions. Many contributors continue to hold fast to various forms of psychological functioning (e.g., intending, thinking, experiencing); others wish to maintain a materialist metaphysics; and still others presume the existence of macrosocial institutions. A radical social construction places all these presumptions in brackets. Avoiding the objectification implied in these accounts, terms of psychology, materialism, and macrosociology (among others) are taken to be integers within discursive practices. They owe their intelligibility to relational process, that is, forms of coordination among two or more persons. Linguistic meaning is born, then, not within the minds of single individuals, but from coordinated action, or "joint-action," in Shotter's (1993) terms. One may speak, but the meaning of the utterance is deferred until granted (temporarily) through another's mode or relationship to the utterance, the meaning of which is open to further supplementation by the speaker, and so on.[2] In effect, from the process of coordinated actions the full array of intelligible utterances is generated, including the account of constructionism itself. The precise meaning of relatedness remains indeterminate and dependent on further coordinations within relationship. We cannot, then, locate relationship within language, but we can through continued dialogue generate the sense of the palpable.

In many respects, as constructionist dialogues have developed, grown strong, and concatenated across the humanities and social sciences, they seemed for a time to be a valuable friend to the humanist. In their critique of the behavioral science rage to reduce human action to scale points, biological urges, response potentials, mental mechanisms, and the host of other scrofulous metaphors with which the profession has attempted to colonize humanity, constructionist writings added a powerful new arsenal of weapons. In this sense constructionist thought played a parallel role to that of existentialism of earlier decades, significantly strengthening the humanist voice in the social sciences. Yet, as the dialogue has unfolded, humanist thinkers have begun to find much at fault in the constructionist expansion. On closer inspection, many conceptions and values central to the humanist tradition seem to be abandoned or destroyed by constructionist thought. In its rampant relativism, it is said, constructionist theory lacks moral or ethical commitment; it offers no reason for rejecting the most vile and inhumane actions. Its "anything goes" mentality seems morally bankrupt, even repulsive.

In the present offering my attempt is, first, to examine the critical implications of a fully extended constructionism for the humanist tradition and, second, to explore the potentials of such thought for engendering humane forms of cultural life. These challenges, in tandem, should succeed in extending the meaning and implications of a particular mode of defining and explaining the social. In the first instance, I will argue that humanists have generally *underestimated* the critical implications of constructionism for their project. "Rampant relativism" is only the beginning of what might be viewed as a wholesale slide into humanist despair. However, as I shall then endeavor to argue, one may locate within the bosom of constructionist writing an alternative horizon of understanding. And if we play out the potentials of this conception of the social, we confront the possibility of redrawing the face of humanism. We locate in a specifically relational *humanism* a new and significant means of realizing traditional visions of human well-being. Further, it is within this elaboration that we acquire a richer elaboration of a uniquely social account of human action.

## Social Constructionism: A Humanist Damage Report

As a general surmise, it is my view that the forms of argument deriving from constructionist dialogues—fully extended—are fully lethal in their potential. That is, they have the capability of undermining, dissolving, or rendering suspicious, even meaningless, any form of advocacy, declaration, authority, or protest—including their own. The forms of argument developed within constructionist spheres, taken together, are little short of "doomsday weapons" in the evolving generation of human meaning. If allowed full expression, there simply is nothing left to say—or do. For present purposes, I simply wish to play out some of the potentials of these dialogues, as they apply in this case to pivotal assumptions in the humanist tradition. I will not attribute responsibility for any of these critiques to any particular individual (which itself would be problematic in light of constructionist arguments) but will simply allow the criticisms unadulterated expression relevant to several pivotal assumptions in the humanist tradition.

### Subjective Experience

In the humanist view individual, subjective experience is of paramount value. One's conscious experience, it is held, is indeed inseparable from one's identity as a human being. (The value of an accident victim who will never recover consciousness, but whose life can be sustained by machines, rapidly becomes marginal.) To prize the subjectivity of each individual is thus to render the project of humanity viable. But, asks the constructionist critic, what is the warrant for the preeminent presumption of private experience, a state of *inner* experience as against an outer reality, a psychological as opposed to a material reality? This subject-object binary cannot be substantiated by virtue of "what there is"; there are no viable philosophical justifications for the distinction. Is this metaphysical commitment not, then, a byproduct of a uniquely situated cultural history? Are there not myriad other ways of conceptualizing human consciousness? And, indeed, are there not multiple characterizations of human action extant in the world that make no mention of human consciousness? And if the concept of human subjectivity is thus optional, a cultural construction of our own making, then what is to be said in support of its collective objectification? Is the concept not a justificatory device for a tradition of self-contained individualism, in which the state of my subjectivity gains paramount importance, and in which narcissism becomes a cultural pastime?[3]

## Human Agency

The concept of human agency is a close companion to that of individual subjectivity. It is within the realm of individual consciousness that responsible deliberation and choice take place. It is deliberative choice that gives consciousness its distinctive character. However, the presumption of human agency adds an important dimension to the traditional humanist project, inasmuch as it places the origins of action, and thus of the good society, within the individual. Because of human agency we may choose the welfare of others, and we may desist in patterns of conduct inimical to them. However, again the pariah of constructionist criticism enters from the wings. In this case ample preparation had been made in other intellectual quarters. Already the presumption of agency had been badly damaged by twentieth century science, arguing as it had that individual action is best understood in terms of its antecedent conditions and that the concept of agency is an unfortunate and mystifying holdover from an obfuscating, medieval metaphysics.

However, constructionist arguments add still further laminations of doubt. The concept of agency begins to lose gravity in our preceding deconstruction of consciousness. So fully conflated are the concepts of consciousness and agency that to dispense with one is virtually to abandon the other. (It is scarcely intelligible to say, for example, that personal agency is beyond conscious control.) Further, the constructionist questions, why should we presume that there is an originary source (a cryptospeaker or Doppelgänger) lying somewhere behind and pulling the strings of public action? Not only are there no compelling grounds for such a presumption, but to make arguments of this form is to create a double problematic—not only that of explaining the public actions themselves but, additionally, that which presumably lies beneath. This would be akin to presuming a god who directs the motions of the clouds or the eruptions of volcanoes. The presumption generates a double concern—with the natural conditions of the weather and, again, with the sentiments of the supernatural being. Must we, however, gain access to these exotic sentiments to predict the weather?

And, the critic continues, in what sense is free and unfettered deliberation ever possible? How can I make a moral decision that is truly my own—beyond the influence of others? If I took away all the cultural language—a language of justice, moral worth, equality, and the like—on what grounds could I deliberate? If we empty the individual of culture, leaving him or her completely free to choose, would we not find ourselves with an empty vessel—unable even to conceptualize what it is to have a choice?[4]

## Individual Liberty

For many humanists the concept of liberty serves as the critical component of the tradition. We must, it is extolled, value the liberty of each and every individual—endowed as we are with unique subjectivities and the capacity for free and responsible action. Oppression in any form is to deny the individual expression of his or her fundamental humanity. It is such thinking that is foundational as well to the view of inalienable human rights, universal rights of free individual action—without interference or control of others. However, with subjective experience now impugned by constuctionist arguments, as well the related concept of individual agency, how are we to rationalize the concept of liberty? If conscious deliberation proves to be a cultural construction, along with the presumption of human agency, have we not undermined the concept of liberty and the associated commitment to fundamental rights of man? And, suggest many feminists, careful note should be taken of the convenient phrase, "rights of man." For has the valorization of liberty not primarily been of androcentric origin? And does it not lend justification to male liberty, in particular, which is to say, freedom from commitment, from family, from community, indeed, all forms of interdependence?

Of course, it may be countered, we need not view the concept of liberty as foundational; we can take a more instrumental approach in which the term and its cognates ("rights," "freedom," "justice") are essentially used to condemn oppressive conditions in society. Liberty, in this case, serves both as a term of moral evaluation and a battle cry of emancipation. This is certainly a reasonable rejoinder, and many would consider the gains of various activist groups (e.g., women, blacks, gays) as supportive evidence. However, this view scarcely suffices. For in a world of pluralistic moralities, oppressions can be claimed from multiple standpoints, and one group's emancipation is another's enslavement. Here we should keep in mind the incremental increase over the past decade in "claims to rights." So pervasive and vituperative are such claims that suspicious if not calloused columnists now speak of the "rights babble." Clearly, liberty as a form of rhetoric is insufficient.[5]

## Moral Responsibility

As intimated earlier, the concepts of subjectivity and agency form close companions to the presumption of moral responsibility. While the individual is fundamentally free to choose, such choice is accompanied by a responsibility for action that will not injure or unjustifiably constrain others. Each individual may thus be held responsible for his or her actions and may be penalized or rewarded by dint of his or her conduct toward others. The ethical or humane society thus rests on the moral responsibility of the individuals composing that society. Yet, as we have explored the problematics of consciousness, individual agency, and liberty, we also find the justification for moral responsibility rapidly dissolving. How indeed is one to be responsible to oneself, when there is no private, unacultured self to offer guidance? How could the morally advanced individual generate a set of personal moral principles, except from the repository of cultural intelligibilities at his or her disposal? And, in matters of moral deliberation, if one does hearken to the cultural installation within, then which of the voices should be favored? For are we not all, in a Bakhtinian sense, akin to polyphonic novels, speaking in multiple voices, reflecting multiple traditions? If we inherit a pluralism of moral intelligibilities, on what grounds could we select among them save from the standpoint of yet another inherited intelligibility? And, finally, if moral deliberation is inherently cultural, then in what sense are we justified in holding individuals responsible for the humane society? Is not individual blame thus a mystification of our condition of interdependence? I shall return to this issue shortly.

## From Individual to Relational Humanism

These accumulated arguments—all common within constructionist dialogues more generally considered—erode the very foundations of traditional humanism, grounding assumptions on which many have placed our hopes for encouraging a moral, humane, and solidary society. Further, there are no easy counters to such arguments—other than an ostrich-headed antipathy—inasmuch as the rebuttals stand as well to be undone on grounds of their ideological, rhetorical, and constructed character. And, should we succumb to the powers of deconstructive arguments and turn them reflexively on themselves—essentially deconstructing the deconstruction—then we simply have no room for further conversation. All dialogue terminates. But we need not conclude the present discussion in this dolorous condition. Indeed, the sense of nihilism is warranted only from within the humanist tradition itself. If for the nonce we can bracket the humanistic perspective, that is, consider it one possible account among many, we may then inquire into (1) the potential of humanist thought to engender the humane and solidary society and (2) the positive potentials inherent in radical constructionism.

In the initial case, it is not at all clear that the humanist legacy can deliver as hoped. Surely there is little evidence that beliefs in individual agency, freedom, and moral deliberation central to the Western tradition from at least the Enlightenment to the present have contributed to the humane treatment of human beings. Massive obliteration of peoples in western culture has not diminished markedly since the seventeenth century—that epoch often identified with the origins of humanist thought.[6] Further, as we move rapidly toward conditions of a global village, it is not clear that humanistic assumptions can help us to grapple with alterity—others who are not like us in their values and beliefs. Not only does humanism eschew contrary metaphysics (e.g., materialism, constructionism), but it favors a conception of the individual as fundamentally isolated, alone within his or her subjective experience, ideally generating his or her own decisions without the intrusive influence of mere social opinion. The very best that might be hoped from such a perspective is that the coming world condition would allow for peaceful coexistence—each individual and each cultural enclave simply persisting in its own self-determined way—independent of the others. However, world conditions no longer allow us to live in such independence; we now recognize our common existence on a ship that shows every possibility of sinking. Under such conditions, to celebrate the preeminence of the individual is to invite an ingurgitating conflict of peoples seeking to save their own skin.

At this point I wish to turn the discussion in a more positive direction. Rather than ruing and retrenching, let us reconsider the constructionist arguments and, more pointedly, explore the implicative network of assumptions for more promising potentials. When we move beyond the deluge, are there implications for the creation of a humane society? Of course, many lines of constructionist argumentation exist, with substantial differences in their entailments. However, there is one domain of discourse that, in my opinion, harbors significant promise for humane relationships in a shrinking world. Consider in particular the emerging network of interlocking arguments regarding language. Constructionist thinkers generally abandon the view that our language about the world (or the self) functions as a mirror or map or that it bears any transparent or necessary connection to an array of existants outside itself. In contrast, constructionists have largely favored some form of Wittgensteinian or use-based (neopragmatist) account of language. Here the emphasis is placed on meaning as embedded within language use, words deriving their meaning from the attempt of people to coordinate their actions within various communities. In this vein, the meaning of language originates within ongoing relations among people. The individual mind is abandoned as the originary source of meaning and replaced by relationship. Or to extend the implications still further, our capacity to mean (to think, to be intelligible, to count ourselves as individual agents at all) is born of relationship. Relationship precedes individual existence, not vice versa.[7]

If we can grant the preeminence of relationship in fostering human intelligibility, we are positioned to reconsider the foundational assumptions within the humanist tradition. Can we, in particular, re-vision the family of humanist concepts in terms of human relationship, altering our understanding of them such that they are rooted in relationship? And, as we attempt to reconceptualize these concepts in terms of a relational ontology, let us consider their implications for human well-being.

## Experience as Relationally Grounded

Earlier we questioned the subject-object binary on which the concept of a personal or subjective experience is grounded. Let us consider, then, how we might abandon the binary and attempt to reconceptualize experience in terms of relationship. Rather than holding experience to be akin to an internal mirror reflecting an exterior reality, let us consider experience as a form of relational action. Experience in this case is not a specific form of action, separate in kind from all others, but action indexed in terms of relationship—linking what we presume in Western culture to be individual being and other "entities" within the conventional ontology. "To experience," then, is to engage in a relationship or a oneness—*a being with*. This kind of reconceptualization draws importantly from the phenomenological tradition from Husserl to Merleau-Ponty. However, unlike phenomenology, it does not recognize the subject-object unity as foundational. Rather, the very idea of experience as a relational action is itself a construction, deriving in this case from a particular tradition of dialogue.

At the same time, we must expand on this conception in an important way. In particular, we must trace the character of the momentary "experience" to the broader array of relations in which one is embedded. The experiential action acquires its intelligibility within processes of relationship. On this account, to experience happiness or sadness is to manifest a particular immersion in a cultural tradition. My moment-to-moment sense of the real is premised on my history within the culture; in effect, there would be no experience of "happiness" save through a particular array of coordinated practices within the culture (relationships, for example, in which we come to agree that happiness exists and these are the conditions in which we feel it). Thus, the phenomenal unity of experience (what we generally index as "perception" or "experience of the world") would function as an extension of relatedness. Or, to put it otherwise, in significant degree, "conscious experience" is relatedness speaking through us. Relatedness furnishes the forestructure for the condition of our immediate immersion in onrushing life.

If we are successful in recasting "subjective experience" as a relational process, we are no longer invited to consider our subjectivities as isolated, cut away, or alienated from others, beyond the comprehension of others. Rather, we sense ourselves as both constituted by and constituting the other. In a certain sense, *we are each other*, our conscious experience born of each other. For me to make sense here and now is in essence to duplicate you, to act as a partial replication of you. Should I fail in this duplication, I would also fail to achieve a comprehensible action. In a broad sense, I owe all that I value to my relationships, and all that I find grievous can be altered only through relationship. Individual subjectivity, then, is not a mark of differentiation but of relatedness. To seek a better quality of life is not a narcissistic endeavor but a communal one.

### Agency as Relational Engagement

Rather than viewing individuals as originary sources of their own actions (an assumption that casts the individual in the image of God), let us abandon the entire voluntarism-determinism binary. To speak either of these symbiotic languages is optional, and we are not obliged either to choose between them or to sustain one pole at the expense of the other. Rather, let us consider individual action as always already embedded within patterns of relationship. One acquires impetus (indexed as a sense of motive, consciousness of value, or desire) by virtue of the manner in which one is enmeshed in relationship. For example, why do we strive for high self-esteem if not by virtue of our particular location in Western culture at a particular point in its history? We possess telos or direction in life not because of some inner possession of motive, calling, or biological proclivity but by virtue of the forms of relationship of which we are a part. Agency, then, may be more usefully conceptualized as a form of relational engagement. (To want is to "want with," to "choose" is to reflect the condition of one's relatedness.)

If we do envision the impulse toward action as a byproduct of relational engagement, we may also refigure the institutions of blame and responsibility. For if we hold single individuals responsible for their actions, we again position ourselves symbolically as God—here the supreme judge of good and evil. And in our godlike form, we effectively deny our participation in the culture, treating ourselves as the overseeing eye, suspended above the acts of mortals. In contrast, if we envision action as a relational outcome, our sensibilities are horizontally recast. Specifically, a stance of *relational responsibility* is invited, one in which we approach heinous and egregious action with a curiosity of context. That is, we broaden the network of participation, to consider how the relationships in which the erring individual was involved (personal, mediated, and environmental) have brought about such an end. As we broaden the relational context so as to include multiple others, so should we consider their relationships and how they impinge on the actions in question. And, if our concern is sufficiently great, we may eventually reach the point at which we realize our own complicity in the action. Blame and responsibility are thus distributed within the community, and indeed the culture. We are all invited thereby to join together in actions that would establish a more promising future. (Here, for example, we might consider our own participation in the problem of drugs, rape, homicide, and joblessness.)[8]

### Liberty as Polyphonic Expression

In the traditional humanist view, the concept of liberty functions as a condition of free-floating individuality, an expression of pure and unencumbered agency. The individual may *choose* irrespective of, and indeed with some suspicion of, the remainder of the culture. If conditions seem oppressive, they are distended from the self typically attributed to blameworthy others. If a marriage, a friendship, a community, or even a political condition becomes disagreeably binding, we are moved by humanistic discourse, to "free ourselves from the shackles," to liberate ourselves from social constraint, and to restore the state of pure freedom or independence. As Bellah (1985) and his colleagues have argued, such thinking strongly encourages the dissolution of marriages and the avoidance of communal or political participation. "If the relationship does not benefit me, if it harms my development, then I will chose freedom."

In contrast, the relational view proposes that we cannot escape the requirements of relationship to locate a condition of pure agency. We are never free of relationships. And, indeed, the very sense of being an individual agent, the senses of pleasure and anguish derived from daily interchange, and the motive to seek freedom are all premised on a history of relatedness. Invited, then, is first a diminution in the tendency to blame the other or the conditions, and then an increased concern with the ways in which we participate in the conditions deemed oppressive. Further, attention is directed to the broader patterns of relationship that figure in or contribute to the present condition (e.g., economic relationships, person-machine relationships). Finally, consideration must be directed to the alternative forms of relationship into which one would be propelled should "freedom" be achieved. A condition of free and autonomous action, disconnected from the ongoing social world, simply leaves one spinning in the residues of relationships of the past—in the long run potentially incapacitating one from full participation in the unfolding of cultural life. We do not move from the pressures of engagement to freedom but from one set of relational requirements to another.

## Morality as Infinite Conversation

Earlier I questioned whether several centuries of commitment to the idea of moral principles have actually contributed to humane circumstances. Although it would be difficult to draw an affirmative conclusion, we could, in a very rough way, view moral deliberation as superior in its effects on humankind to the force of arms. The use of moral discourse in settling complex problems of conflict and anguish represents, in this sense, a positive step in cultural evolution. However, moral principles also stand as justifications for the most brutal actions—from the Crusades and the Grand Inquisition to the slaying of abortion specialists by pro-life advocates. Further, as we move rapidly into a world in which we daily confront subcultures or civilizations whose moral principles differ from our own, moral principles reach their upper level of efficacy. With the clash of incommensurables, a resort to moral justification typically intensifies the conflict. The "global village" requires a new step in the evolution of cultural resources.

Let us consider the contours of a relational alternative. As we have seen, the relational emphasis favored by much constructionist writing would first reduce the tendency to place moral judgment on the other (or the self). We are, instead, invited to spread the concern to the network of relations from which issues of conflict or wrongdoing arise. But how, on this account, are we to confront conditions of incommensurable moral traditions, cases in which groups find each others' traditions of the good intolerable? In this case, because of its emphasis on the communal construction of the real and the right, a relational view would place the strong emphasis on altering discursive forms. The problem would not be to "settle the issue" of moral superiority, or rationally to adjudicate territories, but to locate means of mingling the discourses, enabling alterior signifiers to play freely—to form new combinations, new metaphors, and ultimately new forms of interdependence.[9]

The important point here is that the relational orientation does not obliterate moral deliberation and a concern with moral principles. To do so would be to eliminate tradition, and without tradition there would be no intelligibility. Rather, the attempt is to respond to situations traditionally favoring a moral judgment, with an invitation to conversation—to a particular form of relationship. Moral principles have the ultimate effect of terminating conversation. One must ultimately lodge one's rationality in an unwarrantable declaration: "This is where I stand." "Beyond this point I cannot go." "This is right, because it is right." In effect, disconnection. In contrast, the relational view urges us as theorists, human scientists, and practitioners to seek ways— multiple ways—of generating integrative conversation. For if we can but join in the construction of such cultural resources, we stand to make a contribution to the expression and peaceful interpolation of multiple voices, in both the culture and the world at large. In my view, such an imaginary is congenial with the deepest hopes of the humanistic tradition.

## Explicating the Social

The attempt here has been to put forward a rudimentary conception of "the social" within the context of a particular discursive tradition and, from the matrix of tensions thereby created, to press this conception toward further articulation. In this way we avoid a priori and context-free commitments and set out to generate the meaning of "social" within a dialogic space. Within the dialogue we stand to open new vistas of intelligibility. We thus began with a vision of the social implicit in much social constructionist writing, one that holds meaning itself to be a byproduct of communal coordination. This orienting commitment was then placed within the context of the liberal humanist tradition, in which the attempt has been to derive foundations for moral action from conceptions of individual agency. Within this context, the constructionist view seems morally vacuous. So as to explore the weaknesses of the liberal tradition, and to counter its critical asser-tions, a constructionist relationalism was set in motion.

As we initially found, various arguments within the constructionist colloquy could satisfactorily undermine both the legitimacy and the intelligibility of moral foundations based on humanistic individualism. These critiques, in turn, closed out certain descriptive and explanatory options for what would become the contrasting account of the social. Specifically, this view of the social could not be based on traditional assumptions of individual interaction (e.g., individual, conscious, self-determining agents coming together to form a social world). With such forms of intelligibility now bracketed, the attempt was to begin the articulation of a relational replacement for individual humanism. In doing so, a view of the social emerged in which:

1. Recourse to individual beings proved necessary, owing to a tradition in which relationships are inherently made up of inde-pendent parts. The question, then, is how at once to participate within this tradition and simultaneously shed the semantic bag-gage that it imposes. By implication, this was done by using the concept of the individual person as a conversational indexical for physical bodies making up a relationship. However, it is simultaneously to recognize that these singular bodies are, in terms of what we take to be human action (as opposed to physical behavior), manifestations of relatedness. By tradition, we take persons to be independent entities, but it is this tradition that is placed in question. Rather, the individual actor is essentially a

relational integer and gains meaning as an actor through the relational process.

2. It proved necessary to reassert a language of "experience" and, by implication, the full array of mental predicates pivotal to the humanist tradition. Again, however, the attempt was to recast the meaning of experience and its cognates. This was done by deobjectification, pragmatization, and indexicalization. That is, mental terms were first cut loose from their putative objects (or referents in a specifically mental universe). Second, such terms were cast as integers within processes of relational pragmatics. Such terms do not refer, then, to processes that generate relationships but are constitutive of relational patterns themselves. Finally, such terms function indexically within relationships (e.g., ongoing conversation) to refer to conditions of relationship ("myself"/"my environment").

In a broad sense, we began with a conception of the social that feeds from the traditional binary of individual-social. That is, the individualist conception was essential to give meaning to the contrary alternative of a radical relationalism. Yet, as the relational theoretic was further elaborated, so did it begin to absorb the language of the individual, recasting individual attributes and processes in terms of a relational ontology. Slowly the binary moorings were cast off. At the same time, we find that the relational ontology permits neither culminating critique nor completion. On its grounds, all critique is born of relationship, and its terms are given meaning within relationship. Critique can furnish no foundations, no transcendent rationality, or no "good arguments" without collaborative assent. To deny the collaborative process would be to remove the possibility for meaning itself. At the same time, the ontology of radical relationship remains forever incomplete. This state of polymorphous contingency is essential, for to objectify and canonize its suppositions would be to remove the language from the dialogic sphere in which its meaning is born and reborn as the conversation moves on. The quest for intransmutability—immortality for the emanations of individual psyche (spirit/mind)—is to approach the void.

## Notes

1. For an extended treatment of social constructionism, see Gergen (1994).

2. For more fully detailed accounts, see Gergen (1994) and Shotter and Gergen (1994).

3. For further critique of the ideology of self-contained individualism, see Sampson (1993).

4. For a full elaboration of this argument, see Sandel (1982).

5. For a more extended treatment of the problems and limits of human rights movements, see Gergen (1995).

6. For a more extended treatment of the incapacity of ethical suppositions to engender the ethical society, see Gergen (1994).

7. For a more extended treatment of this position, see Chapter 11 in Gergen (1994).

8. For a more extended discussion of relational responsibility, see McNamee and Gergen (1995).

9. For an excellent illustration of this pragmatic form of ethical deliberation, see Chasin and Herzig (1994).

# References

Bellah, Robert. 1985. *Habits of the Heart*. Berkeley: University of California Press.

Chasin, Richard, and M. Herzig. 1994. "Creating Systemic Interventions for the Sociopolitical Arena." In *The Global Family Therapist, Integrating the Personal, Professional, and Political*, ed. Barbara Gould and Donald H. DeMuth. Boston: Allyn & Bacon.

Derrida, Jacques. 1976. *Of Grammatology*. Baltimore: Johns Hopkins University Press.

Gergen, Kenneth J. 1994 *Realities and Relationships*. Cambridge, Mass.: Harvard University Press.

———. 1995. "Social Construction and the Transformation of Identity Politics." Paper presented at the New School for Social Research conference on Social Construction, Politics, and the Practice of Psychology, New York.

McNamee, Sheila, and Kenneth J. Gergen. 1995. "Relational responsibility". Unpublished manuscript. University of New Hampshire.

Quine, Willard V.O. 1960. *Word and Object*. Cambridge, Mass.: Harvard University Press.

Sampson, Edward E. 1993. *Celebrating the Other*. Boulder, Colo.: Westview.

Sandel, Michael J. 1982. *Liberalism and the Limits of Justice*. Cambridge: Cambridge University Press.

Sartre, Jean-Paul. 1977. *Existentialism and Humanism*, trans. P. Mairet. Brooklyn: Haskell.

Shotter, John. 1993. *Cultural Politics of Everyday Life*. Toronto: University of Toronto Press.

Shotter, John, and Kenneth J. Gergen. 1994. "Social Construction: Knowledge, Self, Others, and Continuing the Conversation." *Communication Yearbook* 17:3–33.

## Chapter 11

# Life Beyond the Edge of Nature? Or, The Mirage of Society

### Tim Ingold

Are social relations human relations? This is not a question that social anthropologists often ask themselves, perhaps because a positive answer is already presupposed in the very constitution of their discipline. For only if social relations are human relations can their study be an aspect of the study of humanity. Indeed, I suspect that many social anthropologists would find the proposition faintly tautological. Surely, they would declare, the disposition or capacity to form social relations is an essential criterion of what it means to be human. Almost by definition, it seems, social being is human being. Yet if that were really so, what would we make of the social lives of nonhuman creatures? It is surely absurd to claim that there is something peculiarly human about bees because of their complex association in the hive, or that wolves take on an aura of humanity by virtue of their companionship in the pack. By what right, then, do we dignify such patterns of intraspecific interaction by the term 'society'? In extending the notion of sociality to nonhuman kinds, are we merely indulging in anthropomorphic metaphor, calling on our experience of relations in the human world to model those to be found in the world of nature?

A confirmed social anthropologist, such as Meyer Fortes, would respond unequivocally in the affirmative. One cannot but be struck, he writes:

> by the regularity with which anthropomorphic models taken from anthropology are resorted to in studies of e.g. animal mating, parental, and

general social behavior. This is understandable seeing that more is known
by humans about their own behaviour and social life than about animal
behaviour; and the investigators are bound to draw upon this background,
even if only intuitively. (Fortes 1983:1)

But students of animal behavior—ethologists, primatologists, sociobiologists—make a fatal mistake if, having thus modeled animal life in
the image of human society, they proceed to invert the argument,
concluding that society itself has its foundations in naturally evolved
predispositions such as those that motivate associative behavior in
nonhuman species. For society, Fortes declares, could never have
emerged "without the cultural equipment that distinguished man from
the rest of the animal world" (1983:34).

What is critical, in this regard, is not so much the content or source
of the models by which we seek to understand ourselves and other
animals, but rather the fact that—as Gudeman (1986:37) puts it, "humans are modelers." It is the capacity, apparently unique to our
species, to render the world meaningful in terms of representations
that may be both assembled in the mind and communicated verbally to
others, that forms the basis for society in the strict sense. One may
speak metaphorically of the 'societies' of bees and wolves, but, *literally*, society depends on that very transcendence of nature that marks
out the distinctive condition of humanity and is a prerequisite for
objective knowledge and therefore for the practice of science of any
kind. Sociality does not lie in any resemblances between the behavior
of human beings and members of other species but in the distinctive
way in which human beings perceive such resemblances and put them
to work in their knowledge practices. In short, scientists who claim to
observe 'societies' in the world of nature forget that in reality, it is
society that, in raising them to a level over and above the nature
observed, provides them with the platform for their observations.

Now the argument presented in the preceding two paragraphs is that
of a confirmed social anthropologist. But I am *not*, in fact, a confirmed
social anthropologist—or, at least, not any more. I do not believe that
there exists a separate domain of society, beyond the limits of nature,
within which properly human life is lived. The thesis I want to defend
here is precisely the contrary: namely, that the world in which we
dwell is inhabited by beings of manifold kinds, not just human beings,
and that our ideas about the world—including those that go by the
name of science—are fashioned against the background of our active
engagement with its diverse human and nonhuman constituents. I have

come to this conclusion after at least a decade of worrying about how to draw the line between humans and other animals and about how to define the field of relations that could properly be called 'social', as opposed to relations of other kinds. It has been a difficult road to tread, taking me all the way from a view of human uniqueness that, at least for a social anthropologist, was pretty conventional, through an intermediary position that sought to open up the space of social being to other-than-human persons while still upholding the fundamental distinction between the social and the biophysical, to a much more radical view that dispenses altogether with the distinction, at the cost, however, of having to jettison the contemporary biological concept of species as well as the established theory, going back to Darwin, of their evolution (Ingold 1988, 1994, 1995).

In what follows I want to retrace something of this intellectual journey. I begin by supposing, for the sake of argument, that social relations are indeed uniquely human, and that social life is conducted against the background of an external world of nature. I show how this assumption is reflected in conventional ideas about production, history, environment, socialization, language, and, of course, social interaction itself. Next, I shall explain the reasoning that led me to adopt the intermediate position, which would have the effect of opening up the lives of nonhuman animals to the kind of humanistic inquiry previously reserved for members of our own species. Only subsequently did it dawn on me that the only way to achieve a coherent biosocial synthesis that would not simply replicate the old dualism of society and nature was through a radical overhaul of evolutionary theory itself. What I have written since has been largely motivated by this agenda, and in the final part of this chapter I shall spell out some of its implications for the way we think about people and their relationships. I am still not sure where it will eventually lead, and what I present here as a conclusion is bound to turn out, in retrospect, to be yet another intermediary position on the way to somewhere else. Life is an open-ended business, and that observation must apply to my own thinking and writing as much as to anything else that people do in the world.

## Society against Nature

Imagine a being that, unlike all others, is to be understood as something more than a mere organism. An animal such as, say, the bee or

wolf is all organism: it has no properties that could not be comprehended within an exhaustive biological account of its nature and
functioning. But the being I have in mind cannot be comprehended
within such an account; it is, rather, raised above the run of other
living things by a factor—call it mind or self-awareness—that can be
found not by external observation but only by the knowledge we have
of ourselves as persons with specific identities, feelings, memories,
and intentions. For it is such beings that we imagine ourselves to be,
and it is by that very factor that we measure the scope of our humanity.

Of course we have bodies too, since it is only by way of our
bodies—through the sensations they receive and the movements they
deliver—that we are able to make contact with the external world. But
it is the unique predicament of *human* being, as one philosopher has
put it (Collins 1985), to be 'body plus'. We are, according to this
image, constitutionally divided creatures, existing simultaneously as
organisms with working bodies and as persons with active minds. In
the former capacity, humans are situated in the world of nature and
are necessarily caught up in a matrix of relations with other biotic and
abiotic components of the environment. But bodies, on their own,
'cannot be said to be capable of *acting*'. To be able to act, the body
must be topped up with "some psychological identity, the possibility
of which essentially depends on social relations" (Collins 1985:73–6).
Thus completed, as persons, human beings can convert nature into the
object of relations among themselves, relations that are said to be
constitutive of the distinct domain of society. Social life, therefore,
appears to go on beyond the limits of nature, in a separate, intersubjective world of its own.

Whatever one might think of this way of imagining humanity and
social life—and as I have already indicated, it is one with which I am no
longer comfortable—there is no doubt that it has been extraordinarily
pervasive and influential in the social sciences in general, and in social
anthropology in particular. I would now like to chart briefly the way
this influence has worked to shape a number of other concepts that
have long been part of the regular stock-in-trade of modern anthropological thought. I begin with the concept of *production*.

Like all other animals, human beings have to eat if they are to live.
It is widely supposed, however, that in the provisioning of humans,
the means of subsistence do not pass directly from hand to mouth but
take a detour through society. As Marx and Engels declared over a
century ago, it is in actually producing their food, rather than simply
gathering or collecting it ready-made in nature, that humans distinguish

themselves from the rest of the animal kingdom (Marx and Engels 1977:42). The notion of production, here, has a double connotation—of appropriation and transformation (see, for example, Cook 1973:31). To appropriate is to take hold of some portion of living nature in such a way as to make it the object of relations among persons; to transform it is to alter it from its naturally given state in accordance with a design or plan that issues from a superior source in society. Nonhuman animals may literally take hold of their quarry, whether with tooth or claw, but they do not thereby convert it into property; they may also, through their activities, wreak transformative effects on the environment, but they do not do so intentionally. They have no conception of their task. Human beings alone are said to produce, since they confront nature as a domain of raw materiality external to their socially constituted selves. In short, couched within the duality of society and nature, production figures as the work of social agency against a natural resistance.

Now in their transforming action on nature, their production, human beings are supposed also to transform the relations among themselves that are constitutive of the form of society. And in so doing they make themselves a *history*. This is the second of the key concepts I want to take up. We are, of course, accustomed to speaking of the natural history of animals and plants, but human history is widely acknowledged to be a different matter altogether. It is History, as Maurice Godelier puts it (1989:63), 'with a capital *H*'. We are led to understand that (capital *H*) History exceeds (small *h*) history by the very same factor by which the person exceeds the organism. That is, it comprises a series of changes over time in the forms of human subjectivity—in structures of perception and cognition, in patterns of awareness and response, in the understanding of self and others—that have left the organism virtually untouched. In the course of this History, humans have spread to every habitable region of the earth, great empires have risen and fallen, and developments in science and technology have placed in the hands of at least some humans instruments of control and weapons of destruction of unparalleled magnitude. Through all of this, however, basic human nature is assumed to have remained much as it was in the Stone Age, the product of an evolutionary adaptation to the conditions of life faced by ancestral hunter-gatherers in Pleistocene environments hundreds of thousands of years ago, in the days before History even began. One prominent psychologist has recently gone so far as to define history as "a sequence of changes through which a species passes while remaining biologically stable" (Premack 1994:

350). The very possibility of history, in this sense, presupposes a dimension of existence beyond the purely biological—a dimension that, as we have seen, is commonly identified with humanity itself.

It is somewhat paradoxical that human nature should be considered to be so fixed and immune from the effects of history, when these effects on the nature that surrounds us, in the *environment*, are apparent for all to see. The paradox is resolved, up to a point, by attributing the formal specifications of human nature to an interior program, nowadays known as the genotype. According to the rule first enunciated by Weismann, at the close of the nineteenth century, there can be no reverse influence of the developing organism on its hereditary endowment, thus rendering impossible the so-called 'Lamarckian' inheritance of acquired characteristics. Weismann's barrier, which is fundamental to the structure of modern evolutionary theory, effectively insulates the genotype from the direct impact of historical experience (Ingold 1990:212–3). However, when we turn to consider the human transformation of external nature, as in the construction of the built environment, the relation between form and substance is inverted. Far from providing the form, in the shape of a genetic program, nature furnishes the substance, upon which are imposed forms—cultural or ideational rather than genetic—whose source lies in the exterior domain of human society. The built environment, as it were, wears its forms on its material surface rather than hidden within, and it consequently bears the cumulative imprint of a changeful sequence of historical subjectivities. Surveying the world around us, we see nature not in its pristine state but modified to varying degrees through the inscription of cultural design. That is why we are inclined to speak of buildings, tools, and other artifacts as objects of 'material culture' rather than of nature, even though the stuff of which they are made is intrinsically identical to that which may be found in environments untainted by human activity.

Turning from the nature that surrounds us to the nature within us, the metaphors change. Human nature is conceived not as a surface to be molded but as a receptacle to be filled; correspondingly, culture is understood to consist not in forms to be imposed but in content to be acquired. The acquisition of cultural content is classically described, in the social science literature, as a process of *socialization*. The child is depicted, in this process, as the passive recipient of authorized knowledge descending on him or her from society. So far as I know, the notion of socialization has never been adduced with reference to the young of any other species. The reason, once again, is plain: if there is more to the person than a 'mere organism', then some additional process must be invoked, beyond that of the development of the organism in its environment, to account for the acquisition of this superorganic increment. Although we might agree that the baby born of human parents is a human being itself and can never be anything else, its essential humanity—its potential to become a person—will remain unrealized so long as it is left to learn, as are the young of many other species, solely through observation and imitation. Children, it is supposed, have also to be educated in the moral norms, intellectual achievements, and aesthetic standards of their society. The logic of the argument requires, however, that the process of education be clearly distinguished from the historical drama of social life. For only when novices have been thus equipped with the rudiments of personhood, and thereby 'prepared' for their entry upon the social stage, are they in a position to play their part in the drama itself.

In the conversion of human babies into fully formed social persons, nothing is held to be more critical than the acquisition of *language*. This is a complex topic that I can only touch on here. I want to make just one point, which stems from the observation that every theory that lists language among the essential attributes of humanity also draws a clear-cut boundary between speech and nonverbal communication. And whether the theoretical concern is with the evolutionary origins of language or with its ontogenetic development in the life history of every individual, one invariably encounters the notion of a 'breakthrough', in which the boundary is crossed. My point is that this boundary is none other than the now familiar division between nature and society. Signaling by means of manual, vocal, or facial gestures is common throughout the animal kingdom, as well as in the communication of prelinguistic human infants. But the meanings of these signals are inseparable from the material effects they bring about in the particular contexts of their production. In many cases these effects assume the imperative force of a command, moving those who attend to them to respond in particular ways. The meaning of the spoken word, however, is held to derive from its attachment to a concept, and concepts are the building blocks of comprehensive mental representations (Ingold 1993:452–3). To have made the transition to language is therefore to be in a position to enter that traffic in representations that, in the literature of social science, is known as the 'social construction of reality' (Berger and Luckmann 1966). No longer bound, like other creatures, to an unreflective life in nature, the speaker of language can join the discursive realm of society.

This brings me, finally, to the very notion of *social interaction*. As I have already shown, with human beings conceived as 'body plus', this interaction is understood as an engagement of subjects rather than objects. Thus, according to the developmental psychologists Colwyn Trevarthen and Katerina Logotheti, "human cultural intelligence is founded on a level of engagement of minds, or intersubjectivity, such as no other species has or can acquire"(1989:167). Intersubjectivity, here, figures as the constitutive quality of the social domain as against the object world of nature, a domain open to human beings but not to nonhuman kinds. The common predicament in which subjects find themselves is one of having to make sense, in their discourse, of a material reality from which they are excluded (an exclusion that follows logically from the separation of mind and nature). In their attempts to do so, their thought becomes entangled in ever denser and more richly textured "webs of significance" (Geertz 1973:5). As social beings they are destined to remain permanently suspended in such semantic webs, while their bodies continue to be firmly anchored in the material relations of the object world—relations that may furnish metaphorical resources for social cognition but that are, by the same token, partitioned off from it (see Johnson 1987). The bodily movements of people, as they go about their multiple and interlocking tasks, may serve to *express* what Geertz (1973:19) calls "the curve of a social discourse," but the latter does not *subsist* in the movements themselves. Social life goes on, according to this scenario, and indeed will always go on, beyond the edge of nature; society floats like a mirage above the road we tread in our material life. Is it then, like the mirage, all an illusion?

## The Humanity of Animals

Let me emphasize once again that the picture I have presented up to now, founded on the dualism of the human being as both organism and person, is one that I now consider to be profoundly misguided. I admit that my presentation of this picture is but a thumbnail sketch of a vast literature, and that as such it is simplified almost to the point of caricature. Moreover, I have really set it up only for the purpose of knocking it down. Before doing so, however, and as a kind of interlude, I would like to turn to what I have called my 'intermediate position' and to outline the reasoning that led me to adopt it. The problem I confronted is this: if what makes human beings human is some essential quality of subjectivity, self-awareness, or personhood, then 'being human' can scarcely be the same sort of thing as 'being chimpanzee' or 'being whale'—or even, for that matter, 'being a human being'.

Imagine the world two million years hence: an optimistic scenario in which chimpanzees and whales have miraculously survived the depredations inflicted on them by the twentieth century humans, and have gone on to develop linguistic capabilities and a reflexive self-awareness of their own. Indeed, whales, for all we know, are already there; as for chimpanzees, some researchers have suggested that it would only require the systematic application of selection pressures favoring such capabilities, over a reasonably prolonged period, to 'fix' genetically what has already been demonstrated as a behavioral possibility (Borchert and Zihlman 1990). Would our whales and chimpanzees then have crossed the threshold to humanity? Biologically, this is an impossibility, for biological taxa are defined genealogically, and phyletic lines, once they have diverged at or beyond the species level, can never recombine. But there is no a priori reason why they should not achieve the condition of being human, as defined earlier. And, conversely, just as we cannot rule out the possible humanity of nonhuman animals, nor can we exclude the possibility that beings that are biologically human, belonging to the taxon *Homo sapiens*, might lack the attributes of humanity. Severely autistic children, for example, or people such as stroke victims with crippling defects of speech, memory, or feeling would by no means meet the normal criteria by which the human condition is defined. But they are still human beings, born to human parents.

We seem to be caught in a dilemma. Whatever we take to be the criteria of essential humanity, either some nonhumans are let in or some human beings are left out (Hull 1984:35). The reason for the dilemma is simple. Biological taxa are not natural kinds, so that they cannot be expected to conform to any essentialist system of classification. Indeed, most biologists reject any appeal to essentialism in the definition of species, as fundamentally contrary to the Darwinian principles that lie at the core of their science. The puzzle is why they should nevertheless continue to search, against all the odds, for an essential specification of humanity. And the answer is that the essence they are looking for is a precondition for the project of natural science and for that objectification of nature that allows us to recognize organisms as belonging to species in the first place. Humanity can appear as a species of nature only to a mind that can detach itself from its bearings in the material world. Or, to put it bluntly, you have to be able to set yourself apart *from* nature to see yourself as part *of* it. This is the central paradox of Western science.

My provisional solution to this paradox was simply to disaggregate the biological species, *Homo sapiens*, and the existential condition, of primary intersubjectivity, both of which have conventionally been conflated under the single rubric of humanity, and to regard the project of anthropology as an exploration of the relation between the two: between humankind and its social conditions of existence (Ingold 1994). I did not, at this stage, seek to dissolve the boundary between the mind and the physical world, or between society and nature. It seemed that a threshold had still to be crossed for any creature that would enter the world of meaning. But you did not have to be a human being, I thought, to make the crossing. In principle, nonhuman animals, too, could experience the 'body plus' predicament, could produce, have a history, intentionally shape their environments, educate their young, communicate discursively, and engage with one another on an intersubjective level. By the same token, it seemed to me that the kinds of approaches developed within the humanities and social sciences for interpreting the knowledge and practices of human beings could be applicable to nonhuman animals as well (Ingold 1994: 24). I am no longer satisfied with this solution, for reasons that will become clear in the next section. However, it does point to a matter of some importance that goes back to the question with which I began, of whether social relations are human relations.

If the mark of the social lies in the personal qualities of agency and intentionality, feeling, memory, and speech that are brought to bear in the formation of relationships, and if these qualities are attributed—as they are in the tradition of Western thought—to the intrinsic capacities of a particular kind of being, known as human, then the answer must be 'yes'. We might perhaps want to make an exception when it comes to our closest animal companions: it appears to me, for example, that my pet dog is a character with intentions and feelings of his own, who knows me well and responds intelligently to the sounds of my voice. Yet companion animals may be taken as the exception that proves the rule, for it seems that we can enter into social relations with nonhuman animals only to the extent that, through close association, something of our humanity has 'rubbed off' on them, transforming them almost into honorary members of the human species. Indeed, cynics might argue that in treating pets as persons, we are indulging in an elaborate anthropomorphic pretense.[1] From there, however, it is but a short step to the conclusion that social relations are human relations because they are with individuals who belong, whether in reality or in the imagination, to the same species as we do. To take this step is, in effect, to convert what was a purely contingent aspect of social relations—the species membership of participants—into their defining feature. Having taken it, the path is clear to extend the concept of the social to cover the interactions that any kind of creature, human or nonhuman, may have with its conspecifics. For me, social relations are human relations because I happen to be a human being. If I were an ant, my social relations would be with other ants, not with humans!

It is in just this derivative sense, connoting relations among conspecifics, that the notion of society has been taken up in the writings of sociobiologists and other students of animal behavior. Consider the following definition, from the text that launched sociobiology as a brave new synthesis: "*Society:* A group of individuals belonging to the same species and organized in a cooperative manner" (Wilson 1980:322). Following Wilson's lead, sociobiologists have made it their business to describe and explain the varieties of social behavior across every branch of the animal kingdom. And they insist that human sociality, for all its distinctiveness and complexity, is but one variant of a widespread phenomenon whose study should therefore represent a particular speciality within a much broader, more inclusive science. That science, of course, is evolutionary biology. But whatever successes sociobiologists may have had in accounting for patterns of cooperative or altruistic behavior, in terms of its consequences for reproductive fitness, their explanations take us nowhere in understanding those qualities—of intentionality, sentience, memory, and speech—that seem to us to be so central to the experience of social being. Indeed, sociobiological explanations carry force only to the extent that these qualities can be relegated to the status of epiphenomenal byproducts of more fundamental, behavior-generating programs. It is ironic to reflect that the identification of society with the domain of intraspecific interactions, which underwrites the sociobiological enterprise, came about only thanks to an original assumption, which sociobiologists categorically reject, that society is the unique preserve of humankind.

Sociobiologists are not, of course, the only people to have claimed that nonhuman animals can enjoy a social life. The belief is widely reported, for example, in the ethnography (with which I happen to be familiar) of northern native hunters, that animals form communities of their own, much like human ones (e.g., Tanner 1979:136–8, on the Mistassini Cree). But for these hunting peoples, the sociality of animals owes nothing to the fact that they are of the same species. Animals are social not because they cooperate with others of their own kind but because they are thought to reveal, in their actions, the same qualities of intentionality, feeling, memory, and speech that humans do. A significant implication, as Tanner points out, is that "social interaction between humans and animals is made possible" (1979:137–8). One does not have to regard animals—as people in Western societies sometimes regard their pets—as pseudohumans if one is to have relationships with them. If, however, social relations so readily override the boundaries of species, as these hunters maintain, then the sociobiological restriction of sociality to relations among *conspecifics* would make no sense at all. For them, intersubjectivity, not intraspecificity, is the mark of the social.

It might be argued, following Gudeman (1986:43–4), that the difference between the sociobiologists and the hunters is that the former model the domain of human relations in terms of an image of nature as material, whereas the latter model the animal world in terms of an image of humanity as intentional. Such an argument, however, remains premised on a fundamental opposition between the intentional worlds of human subjects and the object world of material things—or, in a word, between society and nature. In the following section I will suggest how this opposition may itself be dissolved. The result, as I shall show, is to leave no subset of relationships that could be regarded as properly and distinctively 'social'.

## On Growth and Form

I began by imagining a being that is something more than a mere organism, whose nature somehow exceeds the biological. And I suggested that this is how we imagine ourselves to be, while deliberately remaining vague about who 'we' actually are. Suffice it to say that assertions to this effect are legion in the literature of academic social science and above all in my own discipline of social anthropology. I now wish to put my neck on the block by stating categorically that the view of the human being as one part organism, one part person, is simply false. Human beings are indeed all organism, just as are living beings of every other kind. But it is equally misleading to suggest, speaking of nonhuman beings, that they are 'merely' organisms. For there is nothing in the least 'mere' about being an organism. It is precisely here that the trouble lies, for the image of the organism bequeathed by modern biological science is a peculiarly impoverished one. Organic life is depicted as a passive rather than an active process, in which the organism reacts according to a genetically prespecified program to the given conditions of its environment. With this view, personal powers—of awareness, agency and intentionality—can form no part of the organism *as such*, but must necessarily be 'added on' as capacities not of body but of mind, capacities that Western thought, as we have seen, has traditionally reserved for human beings. Even today, now that the possibility of nonhuman animal awareness has arisen as a legitimate topic of scientific speculation, the basic dualism of mind and body is retained—for the question is phrased as one about the existence of animal *minds* (Griffin 1984). Consciousness, then, is understood as the life of the mind, as distinct from that of the organism to which it belongs.

I take a different view of organic life, as active rather than passive, the creative unfolding of a field of relations within which beings emerge and take on the particular forms they do, each in relation to the other. Life, in this view, is not the revelation of prespecified forms but the very process in which forms are generated (Ingold 1990:215).[2] It follows, however, that there can be no specification of the form of an organism that is independent of the developmental context within which it comes into being. Now the possibility of such a context-independent specification is an essential condition for Darwinian theory, since it is this specification—the genotype—that is said to undergo evolution through changes in the frequency of its information-bearing elements. Moreover, it is in terms of the genotypic specification that organisms are assigned to species. Thus, according to orthodox theory, species evolve as genotypes change. If, on the other hand, as I maintain (with Oyama 1985), organic form is an emergent property of developmental systems, then the evolution of form lies not in changing gene frequencies but in the unfolding of a total relational field. And in this process, organisms can play their part as producers as well as products of their own evolution, contributing through their actions to the environmental conditions for both their own development and for that of other organisms to which they relate. Every being, as it is caught up in the process and carries it forward, arises as an undivided center of awareness and agency: an enfoldment, at some particular nexus within it, of the generative potential that is life itself. We do not, then, have to think of mind or consciousness as something added on to the life of organisms, to account for their creative involvement in the world. Rather, what we may call mind is the cutting edge of the life process itself, the ever-moving front of what Whitehead (1929:314) called a "creative advance into novelty".

Taking this view as my starting point, I should now like to return to the key concepts that I introduced earlier—namely, production, history, environment, socialization, language, and social interaction—to see where an alternative approach might lead us.

When Engels (1934:308) declared that "the most that the animal can achieve is to *collect;* man *produces*," he wrote from the perspective of one whose experience lay in manufacturing industry and for whom the notion of production would have referred in the first place to the act of 'making things'—in other words, to the construction of artificial objects through a process of transforming natural raw materials. Had his background been in agriculture rather than industry, he might have recognized the peculiarity of applying such a notion to the production of food. For as every farmer knows, agricultural produce is not made—it is grown. To understand production as a process of growth is to go back to a much older sense of the term, though one that is still in common use. To produce, in this latter sense, is to 'bring forth'. Farmers, thus, assist in bringing forth the yield of the land. The work that they do, in such activities as field clearance, fencing, planting, weeding, and so on, or in tending their livestock, does not literally make plants and animals but rather establishes the environmental conditions for their growth and development. Different regimes of plant and animal husbandry can, I think, best be distinguished in terms of the ways in which human beings involve themselves in establishing these conditions for growth. To grasp this idea, all that is required is a simple change of perspective: instead of thinking about plants or animals as part of the natural environment for human beings, we have to think of humans and their activities as part of the environment for plants and animals.

But behind this switch lies a point of much more fundamental significance. If human beings, on the one hand, and plants and animals on the other, can be regarded alternately as components of each other's environments, then we can no longer think of the former as inhabiting a social world of their own, over and above the world of nature in which the lives of all other living things are contained. Rather, both humans and the animals and plants on which they depend for a livelihood must be regarded as fellow participants in the *same* world. And the forms that all these creatures take are neither given in advance nor imposed from above, but emerge within the relational contexts of this mutual involvement. In short, human beings do not, in their productive activity, transform the world; instead, they play their part, alongside beings of other kinds, in the world's transformation of itself. It is to this process of self-transformation that I refer by the concept of *growth*.

What becomes, then, of the notion of history? More particularly, how can we continue to uphold the distinction between (small h) natural history and the (capital H) History of humanity? It is commonly supposed that whereas the events of history just happen, those of History are 'made' or authored by human beings themselves. "The essence of the distinction between human history and natural history," wrote Marx (with acknowledgment to the *New Science* of Giambattista Vico), "is that the former is the work of man and the latter is not" (1930:392, n. 2). Let us suppose, however, that this work consists in growing rather than making. It is clear that human beings play their part in establishing the conditions of growth not only for plants and animals but also for fellow humans. Indeed, we could reasonably define human history as the process in which the people of each generation, through their life activities, furnish the developmental contexts within which their successors grow to maturity. Defined in this way, however, human history turns out to be but one part of an evolutionary process that, as I have argued earlier, is going on throughout the organic world (Ingold 1995:203). The conventional distinction between history and evolution (or between human History and natural history) is thus dissolved.

The consequences of this dissolution are startling. For it puts paid to the idea that throughout the course of history, conceived as a *social* process, human beings have remained *biologically* the same, universally equipped with a set of structures and dispositions established through a process of evolutionary adaptation in the Pleistocene era. We have to recognize that human differences are indeed biological, in the sense that the particular skills, capacities, and dispositions that people have brought to bear in their lives, in different times and places, are developmentally embodied—in specific aspects of neurology, musculature, even anatomy—through the experience of growing up in particular environments. There is, then, no essential form of humanity, no way of saying what a human being *is*, apart from the manifold ways in which human beings *become* (Ingold 1991:359). I should stress that this is not an argument for the priority of nurture over nature. Most biologists vehemently insist that the nature/nurture opposition is obsolete, yet it obstinately refuses to go away precisely because it is reproduced in the founding assumptions of their theory (Oyama

1985:26). This theory, as we have seen, depends upon the notion that the development of any organism—human or nonhuman—is underwritten by a preexisting (i.e., genotypic) specification of form. In denying the reality of the human genotype I do not mean to suggest that human beings are shaped instead by the given conditions of their environment. My point is that the metaphor of shaping, with its implication that form already exists, whether in the genes or in the environment, as a template, program or design prior to its realization in the material, is inappropriate to describe the process of growth by which the characteristics and capacities of persons are constituted in the course of their lives.

This is no less true with regard to the processes of formation of the environment. I have shown how, in the conventional account, the environment stands as substance to the historical forms of culture, which in turn stand as content to the ahistorical form of human nature. In this account, every environment is sequentially shaped and reshaped through the imprint of one scheme of mental representations after another, each reshaping covering over or obliterating the one before. The material surface of nature is thus supposed to present itself as a palimpsest for the inscription of cultural form. My argument suggests, to the contrary, that the forms of environmental objects, like the forms of organisms themselves, are not superimposed upon a natural substrate but rather emerge in and through a process of growth. Or, to put it in another way, they are crystallizations of activity within a relational field. To grasp this point, one need only think of all the activity that goes on, for example, in building a house. There may have been a building plan, but as a concrete presence in the environment, the house arises from the work of its builders, not from the plan. Nor is the building ever complete, for as long as the house is *there* it will inevitably be caught up in relations with its surroundings, both human and nonhuman. (It is worth recalling that every human house contains a great many more nonhuman inhabitants than we normally see or care to know about, and that their impact upon its developing form can be far from negligible.)

More generally, environments are continually coming into being through the activities of the creatures, human and nonhuman, whose environments they are (Ingold 1992:50). This is a point, however, that tends to be obscured by a pervasive opposition, heavily institutionalized in Western society, between *design* and *implementation*. By attributing form to prior design, we privilege the intellectual process of reason over the process of our bodily engagement with the environment, thus denying the creativity of that very process wherein forms actually come into existence. It is the same in Darwinian biology, in which every organism is seen as the incarnation of a prefigured solution to a particular design problem—though the solution is attributed, in this case, to natural selection rather than rational choice.

What I have to say about socialization follows, quite naturally, from what I have already said about production, history, and the formation of the environment. Children, too, are 'grown.' And the specific contribution of their elders is not to pass on a ready-made body of context-free information, as in the classical model of cultural transmission, but rather to set up the developmental contexts in which novices can acquire their own embodied skills and dispositions. Three points follow from this. First, there is no way in which the socialization process can be separated from the development of the human organism in its environment. Second, although senior people may take the view that their role is to teach the established norms and values of their society to its younger members, what children actually learn are skills of coping with the situations that arise in everyday life—including those in which teachers are prominently involved (Lave and Wenger 1991:97). These skills may be in part improvised, in part derived from the observation and imitation of others. But, contrary to the impression conveyed in standard psychological accounts of enculturation or social learning, observation is no more a matter of having information copied into one's head than is imitation the mechanical implementation of received instructions. To observe is to actively attend to the practices of others; to imitate is to align that attention to the movement of one's own practical orientation toward the environment. This means, third, that the knowledge of practitioners is not so much 'passed on' or 'handed down' as continually regenerated and renegotiated within the interactive contexts of learning (Bruner 1986: 123). Learning is not, then, preparatory to participation in social life; they are rather two sides of the same coin: on the one side, the enfoldment of relations with others in the experience and sensibility of the self; on the other side, the unfolding of the self in situated action. From birth and throughout life we continue to learn, even as we act.

Turning to language, this view of development leads me to reject the conventional wisdom that words differ from nonverbal gestures in that they take their meanings from concepts in the mind rather than from the specific contexts of their production in the world. Both spoken words and other gestures are, of course, rich in meaning, and in any situation of learning the novice will listen to what people say and watch what they do. But there is no 'reading' of words or gestures that is not part of the novice's practical engagement with his or her environment. Far from carrying meanings *into* contexts of interaction, words—like gestures—gather their meanings from the contexts of activities and relationships in which they are in play. Speaking, in short, is an action whose meaning, like that of any other performance, lies in the effects it secures in the world. But supposing that you, the reader, were to accept this view, you might still want to object that these effects must be limited to other human beings who, being speakers themselves, are also capable of being *moved* by speech, as distinct from nonhuman entities that are, in the words of Kenneth Burke, "by nature alien to purely linguistic orders of motivation" (1969:42). Does this not mark out a sphere of distinctively human interaction that we could legitimately call social? If it does, then how are we to understand apparently anomalous situations in which people appear to talk to animals and plants? Conventionally, such situations are labeled (by us) as cases of magical performance.

Bronislaw Malinowski, in his classic work on the Trobriand Islanders, *Coral Gardens and Their Magic*, offers this wonderfully pithy summary of what goes on in magical performance: "words which are meant for things that have no ears fall upon ears they are not meant for" (1935:241). His point was that magical incantations, although supposed to exert a direct effect on the natural objects to which they were addressed, actually worked their effects on any human listeners within earshot, and that it was in terms of these latter effects that the real power of magic had to be understood. But taking Malinowski's observation at face value, it would seem that the significant distinction is not between human persons and nonhuman things but rather between beings with ears and beings without. One is reminded of the classical Roman author, Varro, who distinguished among slaves, domestic animals, and inanimate instruments on the grounds that the first were 'vocal', the second 'semi-vocal', and the third 'mute' (Tapper 1988:59, n. 3). The animal kingdom is, of course, replete with species that employ vocal communication and whose sense of hearing is often highly developed: individuals of these species can and do respond, in more or less intentional ways, to human calls. If there is anything odd about the sort of performance designated as 'magical', it is that action is presented in a sensory register alien to that of the being addressed in it.

Are we to conclude, then, that social interactions are interactions among *hearing* beings? Such a restriction would seem both arbitrary and absurd. It would, for example, exclude the deaf. And even for people with normal hearing, it would artificially isolate one modality, the vocal-auditory, from all the other modalities of action, which may just as well involve body posture, manual gesture, facial expression, touch, or all at once. Just consider the potential for tactile modulation of the simple handshake! There is no necessary reason, therefore, why the domain of the social should be open only to 'beings with ears', let alone to *human* beings in particular. Following this line of argument to its logical conclusion, it would appear that the scope of social interaction should be broadened from the domain of relations among human beings themselves to embrace as well their relations with animals, plants, and all the other kinds of agencies that inhabit the dwelt-in world. It is a world, if you will, not of intersubjectivity but of *interagentivity*. The different kinds of beings that inhabit this world have different sensibilities and capabilities of action, and in our dealings with them we ordinarily adopt those sensory registers that are appropriate in each case. But there is no register that escapes the domain of our sensory involvement in our environment, no discourse that does not subsist in the process of our bodily dwelling. Thus, if some relations are social, then all are, and all life would be social life. What need have we, then, for a concept of the social at all?

## Conclusion

Starting from the conventional social anthropological position that social relations *are* human relations, I moved on to the rather more qualified position that although social relations are human in an *existential* sense, they may nevertheless be open to beings of nonhuman kinds. I have ended up, however, by dissolving the very category of the social. In truth, there are as many different kinds of relationship as there are beings in the environment of an agent, but the differences are relative, not absolute. Imagine a continuum, on which might be placed the knapper's relation with flint, the potter's with clay, the basketmaker's with willow, the gatherer's with forest fruits, the hunter's with animal prey, the horticulturalist's with vegetables, the herdsman's with cattle, the master's with his slave, and the mother's with her child. To be sure, each of these relations will be qualitatively different and will call for distinctive skills and sensibilities, but it is quite impossible to determine any final cut-off point, as we move from a person's relationships with other humans, animals, plants, and apparently inanimate objects, beyond which we can say, without doubt, that we are no longer dealing with a relationship between persons in society but with one between a person and a thing in nature. In every case, whatever we do *to* others is embedded in the context of our relationships *with* them.

I am not, of course, the first to suggest that a concept of the social is something we can do without, but unlike many of my predecessors, my purpose is not to deny the reality of human relationships. It is rather to re-embed these relationships within the continuum of organic life. One cannot get rid of a troublesome dichotomy, such as that between nature and society, simply by collapsing one side into the other. It makes no more sense to assert that human life is suspended in webs of symbolic meaning than it does to claim that it is "entangled in the message of DNA" (Winterhalder and Smith 1992:19). To be alive and in the world is already to be committed to a certain set of relations with constituents of the surrounding environment, and these, in turn, provide the foundation for all our activities, even those that go by the name of 'thinking'. And with this I return, finally, to the question in my title. Is there some region beyond the edge of nature, in which human beings live distinctively social lives? If, as Matt Cartmill (1993:244) puts it, "the edge of nature is a hallucination," then the answer must be 'no'. Understood as a domain of incorporeal relationships overhanging the biophysical world, 'society' is indeed a mirage. But that is not my point. I have rather set out to refute the idea that behind the domain of real, embodied relationships lies a residual biophysicality—a world of discrete, particulate entities and events—that could be called 'nature'. The illusion is to suppose that a world so conceived could harbor any kind of life at all.

### Notes

1. I should also own up to a pretense. As a matter of fact, I do not keep a dog and never have done.
2. This, of course, was the major thesis of D'Arcy Thompson, in his classic work of 1917, *On Growth and Form*, after which I have deliberately entitled this section (Thompson 1961).

### References

Berger, Peter, and Thomas Luckmann. 1966. *The Social Construction of Reality*. Harmondsworth: Penguin.

Borchert, Catherine M., and Adrienne L. Zihlman. 1990. "The Ontogeny and Phylogeny of Symbolizing." Pp. 15–44 in *The Life of Symbols*, ed. Mary LeCron Foster and Lucy J. Botscharow. Boulder, Colo.: Westview Press.

Bruner, Jerome S. 1986. *Actual Minds, Possible Worlds*. Cambridge, Mass.: Harvard University Press.

Burke, Kenneth. 1969. *A Rhetoric of Motives*. Berkeley: University of California Press.

Cartmill, Matt. 1993. *A View to a Death in the Morning: Hunting and Nature through History*. Cambridge, Mass.: Harvard University Press.

Collins, Steven. 1985. "Categories, Concepts or Predicaments? Remarks on Mauss's use of Philosophical Terminology." Pp. 46–82 in *The Category of the Person: Anthropology, Philosophy, History*, ed. Michael Carrithers, Steven Collins, and Steven Lukes. Cambridge: Cambridge University Press.

Cook, Scott. 1973. "Production, Ecology and Economic Anthropology: Notes towards an Integrated Frame of Reference." *Social Science Information* 12: 25–52.

Engels, Friedrich. 1934. *Dialectics of Nature*, trans. from German by Clemens Dutt. Moscow: Progress.

Fortes, Meyer. 1983. *Rules and the Emergence of Society*. Royal Anthropological Institute Occasional Paper 39. London: RAI.

Geertz, Clifford. 1973. *The Interpretation of Cultures*. New York: Basic Books.

Godelier, Maurice. 1989. "Incest taboo and the evolution of society." Pp. 63–92 in *Evolution and its Influence*, ed. Alan Grafen. Oxford: Clarendon Press.

Griffin, Donald. 1984. *Animal Thinking*. Cambridge, Mass.: Harvard University Press.

Gudeman, Stephen. 1986. *Economics as Culture*. London: Routledge & Kegan Paul.

Hull, David. 1984. "Historical entities and historical narratives." Pp. 17–42 in *Minds, Machines and Evolution*, ed. Christopher Hookway. Cambridge: Cambridge University Press.

Ingold, Tim. 1988. "The Animal in the Study of Humanity." Pp. 84–99 in *What Is an Animal?*, ed. Tim. Ingold. London: Unwin Hyman.

———. 1990. "An Anthropologist Looks at Biology." *Man* 25(2): 208–29.

———. 1991. "Becoming Persons: Consciousness and Sociality in Human Evolution." *Cultural Dynamics* 4(3): 355–76.

———. 1992. "Culture and the Perception of the Environment." Pp. 39–56 in *Bush Base, Forest Farm: Culture, Environment and Development*, ed. Elizabeth Croll and David Parkin. London: Routledge.

———. 1993. "Technology, Language, Intelligence: A Reconsideration of Basic Concepts." Pp. 429–45 in *Tools, Language and Cognition in Human Evolution*, ed. Kathleen R. Gibson and Tim Ingold. Cambridge: Cambridge University Press.

———. 1994. "Humanity and Animality. Pp. 14–32 in *Companion Encyclopedia of Anthropology: Humanity, Culture and Social Life*, ed. Tim Ingold. London: Routledge, pp. 14–32.

———. 1995. " 'People like Us': The Concept of the Anatomically Modern Human." *Cultural Dynamics* 7(2): 187–214.

Johnson, Mark. 1987. *The Body in the Mind*. Chicago: Chicago University Press.

Lave, Jean, and Etienne Wenger. 1991. *Situated Learning: Legitimate Peripheral Participation*. Cambridge: Cambridge University Press.

Malinowski, Bronislaw. 1935. *Coral Gardens and Their Magic*. London: Allen & Unwin.

Marx, Karl. 1930. *Capital*. Vol. I, trans. Eden and Cedar Paul from 4th German ed. of *Das Kapital* (1890). London: Dent.

Marx, Karl and Friedrich Engels. 1977. *The German Ideology*, ed. C. J. Arthur. London: Lawrence & Wishart.

Oyama, Susan. 1985. *The Ontogeny of Information: Developmental Systems and Evolution*. Cambridge: Cambridge University Press.

Premack, David. 1994. "Why Animals Have Neither Culture nor History." Pp. 350–65 in *Companion Encyclopedia of Anthropology: Humanity, Culture and Social Life*, ed. Tim Ingold. London: Routledge.

Tanner, Adrian. 1979. *Bringing Home Animals: Religious Ideology and Mode of Production of the Mistassini Cree Hunters*. London: Hurst.

Tapper, Richard. 1988. "Animality, Humanity, Morality, Society." Pp. 47–62 in *What is an Animal?*, ed. Tim Ingold. London: Unwin Hyman.

Thompson, D'Arcy W. 1961. *On Growth and Form*, (abridged ed.), ed. John T. Bonner. Cambridge: Cambridge University Press.

Trevarthen, Colwyn and Katerina Logotheti. 1989. "Child in Society, and Society in Children: The Nature of Basic Trust." Pp. 165–86 in *Societies at Peace: Anthropological Perspectives*, eds. Signe Howell and Roy Willis. London: Routledge.

Whitehead, Alfred N. 1929. *Process and Reality: An Essay in Cosmology*. Cambridge: Cambridge University Press.

Wilson, Edward O. 1980. *Sociobiology*, abridged ed. Cambridge, Mass.: Harvard University Press (Belknap).

Winterhalder, Bruce, and Eric A. Smith. 1992. "Evolutionary Ecology and the Social Sciences." Pp. 3–23 In *Evolutionary Ecology and Human Behavior*, eds. Eric A. Smith and Bruce Winterhalder. New York: Aldine de Gruyter.

*Chapter 12*

# The Reversible Imaginary:
# Baudrillard and the End of The Social

*Raymond L. M. Lee*

The ancient Socratic question that attempts to essentialize the condition of sociality has now been turned on its head. For a long time, modern and modernizing humans had placed unquestioning faith in the linearity of the social and its historical manifestation characterized as progress. The social was not just an abstraction based on consensus and communication elevated by meaning production. It was also an eschatology animated by Hegelian *geist* moving dialectically toward an ultimate state of perfection. The bearers of the Enlightenment were caught in a myth of their own making: that the straight line to which the social was attached was all powerful. Time was not the enemy, for despite the strains inherent in its unfolding, the weaving of human elements into a community, a state, a nation was inevitable. The plausibility of civil society as the development, or even the epitome, of human altruism became the end state of this unfolding, just as words like *asocial* and *antisocial* were disparaged as the unwanted products of the dialectical process.

The social, as it appears in modern discursive form, is very much rooted in the conceptualization of civil society from the eighteenth century onward, the period in which European capital formation gained momentum under private enterprise freed from the collective constraints of medieval society. It was also the era of the European Enlightenment swept by a new confidence in the scientific ability of human subjectivity to wrestle with the forces of nature. This was the core of the modern imagination that emphasized the diremption of the social from the natural and thereafter held out the promise that humans re-created themselves not in the uncompromised state of nature but in the reflexive interaction between themselves, from the social contract of Rousseau to the communicative action of Habermas. The social was therefore premised on the civil, and the "emphasis on civil practices not only made the identification of nature possible, it *actively created* nature" (Tester 1992:12).

It was in the imagination of civil society, peopled and engineered by bourgeois selves, that the fate of the social became enriched by a sense of symmetry and equanimity. What was spoken and unspoken worked themselves into multiple layers of rules of governing behavior in the public and private spheres. From the perspective of political economy, the ideologies underlying liberal democracy and capital accumulation were essential to the construction of civil interests in which reciprocity and volunteer association could only work under the influence of personal gain. What came to be called a social order was none other than an intellectual account of why we are civilized beings even as we act to fulfill specific interests that may jeopardize the fabric of interpersonal understanding and informed consensus. The forerunners of symbolic interactionism offered concepts such as "looking-glass self" (Cooley) and "generalized other" (Mead) to stabilize this account in order to show that social breakdowns were more an exception than the rule. The internalization of norms implied in these concepts gave a sense of unity to civil society, and it is in this unity that we find the objectification of the social as constituting a component of our "natural attitude."

Objectification or reification of what we have come to accept as our natural rights and roles has provided a type of protection for the meaning of the social. The social is thought to be shielded from the anarchic impulses of the irrational because of our faith toward the infallibility of normative forms and formations. But this is a faith that has also produced the "phantom objectivity" spoken of by Lukacs (1971:83) as social relations taking on the character of a thing dominated by commodity structure and exchange. It is as though our very belief in the civilizing qualities of social engagement has given rise to a nondescript irrationality embedded in commodity fetishism.

Thus, civil society is no longer merely about "fundamental experiential and relational connection between individuals going about their own lives" (Tester 1992:5). Within the emerging global commodity form, the notion of the civil (and its social derivatives) includes the intervention and mediation of all the codes generated by commodity structure. Ironically, it was in the imagined symmetry of civil society that the commodity form achieved its global dominance today. As Tester (1992:126) points out, the premodern medieval notion of sociality based on asymmetric reciprocity "collapsed in the face of urbanization, cosmopolitanism and the consequent redundancy of any and all criteria of firm ascription in the context of a world of achieved strangers and strangeness." This was the birthplace of the commodity form, immanent in the strangeness of civil society and the subsequent notions of individual identity that was not only driven by material interests but also the myth of the freedom of choice.

In its journey from *gemeinschaft* to *gesellschaft* to a civil order now overtaken by commodity structure, the social seems to have arrived at a junction of crisis. This is a crisis of Western modernity and all its conceptual inventions encapsulated within the imagined power of linear time. Never before in the history of Western modernity has the critique of the social been supplanted by its thinglike shadow in commodity structure. All the humanist movements of the last two centuries, from romanticism to the sixties countercultures, seem naive in the face of commodity structure. To visualize the social at this point of crisis is to dissolve all notions of interacting individuals with "real" selves. This provides a vantage point to understand why some contemporary thinkers have jettisoned the social to prepare the ground for coming to terms with the powers of the non-social. Jean Baudrillard leads the field in this type of thinking, and this chapter provides an explication and evaluation of his "reversible imaginary" as a discourse on the limits of the social.

## Baudrillard and Modern Social Theory

The history of modern social theory rests largely on European intellectual struggles to understand, interpret, and canonize the principles of civil society from the Enlightenment onward (see Seidman 1994). From Comte to Habermas, the question "How is society possible?" has been driven mainly by a philosophy of the subject. This implies that individual consciousness is prior to all social actions, and the sum of these consciousness provides a possible indicator of a social whole. In other words, the social whole (social order or society) as an abstract entity is imagined to be stabilized by certain principles and institutions resulting from the civil interactions of individual consciousness. But, empirically, the varied interests of this consciousness contradict the notion of a social whole, leading to a conflict school of explanation ranging from Marx and Weber to the contemporary theories of Randall Collins (1975, 1985). It is this school that has transformed the earlier question into "Why should society be possible?"

This question is disturbing for several reasons. First, it challenges the idea of bourgeois civility; that is, the contractual understandings and the notion of mutual trust necessary for the regulation of a society geared toward the enrichment of the self and the progress of the whole are exposed as the fabrications of a particular class of people. The rise of the European bourgeoisie following the end of feudalism made the idea of civil society possible. So, logically, its decline would be marked by a vulnerability to its theoretical position.

Second, to speak of society in conflict does not strictly imply its disintegration but the limits of equilibrium and homeostasis. Conflict is assumed to be a "normal" state of affairs, the dynamics of which can only be understood as patterns of group or class interests characterized by their ascendance and decline. Third, this position threatens the entire notion of civilization and the teleology of progress. It questions the significance of reason as a vehicle to a perfection of the self in the social and vice versa.

Although the conflict school problematized the foundations of civil society, it did not depart from the assumptions rooted in the philosophy of the subject. Groups fought over resources, territories, and honor not so much as groups *tout court* but as collectivities of individuals driven by personal interests. To know how conflicts begin and end is to examine the role of personalities in historical context, the stuff of epics and melodramas. Large patterns of social movement and conflict may be discerned as changes in group structure, but ultimately momentous events marking these changes are reduced to individual explanations, that is, the behaviors arising from specific individual consciousness.

Thus, one could say that conflict represents the dark side of Enlightenment civil society, undermining the possibility of a social development. Instead, it opens the doors to an appreciation of nihilism, strands of which were already present in some aspects of European philosophy such as Nietzsche's. But modern social theory could not openly acknowledge these strands because they were potentially destructive of theory's raison d'être. Modern social theory attempted to represent for its audience the workings of civil society, while straining its logic to accommodate the premises of conflict from the perspective of individual consciousness. It could not afford to absorb nihilism, for that would have meant possible self-destruction. As long as the philosophy of the subject occupied the driver's seat in modern social theory, nihilism could be held at arm's length and kept at bay.

However, the advent of French poststructuralism in the second half of the twentieth century (see Kurzweil 1980) has paved the way for nihilism to be taken more seriously by modern social theorists. Its theoretical impact has been felt largely through the poststructuralist emphasis on relations of difference. By focusing on the instability of meaning and its relationship to power, poststructuralists were able to show that differences and contrasts are never fixed but subjected to contestations. The chief representatives of poststructuralism, Derrida and Foucault, saw the necessity to deconstruct the "genealogies of truth" that masked the assumptions of hierarchy in Western culture. Their writings contained a nihilistic agenda to suggest the absurdity of Western absolutism. It is this agenda that deflates the primacy of the subject and elevates discursive structures (or one could say "codes of dominance") as the driving force of social life. It is in this sense that society is said to be "decentered," without the individual or self-consciousness central to the notion of civil order.

Poststructuralism has, therefore, sought to replace the philosophy of the subject with the philosophy of the object. For the deconstructionists, the object tends to be ultimately a reference to the concealment of a will to power. This is indeed a position that denigrates the promises of rationality and reduces the apparent achievements of civil society to a Hobbesian situation of unending power formations and contests.

The significance of Baudrillard's writings can be located within the influence of poststructuralism on modern social theory. However, Baudrillard's philosophy of the object comprises more than a general concern with the will to power. He sees the importance of describing this will, first, in the system of signs that governs our lives in subtle and not so subtle ways, and, second, as a transhuman condition that mitigates our investment in the notion of value. This is a difficult philosophy to grasp because it requires an abandonment of self, civility, order, and progress as a type of overcoming of the social and a renunciation of subjective control.

The provocative, poetic style of Baudrillard's writings has either elicited an endearing appeal to those who appreciate the artistic form of French cynicism and irony or activated the scoffing attitude of those who see no redeeming value in what they consider as self-indulgent philosophy. At least two sympathetic accounts of Baudrillard's intellectual development have been published (Gane 1991a, 1991b). These accounts comprise insightful descriptions of his transformation from a Marxian social theorist to an exponent of fiction-theory. Unlike writers who are less convinced of the promise of this theoretical venture— Kellner (1989:179) refers to him as "the Walt Disney of contemporary metaphysics," and Arditi (1993:22) wonders why we should care about him anymore—the more positive statements on his works tend to emphasize the significance of his theory for understanding the demise of the social.

Three discernible phases in Baudrillard's writing career reflect a growing disillusionment with the philosophy of the subject, eventuating in an intriguing exploration of the philosophy of the object. By moving toward the object, the notion of the social becomes unhinged and gradually disappears as an overtheorized artifact of the bourgeois self and its pretensions to civility.

Baudrillard treats the philosophy of the subject as banal because it territorializes all our faith in linear time and the purported power of subjectivity. It provides the conditions for the exercise of unspoken terror: that unless we stay within the charmed boundaries of the social, all anchors, certainties, and verisimilitudes will vanish. It is the Novocain of bourgeois doubts. On the other hand, the philosophy of the object lies beyond linear time and subjectivity. It is impervious to all humanist sociality or socialized humanism. It is not inhuman but transhuman, glimpses of which can be attained through the ironic and poetic.

In the first phase spanning the 1960s and 1970s, Baudrillard (1968, 1970, 1972) attempted to deconstruct Western civil society through a critique of commodity structure. Basically, he argued that the social equivalence and reciprocity in civil society were myths masking the asymmetries between labor-use value and commodity-exchange value. In plain language, the productive output of individual labor does not always correspond in exact and equal terms to the final monetary value realized in the exchange of goods and services. People are not easily fooled by those myths, but their awareness of where they stand in the system of production and commodity exchange subjects them to a notion of individuality within a general model of the social (Baudrillard 1981a:147).

Thus, the social is not mere mind stuff but a "real" product in the commodification of labor that identifies consumerism as an "inhibition of change" and "restores actual inequality against the modern egalitarian social fantasy" (Gane 1991a:78). Indeed, Baudrillard reduces the social to the hegemony of commodity exchange value and, at the same time, reconceptualizes his critique in terms of semiological relations—that is, the social as a system and process involving the consumption of signs.

The consumption of signs implies the manipulation and power of the commodity form over the relevance of individual consciousness, or, as Levin (1981:17) puts it, "it is exchange value that is privileged over use value precisely because exchange value is the system's principle of circulation." The meanings that people attribute to things and actions are subordinated to a system of signs linked to commodity exchange.

But this critique is made within the philosophy of the subject, however limited, for there is still a concern for the evolution of the individual from the system of exchange, as though a realization of this may lead to organized resistance. There is an attempt, so to speak, to raise class consciousness through cultural strategy for "theoretical analysis makes a class logic emerge" (Baudrillard 1981a:57).

In this way, Baudrillard advocates an activated agency in cultural knowledge to break through the veil of commodity consumerism held together by class power. However, this is an underarticulated philosophy of the subject that protests against the elite classes and the system of signs generated by consumer culture. Because of his intellectual debt to structuralism that dispenses with subjectivity and to Marxian dialectics, Baudrillard veers in his early writings between the possibility of a reconstituted consciousness and the pessimism of cultural leveling. As he enters the second phase, this ambivalence disappears as he describes the subversion of the social by hyperreal simulation. This is a situation in which all original ideas and actions have become passé because of our inability to make clear distinctions between what is original and what passes as original. In other words, replicas have become "more real than real" (Kellner 1989:83), and our lives are only models even though we live as if (or pretend to believe that) reality is still virginal. The philosophy of the subject becomes irrelevant at this point.

The second phase occurring from the mid-1970s to the early 1980s was heralded by the publication of several books, of which four (Baudrillard 1973, 1976, 1978, 1981b) stand out as important statements of his shift from the concern with ideologies of consumer society to dominance of signs and simulacra. These works in English translation (1975, 1993a, 1983a, 1983b, respectively) have identified him in the English-speaking public as an incontrovertible theorist of hyperreality.

The philosophy of the subject that operated clandestinely in his earlier works has now become dormant, having fallen prey to the far-reaching effects of hyperreality. It is as though Baudrillard imagined the birth of hyperreality from subjectivity (the sphere of capitalist relations of production, consumption, and exchange) but only to result in the former's domination, what he calls the "offensive counterstrategy of the object" as opposed to the "strategy of the subject" (Baudrillard 1985:583). This spells the end of the social (which constitutes the subtitle of his 1978 book) because all use and exchange values have been rendered superfluous by the emergence of the "structural law of value." This is the law that has increased the arbitrariness of meaning production, resulting in the myriad ways in which hyperreality is coded and distributed.

From here onward, the philosophy of the subject fades into oblivion and the social vanishes, sucked in by the "vertigo of serial signs" and the "cool universe of digitality" (Baudrillard 1983b:73). The third phase from the mid-1980s onward marks his profound preoccupation with the object and the power of reversibility. However, the object becomes more desublimated, magical, and transhuman to the extent that it has little to do with the world of hyperreality. The object seems to reside in the sphere of the uncreated, far removed from the subjective elements of the social or the randomness of free-floating signs. Even his style of writing changes, displaying a lucid and ironic quality as if to suggest that access to this level of discourse is fatally poetic.

The central works of this period (1983c/1990a, 1990b/1993b, 1992/1994—the French originals and English translations) are concerned with predestination and the subtle power of reversibility. They take him farther from the miasma of capitalism and codes and into a completely different world of nonrational causation in which the social is totally excommunicated. He writes as though people are peripheral to macroforces that lie beyond mundane human activities. He cogitates on social impossibilities, fiction-theory that takes the reader into another realm of discourse where speculation approximates conceptual seduction. This statement implies that socially or subjectively his views make little sense, but objectively he takes us into a realm that operates on the power of reversibility.

This is a realm that rejects linear causality and its concomitant subjectivity underlying historical agency and sociality. To understand how the social is deconstructed in this realm, we will examine some of his later works that deal with death, seduction, and enchantment.

## Deconstructing the Social

In one of his major works of the seventies, Baudrillard (1993a) launched a devastating critique against Marx in *Symbolic Exchange and Death*. Baudrillard's critique of the Marxian model centered on his assertion that it was tragically trapped within a capitalist mode of discourse. Marxian production was considered a form of social realism that could not rise above its dialectical fiction of capitalist relations and revolutionary labor because it failed to resolve the contradictions between the use value of living labor and exchange value of dead labor.

For Baudrillard, "we no longer work, but merely perform 'acts of production' " signaling "the end of production-culture" for the " 'productive agent' is no longer characterized by its exploitation, nor by its being raw material in a labour process; it is characterized by its mobility and interchangeability, by being an insignificant inflection of fixed capital" (Baudrillard 1993a:18).

To understand Baudrillard's rejection of the Marxian model, one needs to appreciate his "evolutionary" model of social decline. This is a model premised on the social as a locus of materialistic growth initially determined by a logic of counterfeit in the preindustrial era, progressing to a logic of mechanical reproduction in the industrial era. These two phases are characterized, respectively, by a natural law of value and a market law of value. One could say that bourgeois rationality and subjectivity reigned supreme during these stages of growth because they provided a much-needed lubricant for working the engine of progress, in order to maintain the belief in the individual as the prince of the social who autonomously guides these logics to their historical end—the reification of the individual in the social.

However, Baudrillard sees the arrogance of these phases as now transformed into a subjectless and massified level of existence governed by a never-ending series of simulated appearances. The social has now imploded into the mass, controlled by a structural law of value and permitting only the uninhibited play of signs.

In conclusion, Baudrillard declares that the "simulation principle dominates the reality principle as well as the pleasure principle" (Baudrillard 1993a:76). Thus, in this disenchanted and soulless world of codes and digitality, human agency has no power. In the fractal order, the successor to the order of hyperreality, Baudrillard (1993b) posits the emergence of indeterminate mutations resulting from viral proliferations continuing to infinity. Not only are referents totally erased, values are irradiated to the point of indifference and accidentality. This is truly a world of pure delirium and vertigo where any thought of the social is fatally ridiculous. Genosko (1994:54) puts it well when he says that "Baudrillard evokes a world which is a dense mass, and a confusing mess, of indexical collisions and so-called infections."

Yet, in this convoluted world of the sign, the code, and viral dispersion, Baudrillard sees the power of death as a possible force of resistance against simulation. Within the confines of the social, more value is attributed to life than death. Because of this, death walks a tightrope between life's end and the ends of life, acquiring in the process a pariah status that undermines its potentiality in the promotion of the symbolic. Thus, "in a system where life is ruled by value and utility, death becomes a useless luxury, and the only alternative" (Baudrillard 1993a:156). But following the French philosopher, Bataille, he argues that "death itself is without finalities. Death is neither resolution nor involution, but a reversal and a symbolic challenge" (Baudrillard 1993a:156).

To understand this position, we need to distinguish between symbols and signs. For Baudrillard, the symbolic order is binding in the sense that "signs are limited in number and their circulation is restricted. Each retains its full value as a prohibition, and each carries with it a reciprocal obligation between castes, clans or persons, so signs are not arbitrary" (Baudrillard 1993a:50). In other words, signs in feudal and premodern societies are actually symbols which motivate obligatory relationships by virtue of the strong linkage between signifiers and referents (or between the word and the world). However, once this linkage is broken or referents implode into signifiers, the emancipated symbol takes on the characteristics of the free-floating sign that is uninhibited by the social demands of the symbolic order. The freedom of the sign marks the overshadowing of the social by the simulacral.

Thus, Genosko (1994:45) has accurately concluded that "for Baudrillard the symbolic is usually and radically opposed to the order of signs." It is in this struggle between symbols and signs, and Baudrillard's predilection towards a presimulacral existence, that we can situate his discourse on death. For Baudrillard (1993a:166) complains that "we experience our death as the 'real' fatality inscribed in our bodies only because we no longer know how to inscribe it into a ritual of symbolic exchange." Because the symbolic order precludes all simulacral abstraction, life and death are reversible in symbolic exchange (1993a:159). But under simulacral systems of value, life and death are controlled by the law of equivalence in which "the living are separated from their dead, who no longer exchange anything but the form of their afterlife, under the sign of comprehensive insurance" (1993a:177). For it is in the symbolic reversibility of death that such a distinction can' be effectively challenged, "since death is the real sexualisation of life" (1993a:185) and "itself demands to be experienced immediately, in total blindness and total ambivalence" (1993a:187).

In a way, Baudrillard seems to lament the passing of a social holism inscribed in the ambivalence between life and death, but at the same time he turns to the metaphor of seduction to recover the power of the symbolic and its corollaries of reversibility. In *Seduction*, Baudrillard (1990c—French original 1979) portrays death as seductive and sardonic. It is seductive because it is a "play of veils" and "removes something from the order of the visible" (1990c:33, 34). It is sardonic because it has nothing to fear, not even its own existence since it subsists on the fatal.

Thus, seduction is asocial because it is the primary power of the symbolic order from which various socialities spring, or, as Baudrillard (1990c:41) puts it, "the world's workings are the result of a mental seduction." Sex is not equivalent to mental seduction because it is a type of physical and psychological production. "Wherever sex has been erected into a function, an autonomous instance, it has liquidated seduction. Sex today generally occurs only in the place, and in place of a missing seduction, or as the residue and staging of a failed seduction" (1990c:39–40).

As a power of the symbolic, seduction is said to be reversible, disaccumulative, and not of the order of the real (Baudrillard 1990c:46). Essentially, seduction is circular, and what is circular can contain the linear but not vice versa. It is this circularity that gives "rituality" many advantages over sociality, for the

> latter is only a recent, and not very seductive form of organization and exchange, one invented by humans for humans. Rituality is a much larger system, encompassing the living and the dead, humans and animals, as well as a "nature" whose periodic movements, recurrences and catastrophes serve, seemingly spontaneously, as ritual signs. [It maintains] a form of cyclical order and universal exchange of which the Law and the social are quite incapable. (p. 90)

For Baudrillard, this rituality underlying seduction is not merely individual action that by some account aggregates into a larger social picture, but it also comprises a "mastery of appearances" that for all intents and purposes "always seeks to overturn and exorcise a power," particularly through an appearance of weakness which gives it its strength (Baudrillard 1990c:83–8). Seductive rituality is therefore a symbolic arrangement that transcends all the social forms emanating from production and reproduction because it is not premised on a rationality of appearances that gives the modern social world its luster of reality. Rather, it is premised on an analogical system that "brings opposites together" or subjects them to a "duel and agonistic relation" (1990c:105). It is this relation that marks seduction as destiny, not the dry positivistic predictability of the modern social form but the enchantment of "primitivity": "It is what remains of a magical, fateful world, a risky, vertiginous and predestined world; it is what is quietly effective in a visibly efficient and stolid world" (1990c:180) .

How does this enchantment work? In three difficult but poetically crafted books—*Fatal Strategies* (1990a), *Transparency of Evil* (1993b), *The Illusion of the End* (1994)—Baudrillard advances an enigmatically persuasive account of the power of reversibility as the source of enchantment, contrasting it with the power of irreversibility as the source of disenchantment. It is in the latter that most people speak of the social, the space-time continuum that is forward-looking or that taps into the past to feed the present for the good of the future. It is a continuum that disallows the precession of effects over causes. Baudrillard (1990a:37, 84, 114) refers to "the disappearance of causes and the almighty power of effects," "the revenge of the reversible order," and the disappearance of the subject "from the horizon of the object" as inevitable because there is no reason why we should so simplistically accept irreversible patterns of sociality as final.

Reversibility is enchanting because it does not imply the accumulative ends of value. From use value to structural value, human relations bear the stamp of a finite pattern of decisionism, negotiation, and interlocking interests that gives the social its touch and feel of reality. But in reversible phenomena, value is negated by the gift and counter-gift or any form of agonistic relations. The social is replaced by a bewildering concatenation of events that Baudrillard terms "the ceremony of the world" (Baudrillard 1990a:166).

The ceremony of the world rests on a system of rules, not on values or interpretation, because "ceremony is not of the order of pleasure, it is of the order of power" (Baudrillard 1990a:170). It is the intensity and systematicity of rule making and observance that rechannels all personal energy into the operational signs of rituals to effect the movement of predestination.

Thus, ceremony delivers the power of form (signifiers) over the quest for meaning (signifieds), and uses ritual rules to efface all laws of value. In *Transparency of Evil*, Baudrillard asserts that enchantment is ceremonial. It seduces because its rules are always uncompromisingly agonistic (in opposition) to produce an exchange that is never immersed in values but as "a presentiment of total reversibility" (1993b:113). But humanists who only speak of the power of the subject in the social will reject Baudrillard, and yet they will find it odd that he says "when we speak of the 'end of history,' the 'end of the political,' the 'end of the social,' the 'end of ideologies,' none of this is true" (1993b:116). As master of poetic cynicism, Baudrillard declares that "there will be no end to anything because, at bottom, all these things are already dead and, rather than have a happy or tragic resolution, a destiny, we shall have a thwarted end, a homeopathic end, an end distilled into all the various metastases of the refusal of death" (1993b:116). In other words, without ceremony, enchantment, and seduction, there is only an illusion of the end in which linearity is the prime mover.

The common thread running through these works is irony which, as Lemert (1992:22) points out, "is a powerful literary device precisely because in reversing the presumably real order of things it calls everything, including the order of things, into question." Death, seduction, and enchantment are not treated as factual but as ironic in the sense that they draw our attention to a symbolic universe where reversible power dethrones subjectivity and the civil-social order. It is, perhaps, difficult for many humanists to agree with this position because it tends to deny the achievements of the liberal age. But can we say that the liberal age is in decline and that Baudrillard, writing in a postliberal and postmodern mode, is actually advocating a new culture of "rugged collectivism"?

## The Mirror of Poststructuralism

In the myth of Narcissus, the youth only saw and worshipped his own beauty. He became a prisoner of his own illusions, forgetting the mirror that had empowered them. One might imagine Baudrillard drawing an analogy between Narcissus and the smugness of the modern self. Baudrillard's mission was to smash this self and to challenge the reifying powers of subjectivity to recover the lost identity implied in symbolic exchange and primitive collectivism. The mirror of post-structuralism is Narcissus dissolved.

It is therefore not inaccurate for Kroker (1992:62) to label Baudrillard as "the very first of the *postmodern primitives.*" But this is not to suggest a postmodern *return* to a pristine state of primitivity; rather, it is meant as a critical juxtapositioning of technology and symbolic exchange. The primitive state that is implied by symbolic exchange in tension with technology privileges the formation of a dense network of rules and rituals characterized by intense ceremonials and symbolic reciprocities against the hegemony of the structural law of value. Technology is defined by boundaries that regulate the complex relationship between individuals and institutions. For Baudrillard, technology has become autonomous to the point that its codes underlie so many aspects of human transactions. Hyperreality structured by these codes has reduced social interaction to the play of free-floating signs and spectacles. Indeed, the demise of the social implies the birth of an implosive mass. The primitivity of Baudrillard is directed at transcending this mass so that a type of collective consciousness can emerge.

This consciousness implies a Durkheimian collectivism (cf. Greenwood 1994) because it refers to an effort to embed the meaningfulness of human relations within the structure of rules and rituals. All actions become symbolized with reference to a set of organized rules and rituals, such that individual experiences are represented not as fragmented instances of fleeting arbitrary events but as parts of a common whole. However, Baudrillard is not fully satisfied with the intactness of such a vision because a focus on the integrity of the whole could be readily distorted into a discourse on linear progress. In other words, to preserve the synchronicity of the Durkheimian model, Baudrillard has resorted to the idea of reversibility (an inherent idea in French structuralism; see Gardner 1974:24) to resist any intrusion of diachronicity. Thus, death, seduction, and enchantment are all circular and reversible events because they freeze time within the symbolic space of ritualized movements.

This tactic of Baudrillard to dislodge the alleged supremacy of linearity must be seen against the background of the poststructuralist movement whose adherents share a worldview based on "antihumanism," a "subversive spirit of deconstructionism," and "an anarchistic social vision" (Seidman 1994:201, 205). In a sense, Baudrillard wants to deconstruct the social as the dialectical action of individuals that imputes a progression of shared knowledge. Instead, he wants to show that such a person-centric construction of the social has now been superseded by a decentered mass that thrives on imagery, hyperreality, and digitality. For him, the social may not be able to survive the captivating onslaught of hyperreality, but he seems to believe that two types of conceptual action may be taken to undermine the massification of the social.

On one level, Baudrillard invokes the power of rituals and symbolic exchange to reinvigorate the meaningfulness of human existence. This Durkheimian turn has nostalgic elements that remind us of a romantic reversion to an idyllic, primitive past where the sense of bonding is not dictated by any commodity or structural values but by a continuous cycle of exchange. However, this romanticism is not subject centered because it looks to the group as a whole for the creation and maintenance of symbols to challenge the arbitrary universe of free-floating signs.

On another level, Baudrillard's reversibility addresses the teleological and linear assumptions of modernity. By alluding to the objective power of symbols, he provides a countercultural perspective against the modern social form that seeks global recognition in modernization and the establishment of civil society. To speak of the precession of effects over causes implies the failure of modern sociality to confront the power of the object. In this regard, modern sociality is restricted to a history of dialectical relations, beyond which lies the realm of nondialectical reversibility.

Baudrillard's "rugged collectivism" did not appear out of thin air, but, as a product of the poststructuralist movement, it may be construed as a nostalgic and antihumanist reaction to the apparent failure of civil society and leftist politics in Western Europe. We may note that his major statements on the massification of the social or the reduction of the social to mass consumerism and sign control were made in the mid-sixties and early seventies. This was a period of intense rebellion against establishment politics in the West. His writings at that time came to represent the popular dissatisfaction with civil society as a guarantee of contractual equivalence between different segments of society. It was also a period when the social sciences became politicized. Debates raged over whether the social sciences were really scientific or an aspect of the ideological apparatus of the dominant classes.

Generally, Baudrillard's critique of the social as an arena of consumerism, conformism, and ideological control did not separate him from the continuous stream of critical literature coming out of the social

sciences and humanities. What is interesting, though, is his break with
Marxism as the center of leftist politics (Seidman 1992:49) at a time
when Marxism continued to inspire revolutionary politics in the Third
World. His critique of Marxism reflected a skepticism of the basic
premises of revolutionary labor that, in his view, could not offer a
genuine departure from the travails of massification and production.

His works on signs and simulacra, published in the seventies and
eighties, may be interpreted as representing a new politics of resistance
aimed at showing the meaninglessness of the social as a sum of human
relationships. For him, the masses responded only to signs and images
that could be resisted through symbolic actions. This was a period that
saw the intensification of market relations, the increased circulation of
global capital, and the emergence of a yuppie way of life. Baudrillard
sought to recover the primitive bonds of symbolic action that precluded
a social formation based on civil and market relations. This may be
appropriately called "rugged collectivism" in the sense of rituality
and exchange principles diminishing all gains accruing to the self in
interaction. The symbolic form alone provides a source of power for
cultural actions that require no notion of the autonomous self.

However, the tremendous success of Baudrillard's writings in Europe and the United States does not suggest that the social has actually
ended. The notions of civil society and the self as an independent
entity in the constitution of the social have yet to become obsolete. On
the contrary, the renewed role of liberalism (in the wake of commu-
nism's collapse) and the relentless pursuit of modernity in many parts
of the so-called developing world seem to have given the meaning of
the social a complete facelift.

Yet, one could say that this is merely an illusion created by optimists
who believe in the centrality of the self and linear time in the construction of society. The advent of information superhighways and cyberspace at the end of the twentieth century suggests a re-vision of the
world as a playground of the microchip: humans may have created
cyberspace, but the latter has assumed a life of its own to the extent
that the social is superfluous—only bytes of information matter. In
short, Baudrillard's poststructuralism has alerted us to the imminent
transformability of the social into a dense mass of signs from which no
selves can emerge.

## Conclusion

Although the question of what constitutes the social has troubled
philosophers since Socratic times, it was only during the nineteenth

century, at the height of modernity, that systematic theoretical and empirical treatment was undertaken to distinguish individual action from its aggregation into a collective whole, something which animated history and empowered the movement of civilization. From Marx, Weber, Durkheim, Toennies, Simmel, and many other European thinkers, modern social theory was born and continues to be reinvented for the purpose of asking how the social is at all possible.

However, in only a short space of a century modern social theory seems to be on the verge of collapse, not so much because of its rapid fragmentation into many opposing schools of thought but because of the very crisis of modernity itself. Modernity is simultaneously productive and reflexive, pitting the creativity and mastery of forms against the search for ontological meanings. What modernity has created does not seem to answer back with a resonating voice. Instead, the multiple voices—produced by modernity crisscrossed by boundaries and hierarchies—appear to dissipate meaning across the breadth of its creation. In short, modern social theory is experiencing an "identity crisis" just as Frankenstein's monster labored after an identity in the wake of the mayhem caused by his ontological ambiguities.

It is in this crisis that the social has emerged once more to haunt the creators of its foundations. However, Baudrillard wants to persuade us to construe these foundations as fictitious because the paradoxes of modernity cannot liberate us from our creations. Instead, he proposes a reversible imaginary to end our investment in the promises of a linear subjectivity, and he thereby provides a route out of the miasma of modernity. In the reversible imaginary, it is symbolic space, not linear time, that dominates to revive a consciousness of pure form that vanquishes dialectic motion as the producer of the historical and the social. The vision that Baudrillard offers is probably strange and threatening to many liberals, humanists, and positivists, but in the long run it may be a vision that may help us revise our ideas of what society could be like in the twenty-first century and beyond.

## References

Arditi, Jorge. 1993. "Out of the Maze? Twists and Riddles of Postmodern Thinking." *Contemporary Sociology* 22:19–23.

Baudrillard, Jean. 1968. *Le Système des Objets*. Paris: Denoel.

———. 1970. *La Société de Consommation*. Paris: Gallimard.

————. 1972. *Pour une Critique de l'Économie du Signe*. Paris: Gallimard.

————. 1973. *Le Miroir de la Production*. Tournail: Casterman.

————. 1975. *The Mirror of Production*. St. Louis: Telos.

————. 1976. *L'Échange Symbolique et la Mort*. Paris: Gallimard.

————. 1978. *A l'Ombre Majorités Silencieuses, ou La Fin du Social*. Fontenay-sous-Bois: Cahiers d'Utopie.

————. 1979. *De la Seduction*. Paris: Denoel-Gonthier.

————.1981a. *For a Critique of the Political Economy of the Sign*. St. Louis: Telos Press.

————. 1981b. *Simulacres et Simulation*. Paris: Galilee.

————. 1983a. *In the Shadow of the Silent Majorities, or the End of the Social and Other Essays*. New York: Semiotext(e).

————. 1983b. *Simulations*. New York: Semiotext(e).

————. 1983c. *Les Stratégies Fatale*. Paris: Grasset.

————. 1985. "The Masses: The Implosion of the Social in the Media." *New Literary History* 16: 577-89.

————. 1990a. *Fatal Strategies*. New York: Semiotext(e).

————. 1990b. *La Transparence du Mal*. Paris: Galilee.

————. 1990c. *Seduction*. New York: St. Martin's Press.

————. 1992. *L'Illusion de la Fin ou la Grève des Événements*. Paris: Galilee.

————. 1993a. *Symbolic Exchange and Death*. Thousand Oaks, Calif.: Sage.

————. 1993b. *Transparency of Evil*. London: Verso.

————. 1994. *The Illusion of the End*. Cambridge: Polity.

Collins, Randall. 1975. *Conflict Sociology*. New York: Academic Press.

————. 1985. *Three Sociological Traditions*. New York: Oxford University Press.

Gane, Mike. 1991a. *Baudrillard: Critical and Fatal Theory*. London: Routledge.

————. 1991b. *Baudrillard's Bestiary*. London: Routledge.

Gardner, Howard. 1974. *The Quest for Mind: Piaget, Lévi-Strauss and the Structuralist Movement*. New York: Vintage Books.

Genosko, Gary. 1994. *Baudrillard and Signs*. London: Routledge.

Greenwood, John D. 1994. *Realism, Identity and Emotion: Reclaiming Social Psychology*. London: Sage.

Kellner, Douglas. 1989. *Jean Baudrillard: From Marxism to Postmodernism and Beyond*. Cambridge: Polity.

Kroker, Arthur. 1992. *The Possessed Individual: Technology and Postmodernity*. London: Macmillan.

Kurzweil, Edith. 1980. *The Age of Structuralism*. New York: Columbia University Press.

Lemert, Charles. 1992. "General Social Theory, Irony, Postmodernism." Pp. 17–46 in *Postmodernism and Social Theory*, ed. Steven Seidman and Donald G. Wagner. Oxford: Blackwell.

Levin, Charles. 1981. "Introduction." Pp. 5–28 in Jean Baudrillard (1981a), op. cit.

Lukacs, Georg. 1971. *History and Class Consciousness.* Cambridge, Mass.: MIT Press.

Seidman, Steven. 1992. "Postmodern Social Theory as Narrative With a Moral Intent." Pp. 47–81 in *Postmodernism and Social Theory,* ed. Steven Seidman and Donald G. Wagner. Oxford: Blackwell.

———. 1994. *Contested Knowledge: Social Theory in the Postmodern Era.* Oxford: Blackwell.

Tester, Keith. 1992. *Civil Society.* London: Routledge.

# Index

273

# About the Contributors

**Kenneth J. Gergen** is professor of psychology, Swarthmore College.

**Margaret Gilbert** is professor of philosophy, University of Connecticut at Storrs.

**Scott Gordon** is professor of economics, Queens University, Canada, and distinguished professor emeritus of economics/professor emeritus of the history and philosophy of science, University of Indiana at Bloomington.

**John D. Greenwood** is professor of philosophy and psychology, City College and Graduate School, City University of New York.

**Rom Harré** is fellow of Linacre College, Oxford, United Kingdom, and professor of psychology, Georgetown University.

**Tim Ingold** is professor of social anthropology, University of Manchester.

**Raymond L. M. Lee** is professor of anthropology and sociology, University of Malaya.

**Peter T. Manicas** is professor of social science, University of Hawaii at Manoa.

**Joseph Margolis** is Laura H. Carnell professor of philosophy, Temple University.

**Lloyd Sandelands** is professor of psychology, University of Michigan, Ann Arbor.

**Paul F. Secord** is research professor emeritus in psychology, University of Houston.

**Jonathan H. Turner** is professor of sociology, University of California at Riverside.

**Walter L. Wallace** is professor of sociology, Princeton University.